AF531707

Intellectual Property Rights in The Emerging Business Environment

Intellectual Property Rights in The Emerging Business Environment

Edited by

Bharti Thakar

2010

Icfai Books
The Icfai University Press

Overview

Man is the only living being on earth who is gifted with a brain and unlimited thinking capacity. Earlier, he was able to use and take the help of other's creation and invention. Every new thing created fell into the public domain and there was no restriction on the usage. But, with the advent of technology and political barriers and competition, people have started putting a price on their individual creation; such cerebral asset is termed an intellectual property right. Commonly known as IPR, the intellectual property rights bear a great impact on the day-to-day life of the people. This is because each and every single idea or object made, is, in one way or the other, an intellectual property created by an individual for the usage of the people at large. From industrial equipment, to a specific process of growing hybrid plants, or an interior design of a house, an article written by a teacher or the design of a logo of a company can all come under the purview of intellectual property; this list is not exhaustive. Such thoughts and objects, when they are created into a tangible form and are registered, gives them a protection from unauthorized users. The owner acquires a right to sue such user in the court of law and seek justice. The Intellectual Property Rights Law has also been enacted for better understanding and streamlining the usage of Intellectual Property Rights.

The business environment of today has become very concise and dynamic with the access of Internet. It enables the users to access any information throughout the globe. This has become a serious threat to the valuable asset of intellectual property. The book endeavors to identify these areas and probe further into the changing scene of the intellectual property rights.

This book contains three sections, classifying articles and cases containing issues that identify the recent changes and developments happening in the field of intellectual property in India and around the globe. The first section "**IPR: Emerging Issues**" gives an idea to the reader as to how IPR is touching up various complicated aspects of business on a micro level. The section is also supplemented with case studies to explain how IPR is becoming an issue of vital concern for the companies and countries.

The first article titled "**Intellectual Property Rights – A Path to Value Enhancement**" written by *Bharti Thakar* is a curtain raiser on the basic issues of intellectual property. The contents of the article provide a general guide to the subject matter. It explains how the intellectual property rights are based upon the primary issues of capturing the unique ideas of an individual or a group. When the idea is captured into a form of an intellectual asset it gains great value in terms of the company turnover as well as it gives the company a competitive edge. Intellectual properties are primarily in the form of copyrights, trade marks, patents and industrial designs. The article explains in detail the various types of intellectual assets and the fact that they are a path for anyone, be it an individual or a company to enhance the asset value.

The next article "**Due Diligence in Business Transactions Involving Intellectual Property Assets**" written by *Edward Meilman* and *James Brady* explains the due diligence that has to be observed during the acquisition and strategic utilization of intellectual property assets. Intellectual Property forms an integral and crucial asset in the net worth of an organization. So, it holds a strategic importance during the process of acquisition and takeover of a company. It needs to be observed what type of intellectual property is involved in the organization and how much value does it hold in the total worth of the organization. The article also gives an explanation about the precaution that needs to be taken while conducting a due diligence study of such assets and describes in detail the procedure of obtaining and reviewing the information in this regard.

The article "**Practical and Legal Protection of Computer Databases**" by *Ashok Ram Kumar,* explains the importance of protection of computer programs and software that come under the purview of Copyrights. "Seeds" and "Signatures" are inserted in the database to keep the software protected. The article gives further explanation about the ownership of database and implication and key factors concerned in the protection of database under the Copyright Law and areas concerning legal protection of database managements.

The section is backed up with two case studies which try to project the developments taking place at the domestic level in India and abroad and steps taken by various organizations and the government to cope with the emerging complications created by intellectual property rights.

"**Reforms in US Patent Law: Business Implications**" written by *D Gayatri* and *T Phani Madhav,* explains the complicated situation that arose due to increasing patent applications coming to the US Patents and Trademarks Office. The patents were given to ideas without intense investigation. This led to a situation where such patents were filed that restricted the new inventions and created an unhealthy business environment. The case discusses the reasons that led to the situations and such reforms needed to bring in the US Patent Law to lead to a competitive business environment.

While the former case discusses US patent issues, the second case discusses the implications in the Indian pharmaceutical industry with the implementation of International Patent Law. Formerly, the Indian companies used to manufacture cheaper drugs by making small changes in the process of manufacturing patented drugs, which would not be the case when India would enter into the global platform. The case study, **"Nicholas Piramal India: Survival Strategies for International Patent Law Regime"** written by *Senthil Ganesan* and *K Malini,* explains in detail the strategies followed by Nicholas Piramal India Ltd., to cope with the International Patent Law and to remain competitive in the fiercely competitive global environment.

The second section, **"IPR: Indian Perspectives"** comprises articles which give some highlights into the processes of IPR with special reference to the Indian business world. The first article in this section, **"IPRs in India"** sourced from *Dubey & Partners – Advocates* gives a detailed understanding about the legislation, administration, events coming under the purview of the acts, rights and liabilities, people who could apply and related measures and provisions of the Trademark Act, Patents Act, Copyright Act, Design Act and the Geographical Indication of Goods Act. The article covers the legal framework of the critical and essential elements coming under the purview of Intellectual Property.

"An Insight on Copyright, Geographical Indications and Confidential Information Laws in India" written by *Rajkumar Dubey* explains the procedures to be adopted to protect the rich heritage of India built and preserved through centuries. The Geographical Indication Act of India has defined the meaning of geographical indication and has given a detailed framework as to the eligibility of application, the registration procedure and the type and the time of protection available to the geographical indication. The legalities of confidential information have also been explained in brief in the article.

While the first two articles in the section explain the fundamentals and legalities related to the Intellectual Property in India, the next article **"Intellectual Property Rights Protection in India: An Analysis"** by *Zinnov LLC,* discusses the key Initiatives taken by the Indian Government to protect the Intellectual Property. It also explains in detail several steps to be followed which would help reduce the risk of losing our intellectual property while doing offshore businesses. The article also comprises various small case studies which give an idea about the type of IP frauds taking place in the Indian subcontinent concerning the offshoring business.

The succeeding article, **"Trade Secrets Law in India"** written by *Praveen Dalal* explores various possibilities that can help the trade secrets in India. The author has deliberately not touched upon the traditional laws like the Common Law remedies of Torts but has gone into the details of implications of the TRIPS Agreement, the inter-relationship among trade secret, copyright and patents. The clauses and the provisions under the constitutional and statutory rights of the Trade Secret Law in India; the penalties, liabilities and the remedies available under various acts of India have been explained in great detail to help the reader understand the complexities of the trade secrets and their usage.

The next article **"Reflections on the Amendments to the Patent Act of 1970"** written by *Bharti Thakar,* reminisces through various issues of the Patent laws in India. The article traces the facts of how Indian laws have been framed to replace the British law to suit the Indian economic scene. The Patent laws have undergone various amendments to suit the changing environment and recently, with the global cooperation treaties, the Patent laws have again had to undergo changes. Such amendments have had immense impact upon the various industries in India. The article traces the various provisions of all the acts and amendments thereof. Critical analysis highlights some issues which are paradoxical in nature.

"Indian Patent Regime vis-à-vis European Patent Regime – A Comparative Analysis: How Far are the Indian Patent Laws Lagging Behind their European Counterparts?" written by *Deeptarag Mukherjee* and *Gaurav Dasgupta,* studies the difference between the two countries in the specific context of patent laws. This article analyses the Patents (Amendment) Act 2002 of India and the European Patent Convention, 1973 of Europe under three parameters; namely, patentability of the subject, capability in industrial application and the unity of invention. The article tries to explain the strength or otherwise of the present patent laws of India to promote intellectual property and locates the gap between the Indian and the European Laws. The authors conclude the article by suggesting various measures to fill in the loopholes in the present patent regime of India.

The next article deals with the critical issues pertaining to the IP crime. "**India: Intellectual Property Crime**" written by *Sudhir Ravindran* and *S A Chenthil Kumaran,* discusses the major factors responsible for the growth of IP crime. The authors explain the difference between the counterfeit products and copyright infringements as both of them have different implications in terms of violation of law and protection granted. The article also offers the Indian experience with the IP crime.

The last article of the section "**How to Tackle Counterfeiting in India**" written by *Paul, Taj Kunwar* and *Narula Ranjan,* concludes the section by explaining the civil and criminal remedies available in India under The Trade Marks Act, 1999; Indian Penal Code; The Copyright Act, 1957 and The Customs Act, 1962. One should know the basics and the details of intellectual property and its usage in India so as to protect oneself and the organization from the illegal usage of intellectual property.

The third section, "**IPR: Global Perspectives**" contains articles which relate to the Intellectual Property Rights in the international scenario.

The first article "**Recent International Developments in the Area of Intellectual Property Rights**" by *Carlos M CORREA* examines some of the recent international developments in the area of IPRs. It reviews the implementation of the Doha Declaration on the TRIPS agreement with reference to IPRs and Public Health, developments in Patent Law, copyright and the challenge of open access and protection of Traditional Knowledge. The article suggests that WIPO has been strongly led by a legalistic approach, without adequately considering other equivalent economic and social dimensions.

"New Conciliation and Arbitration Initiative for IP Disputes" written by *Woranuch Periera* and *Edward J Kelly,* describes an experience of Thailand wherein a large number of suits were filed relating to Dispute on Intellectual Property. The Department of Intellectual Property has carried out measures to resolve the disputes through the process of arbitration and conciliation. The article highlights the rules and procedure to carry out the two categories of the alternate dispute resolution system relating to IP disputes. More information provided in the form of *Value Addition* pertaining to arbitration issues has also been incorporated. It gives an explanation of this process and highlights the American Arbitration Association's rules which help further this process.

The section is backed up by two case studies-one that discusses the much talked about issue of music piracy and the second describes issues of online research archive. **"Music Piracy and iTunes"** written by *Hansa Iyengar,* gives a detailed view about the global music industry. This industry, as mentioned in the case, is in the clinches of raging music piracy since 1991. It shows how the industry fought back through lawsuits to overcome piracy. It was still not possible to abate piracy to the desired levels. Apple Computers came up with its iTunes Music Store, which tried to change the fortunes of the beleaguered industry. It came up with various schemes and promotion to stop the users from buying pirated CDs. But, iTunes also had its limitations and was up against serious competition. A *Value Addition* has been incorporated in which the case against the company Napster Inc. with regard to the new digital file sharing technology has been explained.

The last article of the book, a case study **"Copyright and Intellectual Property Rights: A Case Study from the Web Face"** written by *William Kilbride,* provides details about intellectual property rights issues relating to an online research archive. It explains the action taken to curb the unlicensed publication of data by a third party. Transparency and clarity in terms of the copyright and the copyright holder with regard to a particular property can make things much easier and can help in the long run.

Section I

IPR: Emerging Issues

1

Intellectual Property Rights – A Path to Value Enhancement

Bharti Thakar

Intellectual property rights are based upon the primary issues of capturing the unique ideas of an individual or a group. When the idea is captured into a form of a intellectual asset it gains great value in terms of the company turnover as well as it gives the company a competitive edge. Intellectual properties are primarily in forms of copyrights, trademarks, patents and industrial design. The article explains in details the various types of intellectual assets and the fact that they are a path for anyone, be it an individual or a company to enhance the asset value.

The swiftness of the movement of ideas and thoughts cannot be measured. They have to be caught and documented in the movement without which they would pass by. A thought or idea may be implemented, practised and later forgotten; unless it takes a tangible shape of a permanent process or a product. The source of new ideas is an individual's mind or collective thinking and acts of a group of individuals within a company. Ideas which are often new in nature have to be captured. Intellectual Property is based upon this cerebral function.

Through this regulation, ideas and thoughts get converted into property giving added strength by way of exclusivity. When such floating thought, ideas and consequent actions are captured and placed into a tangible module it takes the shape of intellectual property. To define this process all intellectual property are cerebral; meaning they have roots in the individual mind.

The essence of the Intellectual Property Act is protection of the property and giving the exclusivity to the person who originally had the idea. When the idea gets coverage of the law it is transformed into an intellectual asset. It gives the strength of ownership to the person, and the consequent competitive edge to the company benefiting from the same. To gain coverage, the intangible knowledge must foremost be transformed into a tangible form.

- It must be expressed in a discernable way to get protection.
- It must be new as would be 'novelty'.
- It must involve an inventive step.
- It must be capable of industrial application.

Creations of mind which are termed as intellectual property are granted protection under various categories like patents, copyrights, trademark and so on. Intellectual property right encompasses a bundle of rights – right to reproduce, distribute, license, sell and exploit intellectual property in any legal fashion.

WIPO as well as TRIPS have classified the intellectual property under various heads. Certain new categories like traditional knowledge have now been included into the realm of intellectual property. Intellectual property in general is a term covering patents, copyrights, trademark, industrial designs, geographical indications, protection of layout design or integrated circuits and protection of undisclosed information.

In practice, many times it becomes apparent that there is a lack of clarity about certain notions of intellectual property rights. Intellectual property rights can be classified into three categories.

1) Intellectual property rights for which registration is mandatory – such as patents and designs.

2) Though these can be registered, formal registration is not necessary such as in the case of copyrights or trademarks.

3) Intellectual property rights for which at present there is neither codified law, nor registration machinery available such as in the case of know-how and/or confidential information.

The major categories of Intellectual property rights, namely copyrights, designs, patents, and trademarks and the recently emerging Geological Indications, have an elaborate administrative set up for granting registrations. There are offices of Registrars and provisions for Appellate authorities. In case of copyrights and trademarks, it is necessary to take strategic decisions as to how such rights should be managed or protected. In case of copyright, for example, copyright comes into existence as soon as one completes the work, or creates a software program or publishes an idea. The High Courts have by and large held that in India a formal registration of copyright is not necessary for its enforcement. However, registration of copyright has certain distinct benefits. A certificate issued by the Registrar of Copyrights is valuable in infringement proceedings. It is also useful when recourse to police authorities is required to be taken. Such a certificate is considered as prima facie evidence of existence of copyright and is also useful in prosecuting applications for interim injunctions in courts. It is, therefore, always desirable to register copyrightable work under the provisions of the Copyright Act.

Trade secrets fall into a distinct category of intellectual property for the apparent reason of it being secret and confidential; whereas, the same would have to be disclosed to enable registration process. It is therefore peculiar in nature. These often comprise of some internal manufacturing process or classified formulae of the product used by the company. They consist of virtually any information developed by the company through research and development with a good amount of investment of time and money. Consequently, it is information that has economic value and gets that value because it is not generally known to the public and where efforts have been made to keep secret confidential. Being unknown to others in competing businesses, it gives a distinct advantage over such competitors. The recipe of Coca-Cola and the Hyderabad fish cure for asthma are well-known examples of trade secrets. The law of trade secrets is derived from the basic principles of the law of torts, restitution, agency, quasi-contract, property and contracts. There is no registration of trade secret, however, companies use reasonable efforts to keep the information in the form of a formula, compound, and chemistry combination of ingredients etc, secretive and closely held. Such information would comprise to be a trade secret. Other steps to take precaution would be using confidentiality agreements to maintain its secrecy in business deals and transactions, allowing only employees who must know the information to have access to it; a confidentiality clause has to be protected by invoking the principles of law of contract. Under a confidential agreement, it is the duty of the licensee to protect the confidentiality of the information parted with by the licensor under the contract. Needless to say, that if intellectual property rights are not protected vigorously, ultimately it is the company which will suffer in the long run. Such agreements give the company legal cause of action for damages or an injunction to stop its use in case required.

Trade secret protection presents no conflict with the patent law, as it is consistent with the patent policy of encouraging inventions. However, for trade secret protection, uniqueness in the patent law sense is not required. Further, the owner of a trade secret, unlike the holder of a patent, does not have an absolute monopoly on the information or data that comprises the trade secret. Other companies and individuals have the right to discover the elements of a trade secret through their own research and hard work. Consequently, inventors of items that may meet the standards of patentability should prefer to seek patent protection because such protection is far superior to the protection afforded by trade secret laws.

Procuring registration of an intellectual property would entail disclosure of information. In the process of registration it is essential to prove that the company has originally created and owned the particular creation or idea. It is therefore vital to maintain dated proof of creation. It can be done by an economical method of mailing the information to the same company address and retaining the postmarked sealed envelope and alternatively a copy of the same can be deposited with a source code escrow company that would maintain a dated copy of the information in storage.

While deciding upon the issue of registering or not the cost-benefit analysis should be made. The cost of registration vs the benefits accruing from getting a patent or exclusivity need to be carefully considered. Are the costs greater than the benefits? Does the investment on the trademark culminate into a brand giving the company a distinct asset value? While undergoing this process the following factors may be taken into account.

- The extent to which the information is known outside the business;
- The extent to which it is known by employees and others involved in the business;
- The extent of measures taken by the company to guard the secrecy of the information;
- The value of the information to the company and its competitors;
- The amount of efforts or money expended by the company in developing the information;
- The ease or difficulty with which the information could be acquired or duplicated by others.

As far as copyright protection is concerned, there is no copyright in ideas and hence copyright law cannot protect confidential information. Section 16 of the Copyright Act, 1957 ("the Copyright Act") states that nothing in the Copyright Act should be considered as restraining an action for breach of confidence or breach of trust. There is thus no copyright pre-emption of trade secret misappropriation claims.

- **Patents Act 1970** replaced the earlier act designed by the British but followed by India. The same has been amended by acts of 1999, 2002 and 2005 ordinance.
- **Trademark:** The Trade and Merchandise Marks Act, 1958. A new Trademarks Act, 1999 has been enacted superseding the earlier Trade and Merchandise Marks Act, 1958.
- **Copyright:** The Copyright Act, 1957 has been amended in 1983, 1984 and 1992, 1994 and 1999.

- **Layout Design of Integrated Circuits:** The Semiconductor Integrated Circuit Layout Design Act 2000. (Enforcement pending)
- **Protection of Undisclosed Information:** No exclusive legislation exists but the matter would be generally covered under the Contract Act, 1872.

In general Patents, designs, trademarks and geographical indications are administered by the Controller General of Patents Designs and Trademarks which is under the control of the Department of Industrial Policy and Promotion, Ministry of Commerce and Industry. Copyright falls under the charge of the Ministry of Human Resource Development.

Registering the ideas constitutes a high level of protection and if any one uses, sells or imports any work or invention that is granted protection under the intellectual property law it would amount to an infringement. However, specific types of copying of protected works do not fall under the definition of "infringements" since they are covered under the doctrine of fair use. The concept of fair use eliminates the need to obtain permission or pay royalties for purposes such as criticism, comments, news reporting, teaching and so on.

Towards Value Enhancement

Every business has its own peculiar characteristics. An individual approach and strategy for developing intellectual property rights is therefore necessary. A company may evaluate its potential intellectual property rights in two steps. The first step is to have a continuous interaction with the major departments of the Company like Research and Development division, Production, Marketing divisions etc., with a look out for possible intellectual property rights which can contribute to the 'IPR Portfolio' of a Company. The next step is to obtain legal advice for potentially viable Intellectual property rights. At this stage, it is also necessary to take into account Intellectual property rights of the competitors. It must be realized that Intellectual property rights are not separate, watertight compartments. A single product may be a product protected by a Patent, its design may be protected as an Industrial Design, its name may be protected as a Trademark etc. Similarly, apart from broad categories of intellectual property rights patents, trademarks, copyright, and industrial designs, there are also other collateral rights such as confidential information and know-how transfer transactions. It is thus necessary to have an integrated approach while evaluating potential intellectual property rights for creating an IPR portfolio.

Trademarks are being licensed or traded in India for crores of rupees. Trademark CIBACA was sold for Rs.200 crores. Another company in the business of manufacture of audio-visual systems and now in telecom business has total assets estimated at around Rs.500 crores. But the value of its trademark is said to be Rs.1100 crores. The Trademark 'Kwality' was sold territory-wise for crores of Rupees. Indian pharmaceutical companies are selling their patents for substantial amounts in international markets. The recent transaction of Sun Pharma agreeing to purchase three brands of an unlisted US company called Women's First Healthcare (WFHC) involving acquisition of three brands for a sum of $5.4 million, without condition of payment of royalty, is also a pointer in the direction that Indian industries are leading to. (Incidentally, the fact that brands were put up in a Bankruptcy proceeding by the concerned US company also indicates the strength of these brands to pay off some of the dues of the company—though such may not be the intention when the brands were developed first.)

Intellectual Property Rights in Global Business

The need to have an international system for securing IPRs internationally has been recognized since last two centuries. The main vehicle for developing IPRs on international level, are International Treaties. Where there is no treaty or where India has not acceded to such a treaty, protection of IPRs is rather cumbersome. The Paris Convention of 1883 for protection of intellectual property rights was the earliest measure for extending intellectual property rights on an international level. Countries to the Convention were said to form a 'Union', which would protect the intellectual property rights of member countries. The basic principle was the principle of reciprocal protection of intellectual property rights by the members of the Union. The General Agreement on Tariffs and Trade or GATT emerged in 1947. In the year 1980, multinational corporations and international agencies began to show their interest for including intellectual property rights under the umbrella of GATT. The Uruguay Round which ultimately led to the final treaty began in the year 1986. The discussions and deliberations continued to such an extent that GATT came to be nicknamed as 'General Agreement to Talk and Talk'. When concluded finally, it contained 28 agreements. TRIPS was one of the agreements of GATT.

The relevant treaties of Intellectual Property Rights are as follows:

1) **Copyright:** Berne Convention and Universal Copyright Convention or UCC.
2) **Trademarks:** Trademark Law Treaty 1994 and the Madrid Agreement concerning international registration of marks.
3) **Patents:** Patent Cooperation Treaty which makes filing of a single application for a patent on an international scale possible. Another relevant treaty is the Budapest Treaty of International Recognition of Deposits of Micro-organisms for the Purposes of Patent Procedure, 1977.
4) **For Industrial Designs,** the relevant agreement is the Locarno Agreement, establishing international classification for industrial designs 1968.
5) **Integrated Circuits:** Washington Treaty of intellectual property rights in respect of integrated circuits.

India is a signatory to the Copyright treaties i.e., Berne Convention and the Universal Copyright Convention. India is also a signatory to the Patents Cooperation Treaty. In case of other intellectual property rights, multiple registrations in other countries is necessary.

In case of Patents, more than 95 countries are signatory to the Patent Cooperation Treaty. Unlike in the past, single application for patents can be filed in India as an application under the Patent Cooperation Treaty. The applicant has a wide choice to designate the countries in which the applicant intends to secure patent. Considerable advantage of this treaty is that the date of filing patent application in India is applicable in all such countries in which the patent protection is to be secured. Another advantage is that feasibility and usefulness of the patent can be evaluated from the reports received in the procedural stages in a PCT application.

Intellectual property rights can be exploited by companies in two ways. Firstly, the Company itself can use them to its own advantage. Secondly, after building up the intellectual property rights a company may assign it as one complete module to a third party for a consideration. The considerations would be the expected revenue for such intellectual property rights. In the event it is to be retained by the company for itself, the cost of protecting such intellectual property rights nationally as well as internationally would be considered. If the projected costs and other considerations are out of proportion to the expected returns from intellectual property rights, it is better to assign or completely sell off such intellectual property rights. However, the most common method for exploiting an intellectual property right is by granting licenses. Licensing of intellectual property rights requires properly thought-out decisions on the part of the Company.

The IPR Portfolio of a company should be periodically evaluated. This has two advantages. Firstly, it gives a perspective of the intellectual property rights which is useful for deciding whether some of the intellectual property rights can be utilized better by selling off or by licensing.

Secondly, it helps in evolving plan of action for the Company. While evaluating the intellectual property rights it is necessary to summarize intellectual property rights portfolio and assign commercial significance to each intellectual property right. This is essential in the changing times when the value of the IPR would undergo remarkable changes too.

In cases of mergers and acquisitions, the intellectual property assets gain exceptional value as has been observed within the world of business. It can be especially difficult to accurately value such assets, most notably in the rapidly evolving high-tech industries. Understanding the factors that create value in intellectual property assets, and the part such assets play in both domestic and international mergers, is vitally important to anyone involved in the process of merger and acquisition.

The extent to which the price proposed to be paid for the relevant acquisition exceeds the value of net tangible assets should be adopted as a 'rule of thumb' for determining the importance of intellectual property to that transaction. The greater the disparity between the proposed price and the value of net tangible assets, the more likely intellectual property is to be important to the transaction, and therefore, the greater the reason to properly investigate the seller's intellectual property.

This 'rule of thumb' derives from examples such as the Volkswagen acquisition of Rolls Royce, where Volkswagen agreed to pay approximately US$790 million for the Rolls Royce business against a net tangible asset value of US$250 million for that business, but where among the significant intellectual property that was not acquired upon closing, was the 'Rolls Royce' trademark. In that case, use of the above 'rule of thumb' would have prompted an early warning to adopt greater rigor in checking the seller's entitlements to the 'Rolls Royce' trademark. Rights to the 'Rolls Royce' trademark were obtained subsequently, but at an additional cost.

As the global economy races towards information based economy, the value of intellectual property will continue to play an increasing role as the driving force behind future merger, acquisition, and other business activity. It is anticipated that intellectual property will be the dominant force in all future commercial transactions. Another reason could be buy-out of a strong brand from a financially weaker company to gain acceptance in a new space for the acquirer. The financial health of a company which can help absorb the cost of acquisition while looking for long-term benefits accruing from better products or intellectual property is another attractive aspect.

To conclude, intellectual Property rights have great potential to contribute to the assets of a company. In many industries, intellectual property rights constitute the backbone of a company. If Intellectual property rights are developed and protected with a national and global perspective, and with a well-defined IPR strategy, intellectual property rights would be a major gateway to corporate globalization.

(Bharti Thakar is a faculty member in ICFAI Business School, Ahmedabad.)

[Note: The content of this article is intended only to provide a general guide to the subject matter.]

References

1. Ganesan, A.V 1999, "The Implications of the Patents (Amendment) Ordinance 1999." New Delhi: Indian Council for Research on International Economic Relations.
2. IIFT 2003, "Article 39.3 of the Trips Agreement: Its genesis and the present Context", New Delhi: Indian Institute of Foreign Trade.
3. *http://www.patentoffice.nic.in/ipr/patent*
4. *http://dipp.nic.in/ipr.htm*
5. *http://www.laws4india.com/ipr.asp*
6. *http://www.freehills.com.au/publications*

2

Due Diligence in Business Transactions Involving Intellectual Property Assets

Edward Meilman and James Brady

The article explains about the due diligence that has to be observed during the acquisition and strategic utilization of intellectual property assets. Due diligence involves understanding the nature of the transaction as well as the companies from a strategic point of view. It has to be observed what type of asset (i.e., patent, trademark, copyright etc.) is involved in the transaction. The article also specifies the dos and don'ts for the team members conducting the due diligence study. It has also described the procedure of obtaining and reviewing information in detail.

The process of gathering information and assessing the merits, issues, and risks associated with a business transaction is called "due diligence". It is a critical exercise in the acquisition and strategic utilization of intellectual property assets. Due diligence is a necessary precursor to funding a new venture, and is critically important in many other business transactions, including mergers, acquisitions, licenses, initial public offerings, and in some instances litigation.

In recent years, the commercial importance of patents and other intellectual property has become highly visible. Courts have imposed large damage awards for intellectual property misuse and infringement. Multi-million dollar judgments are no longer a rarity. Courts have also granted significant injunctions to limit the products which a company can market. For instance, Kodak was virtually eliminated from the instant camera market and subject to an extremely high damage award when it was found to infringe patents owned by Polaroid. As a result of these potential events, and the increasing value of intellectual property assets in today's high technology society, intellectual property matters have become an important aspect of a traditional due diligence study.

Undertanding the Transaction – Identifying the Company's Short- and Long-Term Business Goals

"Due diligence" involves asking questions, interviewing people with knowledge about relevant matters, obtaining and reviewing relevant documents, and obtaining information from independent sources. Before this can be done effectively, it is essential to understand the nature of the potential transaction and the companies involved from both a business strategy and scientific technical point of view, including any time or cost constraints imposed on the information gathering process. Only by understanding the strategic business objectives of the client, can counsel direct due diligence efforts to identify those issues that may be material to the transaction, and work to resolve those issues in a manner that helps the client attain its business goals. Many times weaknesses in a company's intellectual property position can be remedied prior to completing the transaction if these weaknesses are identified by a due diligence counsel who is keenly aware of his or her client's short- and long-term business goals going into the transaction.

The nature of the transaction and the companies involved affect the amount of intellectual property's due diligence that is appropriate under the circumstances. For example, a start-up computer software company will typically require more emphasis on intellectual property than a manufacturer of a well-established commodity. Likewise, the importance of the different types of property (i.e., patent, trade secret, trademark or copyright) can vary widely depending on the nature of the business or industry. If the transaction concerns a publisher or a television news organization, a detailed investigation into its procedures for avoiding copyright infringement would be in order. On the other hand, companies that market consumer products typically require a close look into trademark and design patent issues. Companies in the chemical and pharmaceutical industries typically require an analysis of trade secret and know-how issues. In biotechnology, it is likely that patents will be a major valuable asset under review. The nature of the transaction, the companies involved and their business goals greatly affect the scope of a due diligence study and also the makeup of the team assembled to conduct the study.

Whether the transaction involves international aspects or only domestic aspects is another factor that must be considered. For instance, the United States is generally more liberal in protecting inventions involving living matter (biotechnology) and software (business methods) than many other countries. The diagnosis and treatment of human beings is not considered to be patentable in some countries. Licenses which are enforceable in the United States may need to be recorded to be similarly enforceable and protect the underlying intellectual property in other countries. For instance, use of a trademark by a licensed but unrecorded licensee can lead to the loss of the trademark right in some countries but not in other countries. In the EEC, one cannot prohibit a trademark licensee from challenging the validity of the licensed mark, while that is generally prohibited in the United States. While databases are generally not copyrightable in the United States, the EEC issued a Database Directive in 1996, and some European countries (e.g., Great Britain, France, and Germany) now have database copyright laws in place.

It is impossible to definitively set forth the parameters which will be applicable to every type of due diligence study. Check lists abound. However, no check list can be relied upon blindly without due consideration of the company's business goals and how they relate to the transaction at hand. Every transaction is different. For some due diligence studies, a particular check list will be overly broad or will be deficient; important information may be missed if such a check list is followed without the exercise of independent judgment based on the short- and long-term business objectives of the company going into the transaction. For some transactions, a particular check list may also be too detailed and strict adherence to it could potentially get in the way of consumating an otherwise viable and important transaction. While a sample due diligence check list is provided at the end of this article, it is important to keep these considerations in mind.

Although there is no definitive check list for all studies, intellectual property due diligence generally seeks to gather information to shed light on:

- What intellectual property assets does the company have, and are there any problems relating to ***ownership or control*** of those assets?
- What is the economic and strategic ***value*** of the target intellectual property? To what extent does it provide effective exclusivity in the market for the company's products or services. What are the potential licensing or other strategic uses of the intellectual property?
- Does the company have potential ***liability*** for infringing the intellectual property rights of others? Can it market its products or services without infringing the rights of others?

The ownership of intellectual property assets requires a clear chain of title from the inventor, author, or previous owner, and also the recordation of assignment documents in the appropriate public records. In many transactions, otherwise valuable intellectual property assets are weakened or lost by the lack of an assignment of all interests from all of the correct inventors, creators, or authors, or by the existence of liens or security interests that encumber the assets. These factors also can affect the ability of a company to control the intellectual property. For example, even if there is a very valuable copyright in existence, it may be a joint work where each author owns an undivided part of the property. A co-author who is not an employee or not under an obligation to assign ownership can then diminish the value of the copyright to the company by granting rights to another entity. In addition, contracts granting rights in intellectual property must be reviewed to identify geographic or other restrictions on a company's ability to use what it believes to be its portfolio of current or potential intellectual property assets.

The economic value of intellectual property depends on the type of intellectual property and its scope, including the extent to which it is limited in terms of geography, time, or potential contractual restrictions. The strategic value of the property depends on how well it fits with the company's business objectives and whether it can be effectively enforced against others in the industry. The business decision-maker can evaluate the strategic value after he or she is fully informed of the intellectual property's character, scope, validity, enforceability, and limitations. A due diligence study of intellectual property is designed to provide critical information based on the scientific and business purpose of the transaction so that the business decision-maker can make an informed decision about the potential transaction and, if possible, any weakness can be remedied in order to guide the transaction toward fulfillment of the client's ultimate business goals.

The scope of intellectual property involves widely different substantive issues depending on the type of property. The scope of a United States utility patent, for example, depends on its claims, which are the numbered sentences at the end of the patent document. The number of claims is much less important than the scope of the claims. A patent with a single claim may be more valuable that a patent with 20 claims. Generally speaking, the broader the claims, the broader the scope of the patent. However, breadth, standing alone, can be misleading. The most important aspect and what must be considered, is whether the claims of the patents provide a useful scope of protection, or whether they can be easily designed around. A patent with broad claims may prohibit competition by similar products, yet still not prevent competition by all alternative products. If alternative products can compete effectively with the patented technology without infringing the patents, then the patents might have relatively little value even though they cover a large area. It is important to verify a company's expectation that its patents cover particular products and also to confirm that alternatives are not readily available to compete with these products. In many due diligence studies, this part of the analysis also involves a determination as to the validity of key patent claims.

Patents observe national boundaries. The EEC has a system in which a single patent application is processed until it is allowed, and then individual patents having the same text are registered in individual countries. What is commonly called a "European Patent" is not a patent at all, but rather a publication of an allowed patent application. Similarly, what is sometimes referred to as an international patent, is also not a patent at all, but rather a published application filed under the Patent Convention Treaty (PCT) and which must then be filed as an application in each individual country or the EEC before it can be processed into a real patent which provides a measure of exclusivity to its owner. In addition to being nationally limited, the type of protection varies from country to country.

The value of a trademark depends on the strength of the mark, whether a registration has been obtained, and on a variety of other factors. Similar to patents, trademarks are essentially limited by national borders. In the United States, trademark rights can be acquired either by actual use or by seeking a registration, whereas in many countries the first entity to register the mark may have superior rights to the first user.

Copyrights, on the other hand, tend to transcend borders. A copyright created in, for instance, in Hong Kong can be valid in New York without any need for registration. However, some countries restrict the right to sue for enforcement of the copyright or limit the damages which can be recovered in the absence of a registration. Further, because of the way the statutory copyright law developed in the United States, the date of creation may affect whether or not the work needs a copyright notice when first published, whether the life of the copyright was divided into two segments and required a renewal application, and the extent to which licenses can be restricted. Additionally, a grant of exclusive rights in the United States must be in writing, although what constitutes a "writing" is liberally construed. In general, highly creative works may be given a broader copyright scope of protection than works that involve only a modest amount of creativity.

Trade secrets have become increasingly valuable to many companies, not only as a tool for achieving a competitive advantage, but also as a source of licensing income. It has been reported that IBM derived about two-thirds of its $1.7 billion licensing income in 2001 from licenses that involved trade secrets. A key element in protecting trade secrets is that the effort to maintain secrecy must rise to at least the level of "reasonable effort" under the circumstances (e.g., marking material confidential, providing physical barriers, providing reminders of secrecy, and conducting exit interviews of departing employees). The extent to which such efforts are in place can affect the value of the trade secrets.

The Due Diligence Team

The object of the due diligence not only affects the scope of the study but also the constitution of the team assembled to conduct the study. Due diligence is typically conducted by a team made up of management representatives, company research and development or other technical personnel, attorneys (both inside and outside), accountants, actuaries, and appraisers. Each contributes to the overall evaluation of the company or other assets or venture being considered. The team is frequently led by an experienced corporate manager or attorney. Attorneys with expertise in specific areas of the law, such as intellectual property or international taxation, are engaged as needed. Members of the team need to be able to interact with other members and draw on their expertise as required.

In general, overview discussions should include all team management members. Management's technical representatives and counsel should handle the intellectual property discussions, particularly if the due diligence involves complex patent or trade secret issues with specialized training and experience and requirements. It may even be appropriate for an independent third party to be retained to perform all or certain portions of the technical due diligence, such as determining whether a patented biotech process can repeatably achieve the desired goals or in vivo efficacy.

Inquiries of suppliers and customers should involve management or investment bankers, but contracts with third parties should be reviewed by counsel. Inspection of physical assets and facilities should be conducted by management and its technical staff, investment bankers or accountants, and where appropriate, counsel.

Examination of intangible assets such as patents and trademarks should be conducted by counsel and, for valuation issues, accountants. Review of regulatory approvals and licenses should be conducted by management and counsel.

Title searches, Uniform Commercial Code (UCC) filings of security interests and other liens, Patent and Trademark Office (PTO), and Copyright Office searches, should be conducted through counsel. Major contracts should be reviewed by counsel, although experts may be retained to examine certain types of agreements (e.g., government contracts counsel may be retained if government contracts are a key part of the assets or business).

Due Diligence Procedure – Obtaining and Reviewing the Information

In the context of a corporate acquisition, basic information about the target company needs to be obtained at an early stage. A great deal of such information is publicly available and can be obtained independently through various on-line services and database sources. For instance, in the case of a pharmaceutical company, reference to what is referred to in the trade as the "Orange Book", a Food and Drug Administration (FDA) publication, will identify a company's pharmaceutical products approved for marketing, the key patents which can be infringed by such marketing, and also certain competitive products, if any.

Based on the business goals and objectives of the transaction, additional information is requested directly from the company. In practice, a separate request relating to intellectual property matters is typical, but this may be combined with requests for information about other aspects of the company. It might also be appropriate to conduct initial interviews with appropriate corporate officers, in-house intellectual property counsel, key inventors, engineers, artists, advertising executives etc. In many cases, the individuals responsible for the company's core technology are important; such individuals should be identified and the arrangements with them explored. For instance, do they have employment contracts? have they assigned their rights to the company? have they departed and joined potential competitors? In some countries, inventors can have a right to receive compensation when a patent is assigned or licensed.

The key products, including detailed specifications, chemical formula, biological activity, pharmaceutical indications, manufacturing processes, etc., should be identified so that a determination can be made as to whether any existing third party patents or published patent applications cover these aspects of the company's key products. Any licenses covering an end product or its production, including any intermediates used, should be obtained and reviewed. If any specific or unique materials are necessary to the production process, such as plasmids, constructs, or cell lines in the biotechnology arena, their source and any contractual arrangements involving them must be examined. All supply agreements, research collaboration agreements, distribution agreements, and the like should be reviewed to make sure they are assignable and will survive the transaction, and also to determine whether they are dependent on third party rights.

Independent contractors, consultants, and grants can be a major source of potential conflicts. Outside companies or individuals may have been utilized in developing a product, the method by which it is produced, or obtaining regulatory approval where required. These companies and individuals are usually independent contractors. Likewise, consultants employed in connection with a project are also independent contractors. The arrangements with independent contractors must be reviewed to ensure that any intellectual property resulting from the work done, including clinical trials and consultations, vest in the company.

Disgruntled former employees can also be a source of conflicts. It can be useful to review any patents which have been granted to, or patent applications which have been filed by these individuals to ensure that none of these applications or patents is directed against the products of the company. When doing so, however, it is important to keep in mind that while most patent applications are now being published 18 months after they were filed, not all applications are subject to being published and, even when they are published, there is still at least an 18 month gap measured from the initial application filing date.

Where feasible, personal inspections by technical personnel should be conducted to reveal aspects of the facilities, products, and processes that were not previously fully known to the due diligence team. A plant visit might also reveal whether appropriate physical security precautions and safeguards are in place, which are factors that can affect the value and scope of trade secret protection.

A thorough independent investigation should be undertaken in connection with all key assets. For United States patent assets, not only should a title search be conducted, but also the actual assignment documents should be obtained and reviewed since they can contain special provisions not found in the published abstracts of what was recorded, and the appropriate state and local UCC records should be obtained and reviewed for recorded security interests. Likewise, title searches for registered US trademarks should be conducted both at the Patent and Trademark Office and in the appropriate UCC records; it is especially important to confirm that no mark was assigned apart from its good will. Information about United States copyright ownership and title issues can usually be obtained by searching in the US Copyright Office. However, indexing is based on the information provided by the submitting party and if two competing copyright claimants use different titles for the same work, the conflict may not be evident. For copyrights of special interest, it is therefore generally advisable to confirm that the copyrights were properly assigned from the author to the company, especially in work-for-hire and joint authorship situations.

Safeguarding Confidential Technical and Business Information

Before or concurrently with any information request, a suitable confidentiality agreement between the client and target companies should be in place. Sensitive commercial and technical information is likely to need to be disclosed between the companies and care must be exercised to maintain its confidentiality. The disclosing party will be concerned that the receiving party may improperly use the information if the transaction is not closed, and the receiving party may be concerned about the difficulty of proving independent development if the transaction is not closed. Further, competitors or potential competitors are often involved and this implicates the antitrust laws, namely the Sherman Act § 1 and § 2, the Clayton Act § 7, and the FTC Act § 5 in the United States, or the relevant provisions of EEC antitrust law (Articles 85 and 86 of the Treaty of Rome). This is illustrated by the fact that the United States Federal Trade Commission (FTC) challenged a merger involving Ciba-Geigy because it involved gene therapy technology, even though there was no present or immediate future product competition as no product had reach Phase II testing. The FTC asserted that the merger could lessen competition in the innovation market, and that it could result in a "killer portfolio", i.e., a bundle of patent rights, which would erect a substantial barrier to market entry by other competitors.

Access to competitive information is necessary in order to evaluate the likelihood of antitrust consequences. At the same time, appropriately restricting such access can avoid problems in the event that the transaction is not completed. To the extent practical, information can be compartmentalized and thus only specified members of the due diligence team allowed access to particular categories of information. In this way, the likelihood that such problems will arise is eliminated or at least minimized.

The importance of appropriately restricting access also arises in situations that implicate information which the law protects from disclosure to others under the attorney-client privilege doctrine. Thus, during preliminary or follow-up interviews, and in connection with requests for documents, consideration should be given as to whether to elicit responses that could potentially waive the company's attorney-client privilege.

The Attorney – Client Privilege Doctrine in Due Diligence

By definition, the attorney–client privilege applies to communications from a client where an attorney, acting as such, is gathering information from the client (without the presence of third parties) for the purpose of rendering legal advice or services or is rendering legal advice to the client. Disclosure of opinions of counsel, for example, could be deemed a waiver of the company's privilege with respect to the subject matter of those opinions. A waiver was found to have taken place in one case when the "parties took no steps to safeguard the privilege" and the prospective seller "sought commercial gain, not legal advantage, through disclosure of its lawyer's advice." In other cases the disclosure of information during arms length negotiations between joint venturers waived the privilege.

The definition of the attorney-client privilege (confidential communications between the client and attorney obtaining information for rendering legal advice or services or rendering such legal advice) provides guidance about how to proceed so as to maintain the privilege. It is recommended that the attorney has a written request for legal advice from the client, because this makes it easier to establish the existence of an attorney-client relationship. The presence of third parties during interviews can vitiate the privilege, and this fact will dictate the exclusion of some members of the due diligence team (members who are not the management control group of the client) from certain discussions and information gathering, if only to avoid raising a question about privilege relating to whether information was shared with anyone other than the attorney and the "client".

In the United States, sharing information between entities that have a community of interest is generally protected by the privilege. One court defined a community of interest as situations in which separate corporations "have identical legal interest with respect to the subject matter of a communication [and the] key consideration is that the nature of the interest be identical, and not similar, and be legal, not solely commercial."

Formation of a community of interest may be inferred from merger-acquisition negotiations. In one case, the disclosure of a patent opinion of a target company to a potential acquiring company was found not to have waived the privilege. Both companies involved in a due diligence situation have a legal interest in ensuring that there is clear title to the intellectual property involved, and avoiding infringement of the intellectual property of others. This understood common interest should, in most circumstances, be sufficient to maintain the privilege based on the community of interest between the companies. Nevertheless, it is best not to leave anything to inference. A court found in one case, there was no privilege because of a failure "to prove that the parties to [license] negotiations shared an identity of interests such as to invoke the common interest doctrine". It is therefore, prudent to include an appropriate "whereas" clause in the confidentiality agreement or in other preliminary communications between the companies so as to establish their community of interest. If the contemplated transaction is completed, the acquiring company may of course wish to assert the attorney-client privilege for itself, rather than causing a waiver of it in the course of evaluating the potential transaction.

In matters involving foreign inquiries, care must be taken to understand the scope and limitations of the privilege in other countries. United States courts may apply foreign law in accordance with conflict of law considerations; that foreign law may not provide for any attorney-client privilege. For instance, asking British counsel for information about on-going patent litigation would not likely to be privileged. British law provides that an inquiry is privileged if the inquiry is made after litigation is commenced or in contemplation of litigation, and also it privileged is for purpose of obtaining legal advice in the litigation or obtaining information and evidence for use in the litigation. Due diligence does not typically satisfy the latter requirement.

Conclusion

Before a "due diligence" study can be conducted effectively, it is essential to understand the nature of the potential transaction and the companies involved from both a business strategy and scientific technical point of view. Only by understanding the business objectives of the client can counsel direct due diligence efforts to identify those issues that may be material to the transaction, and work to resolve those issues in a manner that helps the client attain its business goals.

Due diligence seeks to determine existence, ownership and control of intellectual property assets, the economic and strategic value of the intellectual property, and the potential for liability for infringing the intellectual property rights of others. The economic value usually depends on the type of intellectual property and its scope, including limitations of geography, time, or potential contractual restrictions. The strategic value of the property depends on how well it fits with the business objectives and whether it can be effectively enforced against others in the industry.

It is important that counsel conducting intellectual property due diligence, complete not only a thorough investigation, but also one that is guided by an understanding of the client's business goals and a sensitivity to the confidential and privileged nature of the information involved. Conducting due diligence as outlined in this article will maximize the likelihood that material issues will be identified and, if possible, remedied before closing the transaction, a time when such issues are typically most easily remedied. Due diligence as outlined here will also minimize the possibility that the investigation might unduly interfere with consumating an otherwise viable transaction or cause problems based on a lack of sufficient planning regarding the disclosure of privileged and confidential information.

Suitable arrangements as to confidentiality should be made, but even so, some disclosures should be compartmentalized among the team members and limited in order to avoid breaches of confidentiality and waiver of any attorney-client privilege that would otherwise exist. We recommend the due diligence team use the following checklist, modified to fit the transaction under consideration, as a guide to the inquiries to be made.

Checklist

Patents

- Obtain technical description of products, including formulations and manufacturing processes. Review FDA filings.
- Assess the company's procedures for identifying patentable inventions and designs, and for ensuring applications are timely filed. Determine whether the procedures are followed and are appropriate and effective under the circumstances.
- Obtain a complete list of the company's US, international, and foreign patents and patent applications, both utility and design.

- Obtain confirmation that the company has recorded assignments (where applicable) for all US and foreign patents and patent applications.
- Determine whether the company has assigned or granted security interests against any patents or patent applications.
- Obtain patent maintenance and annuity fee records. Obtain confirmation from independent sources. Identify patents that are expired and/or no longer enforceable.
- For patents of special interest, request all prior art in company's files. Determine whether there are any validity issues that would justify further investigation.
- Obtain any correspondence from the company accusing others of infringing its patents and/or offering licenses under the company's patents. Consider whether any matters justify further negotiations and/or litigation.
- Identify any actual or threatened litigation/claims against the company, such as cease and desist letters. Identify all license offers made to the company. Assess the merits of all such allegations against the company. Identify the current status of any ongoing proceedings or negotiations. Obtain copies of settlement agreements and releases.
- Identify and review all license agreements, covenants not to sue, and indemnification agreements.
- Review the results of patentability and right-to-use searches conducted or commissioned by the company. Consider whether to request corresponding legal opinions, keeping in mind that disclosure of such opinions may potentially waive the attorney-client privilege.
- Review all records of audits conducted by or against the company pursuant to any type of intellectual property license agreements and/or research and development agreements.
- For US patents of special interest, obtain assignment records from PTO and conduct UCC searches. Engage foreign counsel to confirm ownership and clear title to foreign patents of special interest.
- Search for patents and patent applications in the names of key personnel, consultants, and principal clinical trial investigators to ensure that they were assigned or licensed to the company.
- For patents of special interest, where further investigation is justified, obtain prosecution histories from PTO (engage the assistance of foreign counsel for foreign patents).
- Check employee, consultant, clinical trial investigator, and officer agreements to confirm obligations to assign US and foreign rights.
- Conduct freedom-to-operate searches for company's products and processes, including contemplated future products and process. Assess the results of the searches.

Trademarks

- Review all products, marketing, promotional, and packaging materials of the company to determine trademark usage.
- Obtain copies of all US and foreign trademark registrations and registration applications.
- Identify all assertions of trademark infringement, trade dress infringement, dilution, or unfair competition made by or against the company.
- Determine whether any trademarks have been recorded by the US Customs Service by or against the company.
- Obtain records of any US opposition or cancellation proceedings and equivalent foreign proceedings.
- Review all material trademark renewal records.
- Obtain results of trademark searches conducted by the company.
- Confirm ownership and clear title to company trademarks, trade names, and domain names. Conduct independent title searches at PTO and in appropriate UCC records.
- Identify and resolve any potential domain name disputes.
- Review assignments, licenses, covenants not to sue, and security documents, where appropriate.
- Identify any marks of the company that may have been abandoned.
- Identify procedures employed by the company for quality control monitoring of licensee use of trademarks.
- Conduct independent searches for trademarks of special interest.

Copyrights

- Identify all copyrights of interest.
- Review all material work-for-hire agreements and consultant contracts.
- Evaluate the company's policy for identifying and protecting its own copyrights.
- Evaluate the company's policy for avoiding infringement and obtaining copyright clearance to protect against infringement claims.
- Identify all assertions of copyright infringement by or against the company.
- Review all copyright assignments, licenses, and other transfers. Review records at US Copyright Office for copyrights of special interest.
- For all transfers of material copyrights, determine which individual aspects of the copyright were transferred.

- Check employee, consultant and officer agreements for acknowledgement of employee status for copyright purposes, etc.
- Identify any moral rights issues, particularly with respect to foreign operations.
- Identify all relevant recordations of copyrights by US Customs Service.
- Assess adequacy of licenses for all software loaded on the company's computers.

Trade Secrets

- Obtain list of material trade secrets.
- Determine whether appropriate confidentiality and non-compete agreements are in place, especially with respect to key personnel.
- Evaluate adequacy of hiring and exit interviews procedures. Review records for key personnel.
- Evaluate secrecy policies, including physical security, employed by the company.
- Evaluate security policies for computer software and electronic data.
- Consider the impact of recent arrivals or departures of key personnel.
- Review know-how licenses and other technical assistance agreements, indemnification agreements, and confidentiality agreements.

Miscellaneous

- Consider any potential improper anti-competitive effect or antitrust scrutiny under the circumstances.
- Review press, SEC, and annual reports.
- Determine whether key technologies and other intellectual property rights have been transferred or licensed to one or more government agencies, e.g., via US government purpose rights provisions.
- Consider applicability of other types of intellectual property, including semiconductor chip protection, right of publicity, plant patents, domain name registrations, etc.
- Assess adequacy of insurance coverage against intellectual property infringement claims.
- Consider the character of key licensed rights with respect to, e.g., exclusivity, field of use restrictions, geographic restrictions, and royalty rate structures, etc.
- Consider appropriate language for public announcements relating to the transaction.

(Edward Meilman is a partner in the Intellectual Property Practice of the Firm's Technology Group in New York City. He graduated with an AB degree in chemistry from the University College of Arts and Science, New York University and with a J.D. degree from New York University School of Law. He focuses his practice on intellectual property as it pertains to patents, trademarks, copyrights, and unfair competition. In the area of patent procurement, he concentrates primarily on chemical, pharmaceutical, and biotechnology matters, but in the areas of litigation, counseling, licensing, and acquisition of rights, he handles matters pertaining to all technologies. Practice Areas: Intellectual Property, Technology Group; procurement, litigation, counseling.

James Brady is a partner in the Intellectual Property Practice of the Firm's Technology Group in Washington, DC. He has a B.S. degree in environmental engineering, with highest distinction, from The Pennsylvania State University, and a J.D. degree from Cornell Law School. James Brady is a Member of the Board of Directors of the Federal Circuit Bar Association, serves on the Continuing Legal Education (CLE) Committee of the Bar Association, and has been responsible for the Bar Association's CLE programs for many years. He focuses his practice on intellectual property law with an emphasis on patent opinions and client counseling, patent procurement, and IP litigation and business transactions. James Brady's technical area of specialization is life sciences, including pharmaceuticals, and all aspects of biotechnology and chemical inventions. Practice areas: Intellectual Property, Technology Group; procurement, litigation, counseling).

3

Practical and Legal Protection of Computer Databases

Ashok Ram Kumar

Computer software is covered under copyrights, a class of intellectual property rights. The advent of information technology has resulted in the developing of new software. The computer program, software is protected as a literary work under the copyrights. The protection of software can be made with the help of "seeds" and "signatures" inserted in the database. The database is a collection of information stored in any device like hard disk drives, diskettes, tapes, CD-ROMs, etc., which can be retrieved and used at any particular point of time. Database is a property of the creator and requires protection under the copyright law. However, the protection of database has other relevant issues like public knowledge, prior use, compilation of information, etc., which requires special attention. This article discusses various attributes of database managements and the legal protection.

In India, the legalities of Computer Software are often poorly understood by the programmers, authors and also the Software Industry. Indian Software Industry, being one of the top-most foreign exchange earners for this country

Source: ICFAI Journal of Intellectual Property Rights, August 2004.

needs to take a close look and safeguard its market and intellect of its many programmers since computer database is a new type of intellectual property of growing importance in today's world. The Indian Software Industry has to change its orientation and stress the protection of intellectual property and only by doing so there is very good scope of original product development.

In this article, I wish to discuss and acquaint you with both the practical and legal methods of protecting computer database from unauthorized copying and use. While Copyright protection is the central topic here, I would also wish to discuss and touch upon the areas of trade secrecy and non-disclosure.

In view of the tremendous opportunities and advantages of cybernetics and phenomenal growth of computer software, Internet, mobile technologies, digital instrumentation, there have arisen serious judicial concerns of techno-legal dimension more specifically in the arena of Intellectual Property Rights (IPR) regime. The Net with the convenience of world wide web (WWW), mass reeling of Hyper Text Transfer Protocol (HTTP) and Hyper Text Marking Language (HTML), has become the most efficient distribution mechanism. While the issue of computer software piracy and copyright violations is itself not a new one, the onset of the digital environment has become the death knell for copyright law, as the jurisprudential foundations and ideological mooring of the copyright, information technology and cyber laws are juxtaposed to each other in many respects. These juxtapositions, if not seriously addressed to by the Lawmakers and the Judiciary may ultimately prove the various IPR and Cyber law enactments an exercise in futility.

Copyright is a unique kind of intellectual property, the importance of which is increasing day by day. It does not fall in the area of Industrial Property. For enjoying Copyright protection the work must be an original creation. Copyright was not regarded as being of much relevance to the sale of products other than traditionally "artistic" products such as books, music compositions, artistic works, literary works, pantomimes, motion pictures and gramophone records. Copyright still remains the principal means of preventing others from copying or selling software as well as literary, dramatic, musical or artistic works. The foremost purpose of copyright law is to foster the growth of learning and culture and the dissemination of information and is meant to induce the creation of as many works of art, literature, music and works of authorship (including software) as possible. Copyright law gives authors limited property rights in their works, but only for the ultimate purpose of benefiting the public by encouraging the creation of more works. The purpose of copyright is not to protect the author, but it is to benefit the public. The balance in copyright law is drawn by limiting property rights to the author's particular method of expressing an idea. Copyright never protects the idea, but instead only protects the expression of the idea. But once the idea has been expressed in tangible form, the copyright protection exists for words, literary work, musical works in which it is encompassed.

Copyrights and Computer Programs

Today, however, in addition to the above mentioned traditional areas, copyright has become an extremely important weapon in preventing piracy of computer software and preventing copying of various useful items to which "art" has been applied. The protection for software has traditionally been restricted to copyrights. Software can only be copyrighted as a literary work.

Copyright infringement is fairly easy to get away with since it can always be claimed that the source codes, algorithms etc., could be used for different implementations. Hence the need for inserting moles of special identities in the software called as "seeds" and "signatures" by the author. The intentional use of "seeds" and "signatures" in a database, when combined with the three main vehicles of legal protection: Copyright, trade secrets and contract can create a powerful defense against the "computer pirate".

For the Indian Industry, low value-added body shopping and data processing constitute the bulk of the software exports. There are a handful of software companies in India who seriously pursue and secure copyright protection for their software. Out of the rest, some are even unaware that their works could be secured by going in for copyrights and the balance does not seriously pursue the process. There is also one school of thought which simply states that it is not worthwhile pursuing a copyright since enforcing and suing for infringement and damages is a long and cumbersome legal process.

Globally, very few of the large companies hold a virtual monopoly on operating systems and no one in the industry is really putting up much of a fight against the one or two software giants who hold monopoly and who are making millions. The only reason being that these one or two companies have done a phenomenal job protecting themselves and their software products by effectively using the different intellectual property protections available for computer programs, including trade secrets, copyrights and patents.

Indian Copyright Law

The earliest Copyright statute in India could be traced back to the 1847 Act, which was enacted during the East Indian Company's regime. Not much of information is available about how the Copyright Act operated till 1911. In 1911, Britain codified the Copyright Act of 1911 and made applicable to India. Then in 1914, the Indian Copyright Act, was enacted, which was a modified version of the 1911 Act. The First Act after independence is the Copyright Act of 1957, which took into consideration, the new developments and technological advances and introduced a number of changes and new provisions. The Act was further amended in 1983, 1984, 1994 and 1999. The amendment of 1994 brought computer programs within the ambit of the Act. The further amendment in 1999, apart from others, saw the amended definition of the literary works and meaning of Copyright in respect of computer programs.

What is a Computer Database?

To start with "What exactly is a computer database?" Essentially, Computer database, is a collection of information stored in hard disk drives, diskettes, tape drives, CD-ROMs etc., so that it can be selectively searched and the desired information retrieved using a computer. All computer databases could be a program used by the Computer to run certain applications (like the word processor), or data entered by a person in the computer for purpose of record and reuse, or an image file etc. As society moves further into the informational age the significance and volume of database products is on the increase. Since this is a relatively new type of property, there is a need to rapidly evolve and create new standards and legal principles to try and protect against its misuse, theft, unauthorized copying and use.

Databases have long existed in manual or book form. For example, the Telephone book or directory and many reference books, our own legal reporters which can be termed as Manual databases. The computer database is essentially an information compendium like a phone book, which has been placed in a computer and automated. When information is computerised, however, there are many more ways for the information to be accessed, manipulated and used; the value of the database to users is thereby greatly enhanced. Some popular examples of computer databases include legal databases such as Lexis, Juris, Westlaw etc., and various business and scientific databases such as those found on Dialog and Internet.

An automated database is, "a body of facts, data, or other information assembled into an organized format suitable for use in a computer and comprising one or more files." The Indian statutes are yet to specifically list automated databases as a copyrightable subject matter. For the purpose of copyrights, a computer database can be defined also as a "compilation" which means data formed by the collection and assembling or pre-existing materials or of data that are selected, co-ordinated or arranged in such a way that the resulting work as a whole constitutes an original work of authorship. Examples of compilation include periodical, anthology and encyclopedia, or a reference work such as a directory, index, map, telephone book, guide book, law reporter, catalog, chart, or racing guide.

Why a Database can be Hard to Protect Legally

Under traditional concepts of literary copyright, the data contained in a compilation, and the selection of the data, may not sometimes be protected from copying. Only the coordination and arrangement of the database may be protected, and even then there must be some originality to the collection and arrangement, for it to be protected. When a database is composed of facts, these facts frequently cannot be copyrighted, for otherwise, the public's right to use information in the public domain would be unreasonably limited.

The basic problem in protecting a database is that the information compiled is frequently public knowledge, understandably so, since the user has to know how to use the database. Just facts, or the data is otherwise not susceptible of ownership by the compiler of the database. For example, a person could call every lawyer or solicitor in the country and ask if they are specialized in computer law. The names and addresses of those who said yes could then be put into a database of computer lawyers. The question is "Does the person preparing this database own the names and addresses of these Lawyers or Solicitors?" Understandably, this would be denied by the concerned lawyers or solicitors. Then what does the person preparing this database own? How can he prevent another from copying and selling as his own? The way the information about lawyers or solicitors is arranged in the database might involve little or no originality and, hence this aspect of the database might not fall under the caption "copyright" and hence cannot be sought to be protected.

Since the names and addresses of the advocates or solicitors are not susceptible to ownership, a competitor certainly could call up all of the attorneys in the country and, assuming he got the same answers, come up with the same list. This would unquestionably be fair competition, and the first person who thought of the idea of compiling a list of computer advocates or solicitors would not be able to stop the competitor from coming out with compilation of list of advocates or solicitors specializing in Computer law.

There are, essentially, three ways to legally protect computer databases: Copyright, trade secret and contract. Ideally, all three of these legal means can be employed, along with practical non-legal methods, to provide the maximum protection against the piracy of the database program. There are, of course, other legal theories propounded in the US, such as unfair competition and conversion; however, these theories may be pre-empted by copyright law. Indian Copyright law provides the framework and basic foundation for legal protection by securing for limited time to the authors and inventors the exclusive rights in their respective writings and discoveries.

Copyright Law

Copyright protects the expression of idea and not the idea itself. Originality requires the author of the specific work to contribute something more than a "merely trivial" variation, which is recognizably "his own". The traditional copyright doctrine envisages, that a work must show some "creativity" in order to meet the originality test, and it is not subject to copyright if the work merely copies an existing work. The work should evolve from the intellect of the author and shall not be altered or edited repetition of any other existing work. This essential element of "creativity" is weak or completely absent in many manual reference works or computer databases. For example, what creativity is there in an alphabetical listing of names in a phone book?

Another basic problem in protecting a database is that copyright law does not prohibit the copying of facts, even newly discovered or expensively acquired facts, nor does it prohibit the copying of ideas. Copyright law can only provide protection to the arrangement and coordination of facts in a database. Even then, there must be some originality to the collection and arrangement for it to be protected.

Typically, the preparation of a database requires a significant expenditure of time, effort and money to cull and select information from many different sources, but little or no original creativity to express the facts, or arrange them. In these circumstances, where the compiler gathers and compiles raw facts, he did not create the facts, he just discovered or uncovered them, sometimes at great expense and trouble. Such was the case in our earlier example of the poor investigator who had to call every advocate or solicitor in the country to see if they practised computer law. So, how can you prevent copying of the work?

In order to lend copyright protection to merely factual databases, we have to look to the decisions pronounced by American Courts. They moved away from a strict application of the creativity test, and employed the test of "industriousness" or "sweat of the brow". This was attempted in order to test and determine if the database is an "originality" from the "labor and expense" necessary to make the compilation, rather than from any real "creativity" of the author.

Under the sweat of the brow doctrine, copyright could prevent the unauthorized copying of facts in a database, if the compiler could show that sufficient effort went into the acquisition and selection of the data to make it original. The protection would lie even if the information compiled was public knowledge or otherwise not protected.

The decisions of the American Courts and the above doctrine have to be critically analyzed in the Indian legal perspective before any reference is made or guidance taken from.

Apart from Indian Copyright Law, more than meeting the WTO requirements, it still has weak enforcement, and with the other problems inherent in copyright protection of a database, contract and trade secret law become all the more important to try and prevent the unauthorized copying of factual data in a database.

Trade Secrecy Protection

Secrecy in the software Industry is judged in light of the industry's level of general knowledge, the information's ascertainability, and the offensiveness of the misappropriator's conduct. Secrecy can be destroyed by insufficient precautions, by the marketing of a product that reveals the secret, or by disclosure in judicial proceedings or to government agencies.

Trade secret had long been the favorite protection by the software industry. Trade secrets extend to virtually any concrete information, including formulae, data compilations, programs, devices, processes, and customer lists. Thus, trade secret can protect software against the unauthorized use or disclosure by anyone who obtains it through improper means or through a confidential relationship. Secrecy can be divided into two parts: 1) Prevention of disclosure to external competitors, and 2) imposition of confidentiality on one's employees. Most of the software is protected, at least to some extent, by trade secrets. Adding trade secrecy protection to a database can provide significantly greater legal rights. Unfortunately, the Indian Legal system has not seen much development in this sphere of law. Much needs to be done by the Government and the Judiciary in this field of law.

Following are the facts to consider in determining whether a particular information is a trade secret or not:

- The extent to which the subject information is known outside of the business;
- The extent to which it is known to the employees and others involved in the business;
- The extent of measure taken to guard the secrecy of the subject information;

- The amount of money, time, efforts spent by the Company to develop the said information;
- The value of the subject information to the company and to the competitors; and
- The ease or difficulty at which the subject information could be acquired or duplicated by others.

To obtain the trade secret status two important requirements are to be met:

- The subject information provides a commercial advantage; and
- The information is a secret.

Trade secret protection is a viable and useful tool in protecting software because its protection is immediate and can be perpetual. Indian software companies should use this protection to keep their former employees from stealing the work product that rightfully belongs to the Company. Additionally, trade secret protection can protect the Company against stealing of part(s) of the code in violation of an express agreement.

Essentially, a trade secret is knowledge which a person or company acquires through its own efforts and which has some value to it. Typically, this knowledge is kept secret from competitors because it is felt that this information provides some type of competitive advantage. Trade secret information includes information, regarding a formula, pattern, compilation, program, device, method, technique or process. The information should derive independent economic value, actual or potential, not being generally known to, not being readily ascertainable by proper means by other persons who can obtain economic value from its disclosure or use; and is the subject of effort that reasonably warrants under the circumstances to maintain its secrecy.

Since a computer database is a compilation, which derives economic value, it is a type of intellectual property, which has to receive trade secrecy protection. The common legal device for implementing the principle of trade secret is the non-disclosure and secrecy agreement. It is a common practice with the Indian companies to take a declaration or enter into a non-disclosure and secrecy agreement with its employees. Once having signed this, the employee is obliged to keep as a secret the knowledge gained from his former employment in any future employment, more so with a competitor.

Protection by Contract

A seller of the database can require that any purchaser enter into a written contract as a condition of purchase of the database. Using our example, the surveyor of the computer lawyer database could refuse to sell this information to anyone unless they first sign a written contract. That written agreement could expressly provide that the purchaser will not disclose the list of computer lawyers to anyone but authorized users, nor make any copies or unauthorized use of the information. Typically, this takes the form of a License Agreement between the preparer/licensor of the database and the user/license of the database.

A License Agreement is unlike a typical purchase and sale agreement in that ownership of the product involved, the program, remains with the licensor. The licensee merely purchases the right to use the program. The licensee's right to use the program can be limited in any number of ways. The most important limitations typically are that licensee can only use the program on one or a select number of computers, the licensee may not make any copies of the program, and the licensee has to keep confidential certain information about the program or the database. Many other types of limitations or rights and reservations can be contained within the license agreement between the parties.

Practical Means of Protection

Since the law and Courts in general are struggling to keep up with the rapid changes in technology, the author of a database is well advised to try and strengthen his legal hand as much as possible with certain practical protection measures. There are methods, which a programmer can employ to try and prevent someone from simply copying his work, or if they do, to make proof of this copying in Court far easier. Without the conscious employment of these methods it may be difficult to know whether or not a competitor has "cheated", or simply copied your information, or has come up with the same information as his own.

The solution to this problem is the deliberate placement of errors or omissions in your database. If your competitor's database contains the same errors or omissions, then you have pretty good evidence that your database was copied. The odds are astronomical against a second database happening to come up with the same errors and omissions as the first.

Although a clever "pirate" might detect and eliminate or correct some seeds in a salted database, if the database is large enough and the original compiler/salter author is clever enough, it is unlikely that a pirate will ever catch them all. These seeds will provide the best evidence of copying. They will bloom at the time the pirate is sued and this evidence is placed before the Judge deciding the case.

Even if you do not deliberately salt your database, errors will occur naturally anyway if the database is large enough. So in addition to deliberately adding some harmless errors, when and if accidental errors are discovered, they should also be carefully documented or recorded. When subsequent revised additions of the database are made, not all errors should be corrected. There should always be subtle and harmless errors that are well documented in order to have the seeds necessary to protect a database.

In computer databases, however, there is an additional element, which can be used to prove copying which I refer to as a computer "signature". This signature pertains to the computer code or programming itself used to record the information and the program which manipulates the information. These signatures can be identified by the author as they depict his style of programming. This can be comparable to the style of writing. A programmer has also the opportunity to deliberately implant hidden but recognizable signatures in his work. These deliberate idiosyncrasies can be documented and can again provide excellent proof that there has been a wholesale copying of the program data.

Some database products consist only of the database itself and the user displays this database as his own program. For instance, the names and addresses of computer lawyers could be typed in an MS Word file. The purchasers of a database would thus have to use their own MS Word program in order to view the information. In other types of database programs, the information is sold along with a program which allows you to view and manipulate the data. In this case it is a "stand alone" program which does not require another program to view it. So, instead of having to load a host of the lawyers' names and addresses into

MS Word, under such a standalone program you would simply run the program and it would display the names and addresses by itself.

When the database program is a standalone type with its own display and manipulation capabilities, then there are far more opportunities to place signatures in the programming itself. Further, the copy protection strategy that is applicable to all types of software can apply.

Also, standard non-copying protection can be imposed upon the program itself. This makes it difficult for most users to ever make a copy of the program. Still, as every computer buff knows, for every good copy protection scheme there is another good "unprotection" scheme. In other words, a skilled programmer can find a way around such practical copy protection schemes. The ability of one programmer to rise to the technical competence of another, and frustrate such practical protection schemes, makes legal protection all the more important.

Conclusion

Although copyright protection is important and should almost always be pursued, in any license of a computer database of significant value, copyright protection alone should not be relied upon to prohibit unauthorized copying. Trade secrecy protection and an express written agreement between the vendor and consumer are necessary to try and protect the database. If, as expected, information continues to grow in value and importance as a commodity in our society, then the proliferation of license and secrecy agreements is likely. To make or buy technology, the country needs a strong system of IPR Protection, be it Copyrights, Patents or Trademarks. If we need to stand on par with the developed nations in the world market for knowledge, we need to protect ourselves and this is the only way of converting knowledge into wealth.

(Ashok Ram Kumar is a practicing lawyer in the field of Intellectual Property and Information Technology. He can be contacted at ashokramkumar@yahoo.com).

4

Reforms in US Patent Law: Business Implications

D Gayatri and T Phani Madhav

With the number of patent applications increasing exponentially the USPTO (US Patents and Trademarks Office) found it increasingly difficult to cope with the workload. This resulted in a situation where many patents were awarded to vague ideas without scrupulous review. There were many instances where the approved patents stifled innovation, but subsequently, these have also encouraged further innovation. The patents were used more like a weapon against competition. Many were apprehensive about the suitability of the patent system of the industrial age to the information age and suggested revamping not just the patent system, but also the entire system of intellectual property law. The case provides scope for discussing the conditions that led to the troubles for USPTO, the relevance of business method patents and the viability of patent law in protecting innovators in the information age. This case also helps in analysing the potential benefits that the reforms could bring to the US economy, which drives a considerable part of worldwide industrial growth.

"The patent system added the fuel of interest to the fire of genius."

– Abraham Lincoln,
16th President of United States.

"I think the beauty of the patent law is, it encourages innovation, because it says, look, we challenge you to come up with a better way." [1]

– Heidi Messer,
President, LinkShare.

"The country needs to revamp not just the patent system, but the entire system of intellectual property law. It needs to redefine it for an era that is the information age as compared to the industrial age." [2]

– Andrew S Grove,
Chairman, Intel Corp.

Introduction

During the biotechnology boom of the 1980s and the IT boom of the 1990s, the US Patents and Trademarks Office (USPTO) was overwhelmed with patent applications. The increase in the number of applications for patents resulted in mounting work pressure on the USPTO. As a result, the patent office was reported to have awarded many obscure patents for business methods, vague ideas and computer programs, which had begun to ridicule the competence of the office.[3] Some of the applications were left pending for approval at the office, while others were approved without careful review in order to clear off the backlog that had accumulated.

Business method patents awarded specifically in the case of *Amazon.com*'s One Click system and *Priceline.com*'s reverse auctions had raised alarm against the viability of the US Patent Law and business method patents.[4] Some felt that by patenting business methods and computer codes, further improvements in the field were being hindered. It seemed that the same patent law, which had for long nurtured innovations that had begun to stifle research, leading to concentration of economic power. Lawsuits against patent infringement had also increased over the past few years. While the Federal Trade Commission along with Department of Justice and National Academy of Sciences had recommended reforms for the USPTO, business representatives, economists as well as analysts expressed mixed opinions.

US Patent Law – Background

The Congress as well as the Constitution had been promoting science and arts, giving a temporary protection to the writings, discoveries and inventions through the US Patent Law. Patents encouraged research and development in industries and led to more innovations. The industrial age has witnessed some significant benefits of patents. In the 19th century during the technological boom, nearly 4,40,000 patents were issued between 1860 and 1890. Then in the early 1990s to the late 1990s, the number of patents issued increased steadily. The patents were awarded in various fields from basic industries to ornamental designs and genetically engineered seedlings.

It was only after the 1990s that the business methods began to be considered a subject matter of a patent, as part of sequence of other amendments that had happened in the past (Annexure I). Till then only physical processes in the area of chemical engineering, electrical and mechanical inventions were awarded patents.[5] After the Supreme Court's ruling in favour of the patent applicant in the *Signature Vs State Street Bank*, patenting business methods, or the way of doing business had become an accepted norm for the USPTO.[6] The court ruled that business methods could be patented as long as the end results are unique. A similar rule was passed for software, which until then was considered a mathematical algorithm and ineligible for patent. Calling this change a disaster, a Harvard Law Professor had once remarked, "This is a major change that occurred without anybody thinking through the consequences. In my view, it is the single great threat to innovation in cyberspace, and I'm extremely skeptical that anybody's going to get it in time."[7]

Since 1998, there had been many changes in the US Patent Law.[8] Patents are, by definition, temporary granted monopolies, awarded for 20 years to companies or individuals on some invention so that others are encouraged to improve upon the inventions further. Patents reward inventors who publish their work instead of keeping it a trade secret. As the Law goes, anything that is 'novel, useful and non-obvious' is considered to be eligible for a patent.[9] Instead of defining innovation, which is a future event, and whose benefits would not be visible until some time, the law defined anything that was not an innovation. 'Prior art' the method unique to US Patent Law, uses a database of patent applications already approved, and printed material in journals on past inventions to either approve or reject the patent applied.[10] The Patent Law was still broadened after a patent was approved for a human-made, genetically engineered bacteria. It declared that 'anything under the sun that is made by man' is patentable. Apart from these changes in the law, the following other changes that had occurred in the past led to a lenient patent system making patent approvals easy. The 12 regional courts that dealt with the appeals were replaced by a single specialised court. Again in the early 1990s, the patents office was made a service agency, which collected fees from the clients to cover its operating costs. Earlier, tax payers used to bear the costs.

In the last decade, some of the very abstract ideas had received patents under the US Patent Law. Beerbrella, an umbrella that protects beverages from sunlight was one of them (Annexure II). Similar was a patent awarded to a five year old boy on the way of swinging horizontally on a swing. An examiner who worked in the patent office wished to show his son how the office works and managed to get a patent for him. Other such patents were the sealed peanut butter crustless sandwich, 12-foot long TV remote controls, diapers for pet birds, a method of executing a tennis stroke while wearing a kneepad, etc. These patents began to raise alarms among the patent law professors and analysts.

Meanwhile with the IT boom, came the explosion of patent applications sent for approvals to the USPTO. Initially, lack of 'Prior art' in such emerging high technologies stood as a major impediment for patent review and approval. When Barnes&Noble faced a lawsuit from *Amazon.com* for infringing the patent of 'One-click system', the US Patent Law was questioned for its practicality. Some argued that the law has become obsolete, as the new technologies demanded more standards (Exhibit I).

Moreover, with the absence of such proofs, patent applications for software programs were made vague and complicated thus making it unquestionable even in court.

Patents, considered as a tool for gaining competitive advantage, had in recent times become a tool against competition. FTC[11] Commissioner, Mozelle Thomson remarked that the monopoly awarded by patents was being used in an anti-competitive way, preventing products from reaching the market and preventing people from sharing ideas.[12] Companies began to use patents to stifle competition. After Microsoft had to pay $30 million for a patent infringement suit, Bill Gates embarked on a patent drive as a solution. Microsoft asked its employees to patent as much as they could.

Once, IBM filed a lawsuit against Sun Microsystems claiming that it was infringing seven of its patents. When Sun Microsystems denied it, IBM claimed that with around 10,000 patents in its hand, there might be some overlaps, and forced Sun to pay $20 million and close the case. Patents became a tool for making cash. In a similar case, British Telecom Group claimed that it had patents for the most basic technology on Internet, hyperlinks. Though it was later ruled out in the court, SBC communications-Prodigy had to bear the heavy costs of lawsuits. Analysts felt that by awarding such obvious and broad patents also called the 'kitchen-sink patents', further innovation would be impeded. The number of patent approvals had increased; USPTO granted six million patents by 1999, since its inception. While the number of patents issued was increasing in number, the quality seemed to have largely suffered.

IBM's patent on 'system and method for providing reservation for restroom use', which was filed in 2000 was withdrawn after it faced a petition. While IBM could not give concrete reasons for the withdrawal, it announced that it was dedicating the patent to the public and would concentrate on higher quality patents. The patent protected the restroom reservation system, a computer program that assigns a number to each passenger on a first come first serve basis. Based on the sequence, the program tells who the next person is in the line, without the passengers having to wait in the queue. While the system was useful and unique, many argued if it required a patent and a petition was filed against it asking the patent office to re-examine the patent. By withdrawing the patent, IBM was considered to have avoided a major public anguish. A patent attorney remarked, "We have kept track of who gets to use bathroom next for a long time in our society. By disclaiming it, IBM now relieves the general public of wondering whether they would have been a target of this patent."[13]

Problems with Patents – Patently Obvious?

Everyone agreed that the biggest problem was that the USPTO was under tremendous pressure and was overloaded. The patent examiners reviewed 50% more patents than they did some 25 years ago. Some were apprehensive about the genuine innovations getting delayed because of it. With the companies identifying the hidden benefits of patents and the long-term revenues that came with it, they applied for more patents. Intellectual property began to characterize the health of a company especially in the biotechnology and the IT industry. As a result, the number of patent applications in the Patent Office have increased enormously (Annexures IV & V). USPTO reported that prior to 1992 less than 100 patents were awarded, and subsequently within five years it had issued around 750 patents and in 1999 alone, around 4000 Internet-related patents were issued. However, proliferation of patent applications at the office was not complementing the innovation levels.

Law firms also began to see a business opportunity with patents. They bought patents and then filed lawsuits on big corporations for infringing and claimed heavy licensing fee. Others who took up the risk of facing a lawsuit in court ended up spending heavily on lawyers. For example, eBay had to bear heavy costs spent on lawyers to defend against a lawsuit by a company from Virginia. The company claimed that he held patents for fixed price selling. After the technology boom bust during the late 1990s, the Internet startups had no other asset left except their patents, and royalty fees became an active revenue source. Biotechnology firms, who had nothing to sell for years depended largely on the intellectual property for revenues. For some startups like Walker Digital, which claimed it had patents of reverse auctions that *priceline.com* implemented, buying and licensing patents became the sole business.

Patents were traded online including on eBay, from where companies and individuals bought them and used them for generating revenues through licensing fees. The so-called 'Patent-trolls'[14] had allegedly bought cheap patents and then used them as a defense against competition. It was reported that once a person had bought a patent for $50,000 and claimed that it was infringed by all the Intel processors and claimed $7 billion in damages. Though the case was ruled in favour of Intel, it still had to bear costs of $3 million for fighting the lawsuits.

The Supreme Court wrote in a report, "It creates a class of speculative schemers who make it their business to watch the advancing wave of improvement, and gather its foam in the form of patented monopolies, which enable them to lay a heavy tax upon the industry of the country. It embarrasses the honest pursuit of business."[15]

The patent wars among the companies have in a way led to mergers in the industries. The big corporations exercised their patent, and as a protection against lawsuits, the competitors entered into cross-licensing with the patent holders eliminating the competition in a free market economy. 'Defensive Patents' reduced the need for more innovation to gain a competitive advantage while at the same time created entry barrier for the competition. Biotechnology industry was the most affected by this trend. Pfizer Warner-Lambert merger in 2000, Dupont's acquisition of Hi-Bred stood as some examples of such intellectual-property-triggered mergers.

IBM was the largest patent holder from 1993 to 2002, had received 22,357 patents and had generated nearly $10 billion through licensing fees[16] (Annexure VI). In 2004, Washington Mutual was awarded a patent for a retail banking approach. The claims made in the patent looked like very obvious business process enhancements for many. The patent included certain ideas, which the company called inventions, like removal of the barrier between the teller and the customer to enhance interaction.[17] Other details were like the oval layout of the bank, place for kids to play while their parents banked, etc. Such patents have begun to question whether business ideas really meant inventions, and whether they were eligible for patents. The patent office which was overwhelmed with pending applications saw less costs in approving an application than rejecting one, and as a result was reported to have approved many patents which otherwise should have been rejected.[18]

The backlog that had built up at the office was, in a way also discouraging innovation among the inventors as the average waiting time for patent approval had increased to two years by 2002. This resulted in the venture capitalists becoming uninterested towards investments in research. An analyst commented, "At what point will venture capitalists feel like it's no longer useful to invest in certain technologies because they don't know that they're going to get a patent and actually get a return on their investment."[19] Analysts, academicians as well as the business community called for reforms in the age-old patent law. An intellectual property executive at Google, remarked, "The ambiguity and lack of quality that we currently have really mainly favors those who want to use patents as a tool for harassment. The system, because of the way it works right now, is fairly easy to abuse."[20]

Why [What] Reforms?

National Academy of Sciences,[21] the Federal Trade Commission and others began to criticise the Patent Office for its inability to tackle the 'technology creep' in the 21st century. They expressed the opinion that patents were getting in the way of innovation instead of encouraging it. In 2002, FTC along with the US Department of Justice (DOJ) released its version of recommended reforms for the USPTO. Apart from other major recommendations, it was suggested that the number of reviewers should be increased and fees raised by 20%. USPTO was also contemplating on outsourcing a part of its work to private parties and using electronic applications for faster processing. After a 24 day meeting that was held in November 2002, involving 300 panelists from varied fields, business representatives, leading patent and antitrust organizations and scholars in economic, antitrust and patent law, a comprehensive report was released (Annexure VII). The business representatives were mostly from the high technology sectors like biotechnology, information technology and pharmaceuticals. The report stated, "More patents in more industries and with greater breadth are not always the best ways to maximize consumer welfare. Many panelists and participants expressed the view that software and Internet patents are impeding innovations."[22] The report defined questionable patents that could discourage research by competitors in the areas that were covered by the patents. Assumption of the Patent Law was that inventions are one-time events, but in reality every past invention set the ground for next cumulative invention. This way, patents for abstract ideas or whole processes could restrain the competitors from spending on R&D on further inventions and competition could be suppressed. Traditionally the law believed that every invention required access to one or two patents, which was applicable mostly for industries like pharmaceuticals. In industries like the computer software, companies require access to several intermediate codes that might have been already patented. This could lead to the companies dropping research ultimately obstructing the development of new product. For such industries mostly characterized by incremental innovation yet worth protecting, the contemporary laws proved to be inefficient. Thus, a detailed review with stringent standards was deemed essential. However, at the same time, the committee recommended that instead of reviewing every application by multiple reviewers, only those few challenged and dubious ones could be entitled for a third review by outside parties.

As part of the ongoing reforms, patent applications were published for public, 18 months after they were filed, before they were granted. People were allowed to challenge the claim made by the patents and prove any 'prior art'. Competitors and the public would be free to prove a 'prior art', availability of an already existent patent, or a printed material on the innovation, and could influence the patent approval. But with the open system, the small business and individual entrepreneurs would be largely affected, as the R&D departments of big companies could access their patent applications. It was likely that re-examinations of patents by outsiders would mean that the small innovators would have to bear the costs of defending their patents against big companies while also bearing the cost of speeding up their ongoing research to prove the validity of their patent. Ultimately, the small businesses and independent inventors who have been major sources of innovations in the economy would be under pressure. Open source software developers who came out with freeware were specifically at risk.

The deferred review initiative, which was initially proposed, allowed the applicants to delay the review by PTO till 18 months after the date of filing. This would allow the patent applicants to analyze the patentability and the commercial benefits of the applied patent before the PTO reviews them. This was again revised in 2003 stating that the applicants would be allowed to withdraw their applications before the review, which could be delayed for 18 months and receive a part of fees back.

The other major reform that was recommended was the exemption from some research uses of patent inventions. Accordingly, research institutions and universities were allowed to use the patented technology for further research. Lita Nelsen, Director, Technology Licensing Office, Massachusetts Institute of Technology called this reform a 'tempest in a teapot', while John Cotter argued that the private universities and research houses were trying to convert the patent code into a tax code. Such a narrow definition of exemption was considered to create more confusion, as competitors would be allowed to use a patented invention and still escape claiming that it was using it for research.

To Patent or Not to Patent?

While reforms on behalf of the Federal Commission and the USPTO were underway, companies who applied for patents were specifically expected to play a key role in the reforms. Analysts opined that the conventional wisdom of 'patents as a competitive weapon' must be rethought and the analysts contended that unless the corporate world takes responsible initiatives restraining from applying for vague patents for trivial inventions, the real costs for the economy as well as the society at large would remain. The patent system was considered to restrain trade in a free market economy and pass on the ill effects in the form of high prices to the customers through monopoly. However, the USPTO was not expected to advocate reforms that question its revenue model, by discouraging the number of applications as making the standards stringent would reduce the number of vague and unqualified applications, which in turn would reduce the revenues for USPTO.

The reforms were expected to decrease the pressure on the USPTO, while enhancing the quality of patents issued. However, the same reforms could also exacerbate the situation as the director of USPTO James E Rogan himself stated. Relying on an outside source for 'prior art' search could lead to inefficiencies and affect uniformity of the searches and finally the quality of approvals.[23] Some others opined that the US should follow the footsteps of European Patent Law, in which once a patent was issued, competitors were given rights to oppose it.

From a macroeconomic view, patents have been the cornerstone for the economic development. However, in the information age, patents have begun to stifle innovation spirit, with research for further innovations on the already patented technologies waning off. While analysts agreed that ideas and innovations should be protected, they also argued whether all those really required a twenty-year monopoly. R Jordan Greenhall, chief executive of DivXNetworks Inc. called these twenty-year patents "asinine to the point of ludicrosity".[24] While Jeff Bezos, CEO of Amazon.com recommended that the term should be reduced to two or three years for software patents, it was ruled out considering that this way the law would violate international standards.[25]

Some suggested that software patents and business method patents should be completely expelled. A representative from business community agreed, "If you didn't have any patents at all, people would still be doing the same stuff because of the speed of the marketplace."[26] However citing the examples of biotechnology patents and telephony patents which in past had also faced similar resistance, analysts argued that strong patent protection had always promoted innovation, knowledge sharing and economic growth. They believed that the CEOs should learn to manage the patent assets not only as legal instruments but also as financial assets and competitive weapons to enhance their growth in the market as well as shareholders wealth.[27] Many believed that patents remained the driving force for innovations in any economy irrespective of the industry. As Jay S Walker, Founder and Vice Chairman, Priceline.com Inc., put it, "Protecting intellectual capital is the only way to generate more of it."[28]

(D Gayatri is a research associate and T Phani Madhav is a team leader at ICFAI Business School Case Development Centre, Hyderabad.)

Exhibit I: Amazon.com's One-Click System: A Case in Point

Amazon.com received patent for its 'One-click system' with a patent number 5,960,411 ('411 patent') on September 28th 1999. The system allowed customers to purchase with a single mouse click. With the help of stored information about the name of the customer, the credit card number, customers could make purchases by a simple mouse click. Immediately after amazon.com was awarded the patent, in October 1999, it filed a lawsuit against Barnes&Noble alleging that it had infringed its patent. The Express Lane feature that was already in use by Barnes&Noble, allowed registered users to purchase online by pressing a single button labeled, 'Buy it now with just 1 click'.

In defense, Barnes&Noble put forward the argument that the '411 patent' was invalid as the prior art anticipated the invention and that it was only an improvement over prior art. However after the District Court examined several other shopping sites like the Dr. John Lockwood's Web basket, the Netscape Merchant System and Oliver's market, it concluded that the patent was different from the prior art, which had mentions about online shopping but not about the one click shopping. The case was later settled outside the court and Barnes&Noble had to stop its Express Lane feature for Christmas season.

Later Barnes&Noble added an additional click to its order processing system and was released from the lawsuit. Tim O'Reilly of O'Reilly & Associates, a software book publisher, argued that "To Characterize '1-Click' as an invention is parody"[29] and an *eweek* article ridiculed amazon.com's patenting philosophy in a cartoon (Annexure III).

Compiled by ICFAI Business School Case Development Centre.

Annexure I: The US Patent Law Amendments through the Years

1954		Provisions relating to plant patents were amended to make it clear that cultivated sports, mutants, hybrids and newly found seedlings were patentable.
1964		Commissioner given the power to accept a declaration in lieu of an oath in "any document" and to give provisional acceptance to a defective document. 35 USC 25 and 26.
1965		Presumption of validity applied independently to each claim of a patent. 35 USC 282.
1966		Supreme Court decision in **Graham v. John Deere**[1] set out the proper test for deciding whether or not a claimed invention is obvious.
1968		Patent Cooperation Treaty signed.
1971		Supreme Court decision in **Blonder-Tongue v. University of Illinois** [2] held that once a patent had finally been held to be invalid after full and fair litigation, that finding could be used as a defense in subsequent litigation on that patent even if the parties differed.
1975	1.	Name of "The Patent Office" changed to "The Patent and Trademark Office".
	2.	Amendments to accommodate the Patent Cooperation Treaty. 35 USC 102(e), 104, 351-376.
	3.	Liberalized the law having regard to the writing of claims in multiple dependent form. 35 USC 112.
1978	1.	European Patent Office opened.
	2.	Patent Cooperation Treaty came into effect.
1980	1.	Requirement to pay maintenance fees to keep patent in force introduced. 35 USC 154.
	2.	Special provisions made for inventions made with Federal assistance. 35 USC 200-211.
	3.	Provision made for third parties to cite prior art to USPTO. 35 USC 301.
	4.	Possibility of requesting reexamination created. 25 USC 302-7.
	5.	United States rebuffs attempts by developing countries to amend Paris Convention to permit exclusive compulsory licensing.
	6.	Supreme Court upholds the patentability of a genetically modified bacterium quoting the Congressional report leading up to the 1952 Act that "anything made by man under the sun" should be patentable. [3]
1982	1.	Applications permitted to be filed without signature by the inventor as long as the inventor had authorized the application to be filed. 35 USC 111.
	2.	Law relating to correction of wrongly named inventors liberalized. 35 USC 116.

Contd...

Contd...	
	3. Court of Appeals for the Federal Circuit created. 35 USC 141, 28 USC 1295. [4]
	4. Term of all design patents fixed at fourteen years from grant. 35 USC 173.
	5. Arbitration of disputes relating to patent infringement or validity authorized 35 USC 294.
	6. It became possible for United States applicants to request an international search under the PCT by the European Patent Office.
1984	1. Possibility of extending patent term to compensate for delay in securing marketing authority from FDA to sell new drugs for humans. (Waxman Hatch Amendments) [5] 35 USC 156.
	2. Protection from finding of obviousness over work of co-employees etc. 35 USC 103. (c).
	3. Clarification that to be a joint inventor the inventors did not have to work together or each be an inventor of subject matter of every claim. 35 USC 115(a).
	4. Settlement of interferences by arbitration became permissible. 35 USC 135(d).
	5. Definition of infringement amended to include exports of kits of parts that can be used to make a product which if made in the U.S. would be an infringement of a US Patent. [6] 35 USC 271(f).
	6. Boards of Patent Appeals and Interferences consolidated into a single Board of Patent Appeals and Interferences. 35 USC 141.
	7. Statutory Invention Registration scheme introduced 35 USC 157.
	8. United States succeeds in causing inclusion of intellectual property issues in Uruguay Round of GATT negotiations.
1987	1. United States implements Chapter II of PCT. 35 USC 362.
	2. It became possible for United States' applicants to request an international preliminary examination under the PCT by the European Patent Office.
1988	1. Possibility of extending patent term to compensate for delay in securing marketing authority from FDA to sell new drugs for animals. 35 USC 156.
	2. Requirements for securing permission to file patent application abroad if on file in US for less than six months relaxed to some extent. 35 USC 184 and 185.
	3. Definition of infringement amended to include importation into the United States of products made abroad by a process covered by a US patent and to reverse the burden of proof in certain cases of alleged infringement of a process patent. (Process Patents Amendment Act) 35 USC 271(g), 35 USC 287, 35 USC 295.
	4. Definition of infringement amended to include application to FDA for marketing approval of a patented drug to be effective before the expiration of the patent but to

Contd...

Contd...		
		remove from patent infringement acts relating to collecting data for use in submissions to the FDA for marketing approval of a drug etc. 35 USC 271(e).
	5.	Patent Misuse Reform Act made it clear that patent was not unenforceable for misuse on the basis that patentee had refused to license the patent or on the basis of tying arrangements unless the patentee had market power in the relevant market. 35 USC 271(d).
1990		Extension of definition of patent infringement to acts in outer space on a "space object or component thereof under the jurisdiction or control of the United States". 35 USC 105.
1992		State governments made liable for acts of patent infringement. 35 USC 271(h), 35 USC 296.
1993		Extension of right to prove prior invention to acts carried out in NAFTA countries. 35 USC 104.
1994	1.	Uruguay Round of negotiations for revision of the General Agreement of Tariffs and Trade (GATT), concludes an agreement on Trade Related Aspects of Intellectual Property Rights (TRIPS) which include enforceable minimum standards for patent protection.
	2.	Extension of right to prove prior invention to acts carried out in WTO countries 35 USC 104.
	3.	Introduced the possibility of filing provisional patent applications. 35 USC 111(b) and 119(e).
	4.	Subject to transitional provisions, the term of a patent is now twenty years from its earliest filing date (instead of seventeen years from grant), subject to the possibility of extension to compensate for delays due to interferences or the need to appeal in order to secure the grant of the patent. 35 USC 154.
	5.	Definition of infringing acts extended to include offers for sale and acts of importation. 35 USC 271.
	6.	Reversal of burden of proof in certain cases where infringement of process patent is alleged. 35 USC 295.
1995		Protection of biotechnology processes from finding of obviousness if it is for the production of new and non-obvious product. 35 USC 103 (b).
1996		Removal of remedies for infringement of patents for surgical processes. 35 USC 287(c).
1998		The Court of Appeals for the Federal Circuit in **State Street Bank v. Signature Financial.** [7] holds that there is no prohibition in US law on patents for business methods as long as they are new, useful and non-obvious.
		Contd...

Contd...

1999	1. The 1992 amendment to make state governments liable for act of patent infringement is held to be an unconstitutional abridgement of the states' sovereign immunity in **Florida Prepaid Post-secondary Education Expense Board v. College Savings Bank.** [8] 2. The **Intellectual Property and Communications Omnibus Reform Act** of 1999 is passed. This law makes a number of amendments to the United States Patent Law and also includes provisions intended to curtail cybersquatting and to deal with satellite home viewing and rural local television signals. The changes to the United States Patent Law include providing for early publication of patent applications where equivalent applications are published abroad, the protection of inventors using the services of invention promotion services and first inventor (prior user) defense for prior users of business methods. Other changes were also made to the US Patent Law. You can learn more by referring to the following articles: US Patent Law Amendments 1999 and United States –1999-2000 Revisions of the Patent Law and Rules.
2001	The first publication of a pending United States Patent Application, as provided for by the 1999 amendment, occurs on March 15, 2001.

Source: www.ladas.com/patents/USpatentshistory.htm

Annexure II: The Beerbrella Patent

Patent No: 6,637,447

Abstract: The present invention provides a small umbrella ("***Beerbrella***"), which may be removably attached to a beverage container in order to shade the beverage container from the direct rays of the sun. The apparatus comprises a small umbrella approximately five to seven inches in diameter, although other appropriate sizes may be used within the spirit and scope of the present invention. Suitable advertising and/or logos may be applied to the umbrella surface for promotional purposes. The umbrella may be attached to the beverage container by any one of a number of means, including clip, strap, cup, foam insulator, or as a coaster or the like. The umbrella shaft may be provided with a pivot to allow the umbrella to be suitably angled to shield the sun or for aesthetic purposes. In one embodiment, a pivot joint and counterweight may be provided to allow the umbrella to pivot out of the way when the user drinks from the container.

Source: www.uspto.gov

Annexure III: Patents Stifle Innovation

Source: www.eweek.com, March 11th 2002.

Annexure IV: The Patent Backlog at USPTO

Patent Office Flooded with Applications

Over 3,000 examiners process more than 300,000 applications for patents a year. The average wait time to obtain a patent is just over two years.

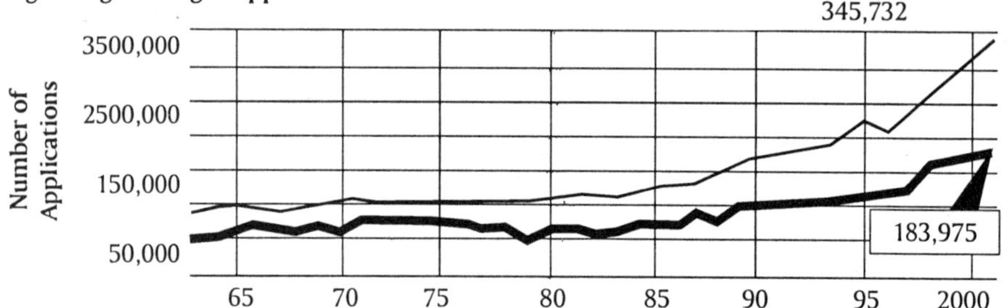

- Backlog of patent applications: 470,000
- Applications received last year: 333,688
- Expected this year: 343,699
- Applications handled by examiners last year: 260,245
- Patents issued last year: 163,221
- Number of examiners: 3,500
- Average wait for patent approval: 24 months

Source: www.usatoday.com

Annexure V: Internet-related Patents and Business Method Patents Increase in Number after 1998

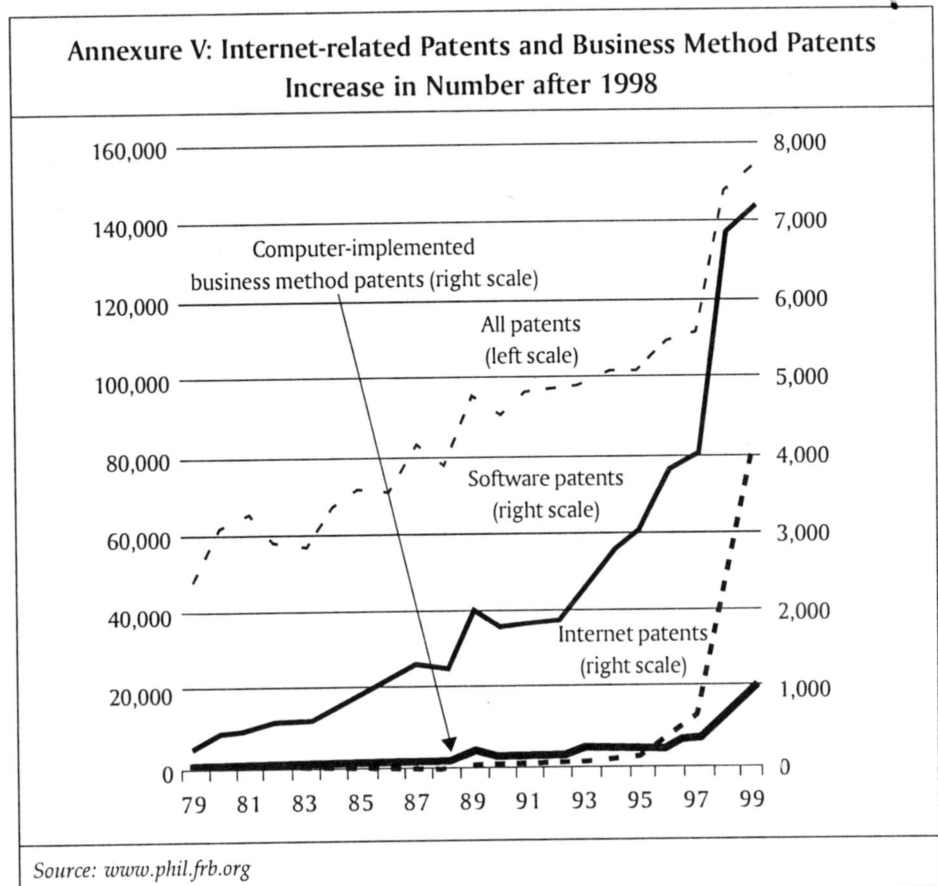

Source: www.phil.frb.org

Annexure VI: Top 10 Private Sector Patent Holders in 2002

Company	Number of patents granted in 2002
IBM	3288
Canon Kabushiki Kaisha	1893
Micron Technology	1833
NEC Corp.	1821
Hitachi	1601
Matsushita Electric Industrial	1544
Sony	1434
General Electric	1416
Mitsubishi Denki Kabushiki Kaisha	1373
Samsung Electronics	1328

Source: http://www.usatoday.com/money/industries/technology/patent-chart.htm

Annexure VII: FTC's Recommendations to USPTO

Title of the report: "To promote Innovation: The proper balance of competition and patent law and policy" October 2003.

Recommendations

Recommendation 1) Enact legislation to create a new administrative procedure to allow post-grant review of and opposition to patents.

Recommendation 2) Enact legislation to specify that challenges to the validity of a patent are to be determined based on a "Preponderance of the evidence".

Recommendation 3) Tighten certain legal standards used to evaluate whether a patent is "Obvious".

- In applying the "commercial success" test,
  1) Evaluate on a case by-case basis, whether commercial success is a valid indicator that the claimed invention is not obvious, and
  2) Place the burden on the patent holder to prove that the claimed invention caused the commercial success.
- In applying the "suggestion" test, assume an ability to combine or modify prior art references that is consistent with the creativity and problem-solving skills that in fact are characteristic of those having ordinary skill in the art.

Contd...

Contd...

Recommendation 4) Provide adequate funding for the PTO.

Recommendation 5) Modify certain PTO Rules and implement portions of the PTO's 21st Century Strategic Plan.

- Amend PTO regulations to require that, upon the request of the examiner, applicants submit statements of relevance regarding their prior art references.
- Encourage the use of examiner inquiries under Rule 105 to obtain more complete information, and reformulate Rule 105 to permit reasonable follow-up.
- Implement the PTO's recommendation in its 21st Century Strategic Plan that it expand its "second-pair-of-eyes" review to selected areas.
- Continue to implement the recognition that the PTO "forges a balance between the public's interest in intellectual property and each customer's interest in his/her patent and trademark."

Recommendation 6) Consider possible harm to competition – along with other possible benefits and costs – before extending the scope of patentable subject matter.

Recommendation 7) Enact Legislation to require publication of all patent applications 18 months after filing.

Recommendation 8) Enact Legislation to create intervening or prior user rights to protect parties from infringement allegations that rely on certain patent claims first introduced in a continuing or other similar application.

Recommendation 9) Enact Legislation to require, as a predicate for liability for wilful infringement, either actual, written notice of infringement from the patentee, or deliberate copying of the patentee's invention, knowing It to be patented.

Recommendation 10) Expand consideration of economic learning and competition policy concerns in patent law decision-making.

- The FTC will increase its Competition Advocacy Role through filing amicus briefs in appropriate circumstances.
- The FTC will ask the PTO Director to re-examine questionable patents that raise competitive concerns in appropriate circumstances.

Source: www.ftc.gov

Endnotes (Annexure I)

1 383 U.S. 1, 148 USPQ 459.

2 402 U.S. 313, 169 USPQ 513.

3 Diamond v. Chakrabarty 206 USPQ 193.

4 The Court of Appeals for the Federal Circuit has *inter alia* exclusive jurisdiction over appeals from decisions of the Board of Patent Appeals and Interferences and over appeals of final decisions of all district courts on actions based in whole or in part on "any Act of Congress relating to patents". The new statute did not, however, abrogate the right of someone denied patent rights or losing an interference from bringing a civil action against the Commissioner of Patents before the District Court in Washington D.C. A major reason for the creation of the Federal Circuit was a sense of lack of consistency in dealing with patent cases in the different regional circuits. During the 1970's there was a growing feeling that certain Circuits were anti patent and others pro patent so that forum shopping was rife.

5 The legislation was a compromise between the ethical and generic drug industries after the Federal Circuit decision in *Roche v. Bolar* 21 USPQ 937 had held that premarketing testing (required by the FDA) by a generic drug manufacturer constituted patent infringement.

6 This was a legislative overruling of the Supreme Court decision in *Deepsouth Packing Co. v. Laitram* 406 U.S. 518, 173 USPQ 769 (1972)

7 149 F.3d. 1368 47 USPQ2d 1596 (Fed Cir 1998).

8 51 USPQ2d 1081.

Endnotes

1 Gleick, James "Patently absurd", *www.around.com*

2 Krim, Jonathan "Patenting air or protecting property", *www.washingtonpost.com,* December 11th 2003.

3 "The cost of ideas", *www.economist.com,* November 11th 2004.

4 Business method patents as defined under US patent law are patents awarded to data processing, financial, business practices, management or cost/price determination.

5 The first patent was awarded in 1790 for potash, soap and a fertilizer ingredient.

6 In the Signature Vs State Street Bank case, Signature Financial group Inc. won a patent on an unique data processing software that helped in saving the customer taxes and cut costs of heavy calculations. State Street Bank filed a lawsuit claiming that business methods that incorporate mathematical formulae are not patentable. Though the Federal High Court accepted the plaintiff's argument, the D.C Circuit Federal Court of appeals gave a ruling that

patents should give an incentive to innovate and as the Congress was also planning to extend the patent law to 'anything under sun made by man,' it ruled the patent valid.

7 Gleick, James "Patently absurd", op.cit.

8 The Law established in 1793 grants patents to unique and novel innovations. The law was enforced keeping in view the industrialization that was active in US. The law defines anything patentable as "any new and useful art, machine, manufacture or composition of matter and any new and useful improvement on any art, machine, manufacture or composition of matter." Thomas Edison's light bulb and Samuel Morse's telegraph were among the initial patents.

9 "Monopolies of the mind", *www.economist.com,* November 11th 2004.

10 Blenko, J Walter "Considering what constitutes a prior art in United States", *http://www.tms.org*

11 Federal Trade Commmission established in 1914 ensures free market system in US, prohibiting anti-competitive mergers and competition-restricting trade practices.

12 Shiels, Maggie "Technology industry hits out at 'patent trolls'", *http://news.bbc.co.uk*

13 Wolverton, Troy "IBM flushes restroom patent", *http://news.com.com,* October 11th 2002.

14 Intel coined the term for people who use patents as a source of business revenues.

15 Gleick, James "Patently absurd", op.cit.

16 Krim, Jonathan "Patenting air or protecting property?", op.cit.

17 "Washington Mutual receives patent for its retail banking approach", *www.wamunewsroom.com,* June 23rd 2004.

18 "Patenting air or protecting property?", op.cit.

19 Schoen, W John "US patent office swamped by backlog", *http://msnbc.msn.com,* April 27th 2004.

20 "Technology industry hits out at 'patent trolls'", op.cit.

21 An organization of top scientists that advises the government on science policy.

22 Krim, Jonathan "Patenting air or protecting property?", op.cit.

23 Carroll, J. Kevin "The plan to reform the US patent system: Will it meet the need of high tech companies?", *http://ipmall.info,* September 2002.

24 "Patenting air or protecting property?", op.cit.

25 Ross, E, Philips "Patently absurd", *www.forbes.com,* May 29th 2000.

26 Davidson, Paul "Patents out of control?", *www.usatoday.com,* January 13th 2004.

27 "Rembrandts in Attic: Unlocking the Hidden Value of Patents", *http://hbsworkingknowledge.hbs.edu,* December 21st 1999.

28 "How patents spur innovation", *www.businessweek.com,* November 16th 1998.

29 Bicknell, Craig "Cashing in one bogus patents", *www.wired.com,* October 19th 2000.

5

Nicholas Piramal India: Survival Strategies for International Patent Law Regime

Senthil Ganesan and K Malini

The Indian pharmaceutical industry is on the verge of a major turnaround with the proposed implementation of international patent law (IPL) from January 2005 onwards. This means that India's pharmaceutical companies will have to strictly adhere to product patent laws and not the process patent laws that it has followed to date. Indian companies were reverse engineering the patented drugs and, with minor changes in the process, launched them in the domestic markets at cheaper rates. The new law will stipulate that Indian companies have to compete with global pharma majors to stay competitive. So, Indian companies have increased investments in research and development (R&D), joint ventures and also have elaborated their marketing efforts. This case chronicles the various efforts taken by Nicholas Piramal India Limited (NPIL) to stay competitive in the post-2005 period. The case focuses on the multifaceted strategies adopted by Nicholas Piramal India Limited to cope with the oncoming implementation of international patent law from 1 January 2005.

Source: ICFAI Business School Case Development Centre, 2004.

We are putting in place major plans to emerge as one of the most focused, cost-effective and leading research pharma companies in the country. These initiatives would now render the company an ideal launch pad for new products.

– Ajay Piramal,
Chairman, NPIL[1]

Introduction

Nicholas Piramal India Ltd. (NPIL),[2] one of the leaders in the Indian pharmaceutical industry, had expertise in bulk drug[3] manufacturing (both for domestic and export markets), specialty labs and chemicals, formulation[4] development, providing genomic information and herbal products. NPIL was also a competitive player in contract manufacturing and excelled in (both on- and off-) patent APIs[5] in the regulated markets of the US, Europe and Japan. The key export markets for NPIL were the US, Europe, Asia, including Japan and South East Asia, the Middle East, Africa and Latin America. NPIL's revenue for 2003 was Rs.9,642.2 million (Rs.8,038.5 million in 2002) and earnings were Rs.1,181.1 million (Rs.482.4 million in 2002)[6] (Annexures I and II).

Over the years, NPIL had engaged in a multi-pronged strategy of acquisitions, brand building, focused selling and manufacturing, expansion of R&D and new recruitment policy for core functions. The company had implemented these strategies as it had realised the implications of the International Patent Law (IPL) proposed to be implemented from January 1st 2005 onwards.

IPL was designed to allow drug companies to obtain patent[7] on processes, machines, manufactures, and compositions of matter as opposed to the Indian Patents Act, 1970[8]. This meant that after 2005, there would be a ban on producing and marketing patent protected new drugs. This posed great challenges for the Indian pharmaceutical industry as majority of the Indian companies had solely concentrated on reverse engineering of patented drugs and had failed to adequately build their R&D expertise. NPIL too was faced with such challenges, but had taken adequate measures to remain competitive.

The Indian Pharmaceutical Industry

Until the late 1960s, public sector firms such as Hindustan Antibiotics Ltd. and Indian Drugs and Pharmaceutical Ltd. and a host of global companies dominated the Indian pharmaceutical industry. 90% of the industry was dominated by the global companies that imported most of the drugs (Annexures III and IV). During the early 1970s, the Indian players slowly gained prominence as a result of the Indian Patent Act (1970), which allowed Indian companies to reverse engineer patented molecules and launch them in the domestic markets. IPA allowed only process patent, and not product patent, so manufacturers would copy foreign patented drugs and, with a minor change in the process, they, could make them available to the common man at an affordable price. As a result, by the mid-1980s, imports reduced drastically and, by the 1990s, exports gained prominence.

Globally, the Indian Pharma industry emerged as the 4**th** largest in terms of volume and 13**th** largest in terms of value by the 2000s. It was worth about $4.5 billion[9]; growing annually at 9.5% and with over 20,000 registered units in 2000. The industry was expected to grow at a compounded annual growth rate (CAGR) of 14%[10] and reach Rs.387,300 million by 2006[11] (Annexure V). The industry provided employment to 2.86 million people, of which over 0.46 million people were directly employed in the industry (Annexure VI).

The major players in the industry were categorised into two types: Companies with Indian origin (Domestic) and MNCs. In 2001, Ranbaxy, Cipla, Dr. Reddy's Laboratories and NPIL were the top four domestic companies in terms of gross sales, while Glaxo-Wellcome, Hoechst-Marion-Roussel, Novartis India Ltd., and Knoll Pharma were the major MNCs (Exhibit I).

Exhibit I: Sales of Major Domestic Companies and MNCs in Indian Pharmaceutical Industry

Rank	Company name	Gross Sales in 2001 (Rupees in Million)
	Domestic Pharmaceutical Companies	
1.	Ranbaxy	17,459
2.	Cipla	10,475
3.	Dr. Reddy's Lab	9,841
4.	Nicholas Piramal	5,667
5.	Wockhardt Ltd.	5,583

Contd...

Contd...		
6.	Lupin Labs	5,437
7.	Cadila Healthcare Ltd.	5,087
8.	Sun Pharma	4,764
9.	Alembic Ltd.	4,738
10.	Morepen	4,297
	Multinational Pharmaceutical Companies	
1.	Glaxo-Wellcome	9,346
2.	Hoechst-Marion-Roussel	5,505
3.	Novartis India Ltd.	4,384
4.	Knoll Pharma	3,333
5.	Pfizer	3,272
6.	SmithKline Beecham Pharma India	3,195
7.	E Merck India Ltd	3,134
8.	Wyeth Lederle Ltd	2,947
9.	Rhone-Poulene India Ltd.	2,629
10.	German Remedies Ltd	2,307

Source: Hemant Joshi, "Analysis of Indian Pharmaceutical Industry", www.pharmtech.com, January 2003.

The Indian pharmaceutical industry was in a state of transition, with the proposed implementation of the International Patent Law (IPL) in 2005, administered by the WTO. The Agreement on Trade-Related Aspects of Intellectual Property Rights (TRIPS)[12] set rules on intellectual property rights/ patents and required member countries of the WTO to reflect in their domestic laws. IPL, being one of its products, enforced the implementation of patents on products, i.e., drugs.

Before the TRIPS Agreement, most of the developed countries granted patents on drugs, but many developing countries, including India, only granted patents for the process of producing an invention (for example, the method of producing a drug) but not for the product (i.e., the drug itself). As a result, generic copies of original drugs (i.e., generic drugs[13]) were made or imported into those countries without getting permission from the patent holder. Hence, the prices of medicines were often lower because of generic competition against the patented drugs. The TRIPS Agreement attempted to end this by implementing the IPL.

Under IPL, governments were required to recognise patents on products and processes in (almost) all the fields of technology, and to give the patent holder the exclusive right to make, use, sell or import the product in their country for a given period of time. (During this time, a patent holder may choose to grant another individual or corporation the right to do these things. This authorisation was called "voluntary license"). All WTO member countries were now required to grant patents on pharmaceutical inventions for at least 20 years from the date of filing for the patent (Article 33). In other words, if patent approval took approximately 10 years from the first disclosure of the molecule, a pharmaceutical company (patent owner) would get only 10 years of exclusivity to market the formulation. Thus, the patent owner's monopoly would result in significantly higher prices for patented medicines than in a situation of market competition.

In January 1995, India too became a signatory of GATT under WTO and accordingly, India had to start recognising the product patent, instead of process patent, by 2005. It implied that India could no longer rely on reverse engineering or embarking on "discovery" or "analogue" research[14]. Hence, Indian companies now faced an uphill task of redoing their business models to remain competitive in the market place. According to Pankaj Patel, MD, Zydus Cadila Healthcare:

"The competitive dynamics of the Indian pharma industry are all set to change. Beyond 2005, Indian pharma companies will have to focus on basic research or collaborate with patent holders to launch new products. The criteria for success will then depend on competitive pricing, product development skills, product portfolio leadership, a highly motivated and efficient field force, superior brand management skills and a strong distribution network. To my mind, the watchwords in the coming era will be R&D, innovative marketing strategies and cost leadership."[15]

Sensing the need to boost the industry's competitiveness, the Indian government encouraged private, public as well as foreign investors to increase investments in R&D. The government recognised the industry as knowledge-intensive and reduced interest rates for export financing and brought about additional tax deductions for R&D expenses. The industry slowly graduated into activities like drug discovery, development of drug delivery systems[16], biotechnology research and bioinformatics to cope up with the impending challenge. In addition to R&D, local companies also started doing contract manufacturing of drugs for MNCs who desired to capitalise on India's cost advantages (Annexure VII).

Evolution of Nicholas Piramal

Nicholas Piramal India Limited (NPIL) was one of the largest pharmaceutical and healthcare companies in India that operated in cardio-vascular, antibiotics & respiratory, pain management, neuro-psychiatry and anti-diabetics segments. NPIL's main strength were its 2000-strong field force, powerful brands (16 of its brands were among the top 300 in the Indian pharmaceutical industry in 2003), state-of-art manufacturing plants (in 2003, NPIL's Hyderabad plant was the only plant in India to have USFDA[17] approval for the entire facility) and the several partnerships it had entered into, with world renowned pharmaceutical organizations.

NPIL's roots could be traced back to India Schering Ltd., which was set up in April, 1947. India Schering was a subsidiary of the British Schering Ltd. (UK), whose main activities were in the healthcare industry. In 1957, British Schering was taken over by Aspro-Nicholas Ltd., a pharmaceutical major in the UK[18]. The name Indian Schering Ltd. was changed to Nicholas Laboratories India Ltd. in September, 1979.

The Piramal Group of Companies, one of India's largest diversified business houses with interests in retailing, textiles, auto-components and engineering, acquired Nicholas Laboratories in 1988. One of the group companies Gujarat Glass Ltd., which manufactured glass bottles and vials for the pharmaceutical industry, was merged with Nicholas Laboratories in April, 1990. During 1991 and 1992, two manufacturing plants were commissioned at Pithampur, Madhya Pradesh, India. In December 1992, the company was renamed as Nicholas Piramal India Limited (NPIL).

In 1993, NPIL acquired Roche Products India Ltd. (affiliate of Roche, UK) and renamed it Piramal Healthcare Ltd. (PHL). In 1995, the company acquired 40% stake in Allergan of the US, a leading manufacturers of ophthalmic[19] products. Also that year, the company merged with the bulk drugs unit of Sumitra Pharmaceutical and Chemical Ltd. (SPCL), Hyderabad. In 1997, NPIL went into a series of joint ventures (JV), which included: Boehringer Mannheim India Ltd, Ambalal Sarabhai Enterprises (ASE) and alliances with Reckitt & Coleman

Plc[20]. NPIL also had entered into a marketing agreement with Stryker Corporation (US), Scholl (UK), and Cytran (US)[21].

In 1998, NPIL entered into a JV with Boots Plc. to form Boots Piramal Healthcare Pvt. Ltd. During the same period, NPIL acquired Hoechst-Marion-Roussel's research center in India, which mainly focused on productive drug innovation. This center was renamed as Quest Institute for Life Sciences. The company also ventured into herbal medicines by forming an alliance with Central Drug Research of India, for conducting original research. NPIL formed a 49% JV with Laporte Plc. in 1998 to manufacture fine chemicals, including pharmaceutical intermediates and food additives.

In 2000, NPIL's research center entered into an agreement with Norton Healthcare (UK) to develop three formulations for cancer treatment. Soon thereafter, NPIL acquired Rhoune-Poulenc India Ltd. (held by Aventis Global), which gave it access to brands such as Phensedyl, Sternetil, Gardenel and Flagyl. The company had also entered into an alliance with Hindustan Lever Ltd. for developing "Cosmoceuticals"[22] and personal care products. It signed an agreement with Center for Biochemical Technology, an affiliate of CSIR,[23] for shared research in the field of Gene Technology (Genomics).

In 2003, NPIL expanded to foreign markets, such as the US and South East Asia, by opening up subsidiaries. NPIL entered into an agreement with Minrad Inc. of the US for distribution and marketing of a new generation of inhalation anesthetic products. The products, Isoflurane, Enflurane and Sevoflurane, were marketed exclusively by NPIL through dedicated distributors and marketing agents in Russia, Ukraine, Nigeria, Kenya, Sudan, etc. NPIL also had plans to market these products in the domestic market starting with Isoflurane. In 2004, NPIL entered into an alliance with Imperial College of the UK, to conduct research in the field of rheumatoid arthritis.

NPIL's Business Strategy

NPIL had developed a business model which was built on manufacturing, marketing, brand building, R&D and Human Resource (Exhibit II). NPIL was a strong believer of "May I be the Highest, having gained your strengths in war, your skill in peace: my feet have trodden on your heads" – Rig Veda.[24] So, the company adopted the policy of merger and acquisition, alliances and JVs with those companies which could add value to its core business.

Exhibit II: Nicholas Piramal's Strategy Model

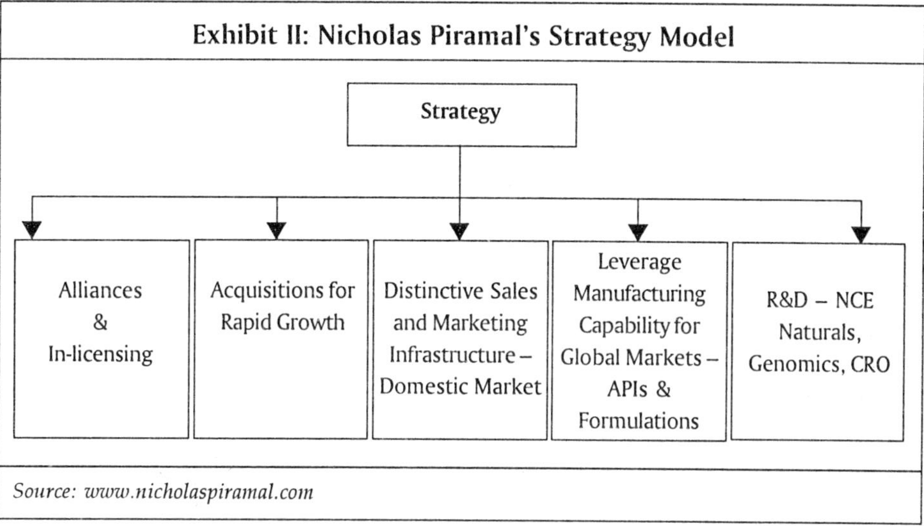

Source: www.nicholaspiramal.com

Joint Venture/Alliance and Partnerships

NPIL's first major step towards growth was a string of JVs, alliances and partnerships (Exhibit III). By 2004, NPIL had JVs and alliances with most of the premium global companies in the pharmaceutical and healthcare industry. The company chose its partners based on what value addition it could derive from them. NPIL

Exhibit III: NPIL's Joint Ventures along with their Activities

Year of JV	Joint Venture	Partner	Activity
1990	GGPL-Piramal	Gujarat Glass Pvt. Ltd, India	Manufacturing & Marketing of Flaconnage
1993	PHL	Roche, UK	Focus on research in biotech
1995	SPCL-Piramal	SPCL, India	Manufacturing & Marketing of bulk drugs
1995	Allergen India	Allergan, US	Manufacturing of eye-care products
1997	PHL	Boehringer Mannheim, Germany	Manufacturing & Marketing of bulk drugs
1997	Stryker-Piramal	Stryker, US	Manufacturing of Orthopedic devices

Contd...

Contd...			
1997	Reckitt Piramal	R&C, UK	Marketing of OTC products
1997	Scholl Piramal	Scholl, US	Marketing of OTC products
1997	Sarabhai Piramal	Ambalal Sarabhai, India	Marketing of Formulations
1997	Cytran-Piramal	Cytran, US	Marketing of anti-TB brands
1997	US Sur-Piramal	US Surgicals	Distribution of surgicals
1998	QILS	Hoechst Marion Roussel's	Research on productive drugs & co-marketing of anti-diabetic drugs
1998	Alliance	Central Drug Research	Research in Herbal Drugs
1998	Boots Piramal	Boots, UK	Marketing of OTC products
1998	Laporte Piramal	Laporte	Manufacturing & Marketing of products of Cultor Food Sciences
2000	RPIL-Piramal	Aventis Global	Marketing of Formulations
2000	Alliance	CBT	Research in Genomics
2002	ICI-Piramal	ICI Pharmaceutical, India	Manufacturing and Marketing of CVS & Critical Care Drugs.
2004	Canere Piramal	Canere Actives & Fine Chemicals Pvt Ltd.	Custom Manufacturer
Source: www.indiainfoline.com			

started its acquisition spree in 1990-1991, when it merged with Gujarat Glass Pvt. Ltd (GGPL)[25]. In 1998, GGPL was formed into an independent subsidiary with NPIL having 54% of the shareholding. GGPL focused on being the leading provider of 'flaconnage', which were the glass containers for pharmaceuticals and cosmetic industry; its products were strategic for healthcare industry only and had a CAGR of over 35%. GGPL's export had increased by 51% from Rs.215.4 million in 2001 to Rs.325.2 million in 2002.[26]

NPIL entered into JV with Allergan (US) in 1995, in order to venture into the Eye Care segment. Allergan was the leading manufacturer of ophthalmic products and the market leader in India with 17.6% market share in 1993. The JV had achieved a turnover of Rs.765.3 million in 2003 with profit after tax (PAT) being Rs.84.3 million.

In 1998, NPIL acquired co-marketing rights' license from Hoechst-Marion-Roussel for two anti-diabetic products – glimepiride and human insulin. The other anti-diabetic brand portfolios held by NPIL were – Euglucon, Semi-Euglucon, Gluformin and Diabetrol. Of these, only Diabetrol was introduced by NPIL, while the other three products were inherited from Boehringer Mannheim in 1996[27]. NPIL had the largest number of anti-diabetic brands under its name. The Sarabhai Piramal Pharmaceutical Private Ltd. (SPPL) was a 50:50 JV between NPIL and Ambalal Sarabhai Enterprises Limited. NPIL's move was aimed at consolidating both the pharmaceutical businesses under one entity. At the same time, NPIL aimed at building up stronger product portfolio in various therapeutic[28] segments by bringing together all the brands of the two companies. According to company sources, the merger helped NPIL become the fourth largest player in the domestic formulation market, with a total market share of 4.4%. GlaxoSmithKline was at the top position with 5.6% market share in 2003[29], the second and third positions being held by Ranbaxy Laboratories and Cipla respectively. Post acquisition, NPIL was expected to get the Top-3 positions in Pain Management, Central Nervous System (CNS) and Respiratory Segments.

Exhibit IV: Ranking of Segments Pre- and Post-Acquisition of SPPL

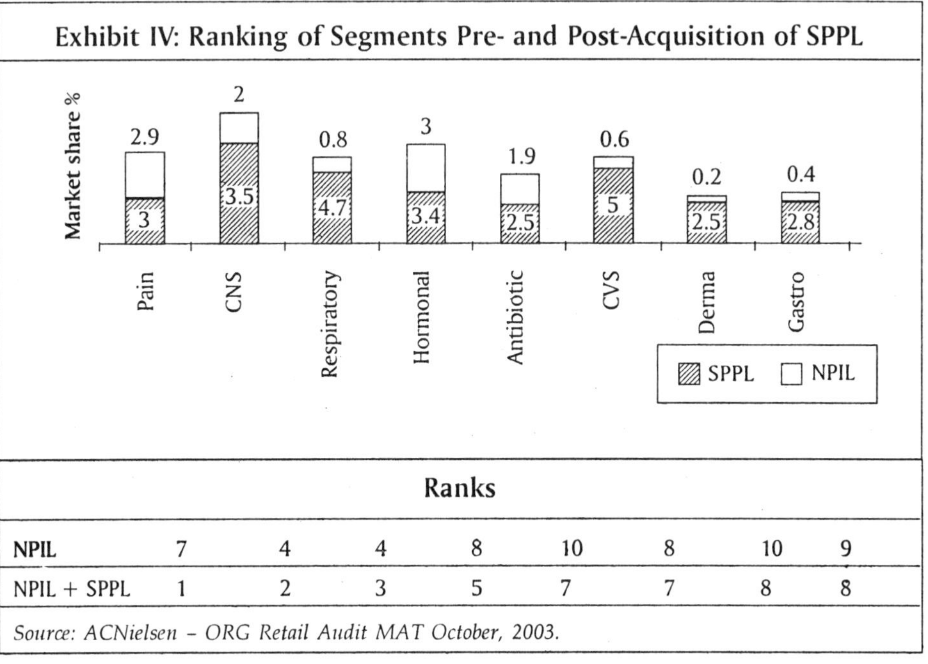

Ranks

NPIL	7	4	4	8	10	8	10	9
NPIL + SPPL	1	2	3	5	7	7	8	8

Source: ACNielsen – ORG Retail Audit MAT October, 2003.

NPIL had increased its equity stake in the JV – BPHL, formed in 1998, from 40% to 49%, effective from 2002 in order to consolidate its position in the OTC segment. NPIL had transferred Aspro (an analgesic) and Lacto Calamine (a skincare lotion) to the JV, while Boots brought in Strepsils (medicated sore throat lozenge) and Sweetex (artificial sweeteners)[30]. BPHL had recorded sales of Rs.678 million in 2003 compared to Rs.403.8 million in 2002.

Laporte Piramal formed in 1998, in which Laporte held 51% and NPIL 49% share, was managed by Laporte Fine Chemicals. The merged company manufactured and marketed products of Cultor Food Sciences, a leading global manufacturer of food flavor ingredients like maltols.[31] Cultor supplied maltol and ethyl maltol products to Laporte Piramal. The merged company also developed products such as Veltol and Veltol-Plus, a new family of maltol-based flavoring agents.

In 2000, NPIL acquired a 40% stake of Rhone Poulenc India Ltd. (RPIL) for a sum of Rs.2,400 million.[32] NPIL had chalked out a strategy to optimize the benefits of the merger; it included the integration of the CFAs[33] and depots, while the marketing and sales functions operated independently to strengthen the brand portfolio of the two companies with a presence across a wide range of therapeutic segments. The leading brands from NPIL's stable included Phensedyl, Gardenal, Phenegran, Tixylix and Flagyl.

In 2002, NPIL acquired ICI India's pharmaceutical business for about Rs.700 million. ICI Pharmaceutical's Indian brands were the market leaders in the cardiovascular segment and manufactured well-known brands such as Tenormin, Inderal, Zestril, Tenochlor in the cardiovascular segment and Fluothane and Diprivan in the critical-care segment. The merged company emerged as the leader in the cardiovascular and critical-care segments. The cardiovascular segment (CVS) of NPIL had a growth rate of 23.9% compared to the market growth rate of 16.2% in 2003[34] . The ICI acquisition also provided a readymade export market to NPIL for specialty bulk drugs like Halothane and Monosulfiram, which had only limited international competition and none from India.

NPIL's another growth strategy was to exploit the increased demand for accredited high quality healthcare testing. Hence, it decided to venture into the Pathlabs market through acquisition of three established and reputed labs in

2002 – Drs. Tribedi & Roy Diagnostic Laboratories, Dr. Phadke Pathology Laboratory & Infertility Center and Dr. Gowlwilkar's Labs in 2002. The first two had accreditation from the National Accreditation Board for Testing and Calibration of Laboratories (NABL), Government of India, and the third was expected to get accredited by 2004.

In 2003, NPIL entered into strategic alliance with Biogen Idec (US) to market Avonex (a leading life-saving therapy for multiple sclerosis) in India. Announcing the alliance, NPIL director Dr. Swati Piramal said:

> *"The tie-up with Biogen Idec is in line with our strategy of being the 'Partner of Choice' and to bring new, innovative therapies to the Indian market. 'Avonex', will further accelerate our already vibrant growth in the biotechnology segment."*[35]

Canere Actives and Fine Chemicals Pvt. Ltd. and NPIL were merged in the first quarter of 2004. Canere was a new API facility setup for USFDA inspection and had capacity to produce 350 tons[36] of high-end API per annum. According to ORG-MARG, a market research firm, with the merger, NPIL would emerge as a leading Custom Manufacturer, as its pipeline ranged from Custom Chemical Synthesis to finished goods. The merger was expected to yield fiscal benefits as Canere's facility was an Export Oriented Unit (EOU) and post-merger with NPIL, it would help expedite contracts and save time on Drug Master File (DMF)[37] and regulatory clearances.

Apart from the partnerships mentioned above, NPIL had a 50:50 JV agreement with BUPA (British United Provident Association), the largest provider of health services in the UK, to introduce a "One-stop" health facility in India. BUPA Piramal Healthcare Limited was aimed to provide a full spectrum of primary care and diagnostic facilities with comprehensive computerized medical records. The first such hospital was started in 1999 at Lower Parel, Mumbai; named "Wellspring", spread over an area of 40,000 sq.ft. The hospital provided modern ambulatory care facilities for a variety of medical consultations with general practitioners, consulting physicians, cardiologists, gynaecologists, paediatricians, dentists, orthopaedicians, etc. The hospital also housed a comprehensive pharmacy outlet for dispensing regular medicines and also stocked life-saving medicines that otherwise needed to be imported.

NPIL had an unmatched record of Joint Ventures/Alliances/Partnerships. This strategy had helped NPIL to emerge as a stronger entity to cope with the IPL challenge. Most companies that NPIL took over had shown a significant turnaround posting a huge increase in sales and profitability (Exhibit V). As a result of this strategy, NPIL had recorded a sustained growth rate of 18% to 20% annually in terms of turnover by 2003[38] . The M&A had allowed NPIL to enter the high volume and high-growth lifestyle drug market of cardiovascular, diabetic and CNS, while at the same time had provided a strong base to focus on R&D activities.

Exhibit V: NPIL's Major Subsidiaries and JV Companies

	Company	Share %	Growth %		2003		2002	
			Sales	PAT	Sales	PAT	Sales	PAT
Subsidiaries								
Pathlabs	Drs. Tribedi & Roy	100	13.8	(47.6)	127.8	15.2	112.3	29.0
	Dr. Phadke's Labs	60	40.5	16.5	53.6	9.2	38.1	7.9
	Dr. Golwilkar's Lab*	70	349.2	161.5	27.6	3.4	6.1	1.3
Gujarat Glass Pvt. Ltd.		53.8	5.7	–	2,609.0	54.7	2,469.1	93.0
Joint Ventures								
Sarabhai Piramal		50	(2.8)	(12.8)	1,798.1	176.5	1,849.2	202.5
Allergan India		49	15.4	41.2	765.3	84.3	663.4	59.7
Boots Piramal		49	67.5	64.5	678.0	94.9	403.8	57.4

Note: ( ) indicate De-growth, * The figures for FY2003 are not strictly comparable with FY2002 as this was the first full year of operations after acquisition of stake by NPIL. NPIL owns 70% of the equity of Dr. Golwilkar's Labs.

Source: www.indianinfoline.com

Research and Development

Investment in Pharmaceutical R&D had steadily been rising in India since 1997-1998. R&D investment was projected to jump from Rs.3.2 billion in 2000 to Rs.15 billion in 2005, while R&D as a percentage of sales was expected to reach 5% by 2005 from 2% in 2000[39] (Annexure VIII). Indian R&D initiatives were mainly in the fields of dosage forms, APIs and recently into novel drug delivery systems (NDDS), New Drug Discover Research (NDDR) and new chemical entities (NCE) (Annexure IX). According to industry experts:

"The Investigational New Drug stage may cost $100 to 150 million overseas but costs only around Rs.40 to 60 crores in India and that the clinical trials cost approximately $300 to 350 million abroad, costs about Rs.100 crore in India."[40]

NPIL with an intention to harness India's low cost manpower started engaging in R&D activities. The company did clinical research on contract basis for various MNCs like Allergan Inc. (U.S), Baker Norton (UK) and domestic players like HLL and had earned Rs.40 million from contract research business during 2002-2003[41].

NPIL engaged itself in major R&D activities, in order to discover and develop new and innovative healthcare products only when IPL implementation was foreseen. NPIL's comprehensive R&D efforts covered New Drug Discovery Research, Herbal Drug Research, Chemical Process Development, Formulation Development, Genomics and Clinical Research. The activities of the company were multicentric with Dr. Somesh Sharma (Dr. Sharma), as the Chief Scientific Officer. The research functions included independent as well as collaborative research projects. The activities of the research functions were guided by internal core teams with inputs from external consultants – both national and international.

NPIL made strategic investments in four areas – Basic Research (focusing on new drug discovery); Naturals Research (focusing on developing safe herbal products); Clinical Research (focusing on providing quality clinical and bioanalytical support to facilitate the international introduction of generic[42] products and to support research on NDDS and clinical development of NCE); and Genomics Research (focusing on translating cutting edge research into innovative applications). NPIL's R&D expenditure had risen to Rs.195.9 million in 2003[43] and the percentage to sales was 1.63% in 2003.

The R&D expenditure of NPIL was meagre compared to its major competitors (Annexure VIII), so it had planned to increase investment in R&D to Rs.750 million in 2004-2005 and Rs.400 million for subsequent years for expansion of the R&D center. It had started with a new R&D facility in Goregaon, Mumbai, which spread over an area of 200,000 sq.ft., focusing on rheumatology and cancer research, apart from NDDS and NCE[44]. NPIL had worked out a multipronged expansion plan to strengthen its position in the area of clinical trials and R&D in India, with plans to setup R&D centers each in Mumbai, Chennai and Bangalore. According to Dr. Sharma:

"These centers will focus on development of drugs where scientists would be involved in making drugs in small quantities."[45]

The focus on R&D had started paying off; NPIL had filed for its first patent in 2000 for its own NCE, an anti-cancer molecule NP102, in India and the US. It had also entered into developmental partnership with Norton Healthcare (UK) to develop three formulations in 2000. NPIL, in 2003, had seven new molecules in trial stages of which, one in anti-malarial (the anti-malaria drug – bulaquine) and another in the cardiac segment were in advanced stages. The company had also entered into a JV with the CBT for collaborative research in the field of Genomics in 2000. The Genomics research group, GenoMed was engaged in progressive research in asthma, schizophrenia, diabetes, and pharmaco-genomics diseases. The new products developed included newer antibacterials, cardiovasculars and anti-diabetics. The clinical research organisation (CRO), Wellquest of NPIL, offered clinical trial services to several Indian and overseas pharmaceutical companies. In 2003, Wellquest CRO received approvals from DCGI (Drugs Controller General of India) as the center for conducting bioequivalence studies.

The R&D focus of NPIL accelerated with the acquisition of Hoechst Marion's R&D division in Mumbai in 1998. The new entity, Quest Institute of Life Sciences (QILS), worked on 54 formulations[46] comprising NDDS, process development and NCEs. According to Swati Piramal, Director, NPIL:

"...the focus will be on R&D in four high potential areas – vaccines, functional genomics, cancer research and arthritis. We are talking to many likely partners in R&D including MNC pharmaceutical companies, foreign research labs and even group of scientists."[47]

QILS was actively engaged in the synthesis of patent-free NCE's in the segments of cardiovascular conditions, diabetes, antimycotics, and oncology. The Herbal Drug Research unit at QILS focused on developing standardised, clinically proven and safe herbal products for therapeutic and cosmetic use. NPIL had dedicated scientists with expertise in botany, pharmacognosy, phytochemistry, analytics and pharmacology, as well as consultants who had experiences in the herbal drug industry, on its roles.

NPIL had planned research programs in the fields of immuno-modulation, musculo-skeletal disorders, particularly inflammatory disorders, diabetes, hepato-toxicity, gastrointestinal disorders, cold and cough as well as antioxidants,[48] for 2004 and later. It had also planned to enter the areas of cognition and memory enhancers.

Marketing and Branding Strategy

NPIL had formulated a new business strategy to leverage on brand strength. It developed products in seventeen therapeutic categories (Annexure X). The company had rationalised the product and business mix, according to Ajay Piramal:

> *"This process has resulted in dropping unprofitable brands, divesting non-core brands, introducing only products where the company would be in the first five in the respective market and divesting unprofitable business tie-ups with multinational companies like Stryker and the US Surgical and Scholl Pharma."*[49]

The company had already started discarding drugs like Carvetrend, Oricar, Cardules, Bezalip and Acinopril as they were low potential brands in cardiovascular segment. The basic philosophy of the company about the new products was to introduce only those brands, which were listed in the top five groups and had an earning potential of Rs.50 to 80 million, in the initial years itself[50].

The company had one of the widest product portfolios in India, across nine key therapeutic areas including cardiovascular, neuro-psychiatry, oncology, diabetes management, respiratory anti-infectives, gastro-intestinals, dermatology and NSAIDS (Annexure XI). NPIL had implemented a new strategy in 2001-2002 to divide the products into three categories – Primary, Secondary and Tertiary. The primary category comprised of the top 10 brands that contributed about 36% of the company's revenues. The company focused on marketing of the top 10 brands resulting in a growth of 16%. The primary brands, which were 26 in 2002, had increased to 60 in 2003 (which included new launches constituting 7.2% of formulation sales[51]). The secondary category products were those that were less aggressively marketed, while the tertiary/tail-brands were marketed to semi-urban and rural markets. The primary brands included Phensedyl, Ismo Supradyn, Gardenal, Stemetil, Haemaccel and Rejoint which accounted for 67%

of the company's turnover and the secondary category included Paraxin, Flagy and Omnatax which accounted for 24% of its turnover[52].

The company had planned another strategy to widen its portfolio by entering into unexploited drug range such as anti-oxidants segment, dietary supplement for osteoarthritis[53] and an anti-allergic drug. NPIL launched drugs in all therapy areas (cardiology, dermatology, diabetics, CNS respiratory medicine, surgery, pain management, orthopaedics, gynaecology and oncology) it could cater to with anti-oxidant segment. NPIL had a value generation of Rs.150-200 million from anti-oxidants segment in 2003 and grew at a rate of 35%, which was much higher than the industry growth rate of 8-12%[54]. NPIL also targeted the global markets of Latin America, Africa, Asia and parts of Europe to build its own brand image. NPIL had launched a dietary supplement – Rejoint (containing glucosamine and chondroitin capsules, which provided nutrition to the cartilage and helped the body to naturally restore the cartilage repair mechanism) for osteoarthritis in 2000. The effect of the supplement was yet to be proven.

NPIL had planned to launch ten new anti-allergic products through its respiratory division, ACTIS (formed when NPIL acquired Rhone-Poulenc). According to Sainath Iyer, President—Sales and Marketing:

> *"The company is looking towards synergizing the expertise of Rhone-Poulenc in the cough and cold market and extend it to the entire range of respiratory critical care. The focus would be on the Rs.350-crore anti-allergic market which is growing at 20 percent every year. Of the company's total marketing expenditure, 25 to 30 percent would be spent on anti-allergic drugs' awareness campaign."*[55]

The company also had field forces, amounting to more than 2000 by 2003, which were segregated into discrete divisions with a disease-focus like cardiovascular, etc. to widen the customer coverage. The company had hired a contract field force of 250 persons[56] for marketing of tertiary brands to semi-urban and rural markets (Exhibit VI).

HR Practices

'Unity in Diversity' had been the key mantra of NPIL, as it had to maintain a multi-cultural workforce of about 4,000 emerging from M&A. The company

Exhibit VI: Sales Breakup of NPIL

(Rupees in Million)

	2003	2002	2001	2000
Bulk Drugs (Intermediates)	401.2	12.6	11.986	19.058
Creams & Powders	266.9	268.057	49.173	–
Feed Supplements	109.1	44.917	51.803	18.439
Formulation (Capsules)	500.5	546.811	435.961	362.113
Liquids	2,823.8	2,680.48	934.09	716.533
Liquids, Drops & Solutions	376.9	188.993	49.276	29.396
Others	1,067.7	951.616	777.828	–
Powders, Ointment & Cream	124.2	144.34	199.907	128.246
Tablets	2,612.4	2,436.554	1,848.495	1,914.865
Tablets & Capsules	1,486	1,003.892	333.741	–
Vials	329.2	278.141	184.663	119.505
Vitamin A In Different Forms & Concentrates	445.4	0.854	480.449	521.572
Total	10543.3	8557.255	5357.372	641.077

Source: www.indiainfoline.com

had developed its own people practice that imbibed the best of all the cultures involved and as a result, had attracted the finest talent in the industry. The work culture was focused on high performance, innovation, entrepreneurship and empowerment. NPIL's empowerment strategy was to combine performance and consequence management element, i.e., the company used a proprietary formula to convert employee 'Key Result Areas' into a performance-based pay system. NPIL's empowerment policy included performance-based pay system which was on par with the industry. It had also designed its HR policy with transparency and feedback as the base for employee evaluation and growth. The company encouraged employees to continue the learning process. Organisational learning and study opportunities were provided by the company, throughout the year for all the members of sales, marketing and research teams. The work culture, created by integrating the acquisitions quickly, was working efficiently and could be traced to the fact that the attrition rate within the acquired companies was lower compared to the industry norms.

Apart from the successful HR system, it had become necessary for NPIL to develop new strategies to cope with tough competitors and the IPL. The company had realised that old strategies could not continue to reap the expected benefits in the new environment, and it had started making significant changes in its recruitment policy since 2001. One of the major moves was to appoint former consultants from different industries to key positions of the company in order to have a good mix of professionals.

The company had hired Praneet Singh as Head of Domestic Formulations Business, who had worked as consultant with McKinsey and Co. for seven years and prior to that as brand manager for five years with Procter and Gamble. The next appointee was Shailesh Gadre in late 2001 as Head, Strategic Marketing Team and later promoted as Head of ACTIS[57]. Gadre had prior experience with Accenture and was qualified to be a chartered accountant, cost accountant and company secretary. Similarly, NPIL hired Neeraj Garg with two-year experience at A T Kearney and four years in marketing at Hindustan Lever Ltd., as the Vice-President, Strategic Marketing in 2003. The new recruitment policy was justified by Ajay Piramal:

> *"The current crop of managers (in the pharmaceutical industry) don't come up with new ways of doing things. If you have to grow faster, you have to think differently."*[58]

The company also planned to hire around 200 scientists[59] in 2003-2004. Significantly, the company had hired Sir Ravinder Maini, recipient of the coveted Albert Lasker Award[60], 2003 for clinical medical research and pioneering in new and better treatments for rheumatoid arthritis, and Dr. Bob Chaudhuri, a senior research manager at Novartis, Switzerland, who had research interests in molecular basis of cancer and neuro-degenerative diseases. According to Dr. Sharma:

> *"The inclusion of eminent scientist like Maini and Chaudhuri will add a lot of impetus to our efforts at the R&D centre. The close collaboration between eminent academic researchers, scientists and doctors in a stimulating environment will lead to major discoveries and improvements in treatment for patients."*[61]

Competitors of NPIL

NPIL's major competitors were Ranbaxy Laboratories Ltd., Dr. Reddy's Laboratories Ltd., GlaxoSmithKline and Cipla Ltd.

Ranbaxy Laboratories Ltd.

Ranbaxy, which was incorporated in 1961, was the largest pharmaceutical company in India with net revenues of Rs.34,898 million in 2003, an increase of 26% from 2002. PAT was at Rs.7,837 million as compared to Rs.6,236 million in 2002. Ranbaxy increased its R&D expenditure from Rs.1,977 million in 2002 to Rs.2,830 million in 2003, an increase of 43%. The R&D expenditure stood at 6.3% to net sales as against 5.3% in the previous year. Ranbaxy had outperformed with a growth of 9.6% compared to the Indian pharmaceutical industry growth of 7.9%. It was ranked amongst the top 100 pharmaceutical companies in the world and was rated as the ninth largest generic company worldwide. The company exported to over 70 countries with ground operations in 34 and manufacturing facilities in seven countries. It had a multi-cultural workforce of about 8,500.

The company operated in anti-infectives, nutritional, gastro-intestinal, non-steroidal anti-inflammatory systems, dermatology, orthopedics, CNS and cardiovascular segments. Apart from this, the company was also involved in animal health, diagnostics and specialty chemicals. The company's mission was to become a research-based international pharmaceutical company and had built its expertise in Chemical Research (Synthetic Chemistry, APIs); Pharmaceutical Research (Dosage Forms); Fermentation Research (APIs); NDDS and NDDR. The therapeutic focus at R&D was on urology, respiratory, anti-infectives, anti-inflammatory and metabolic disorders segments. Breakthrough BPH (Benign Prostatic Hyperplasia),[62] anti-asthma and anti-bacterial New Chemical Entities developed by the company were at different stages of drug discovery.

Dr. Reddy's Laboratories Ltd.

Dr. Reddy's Laboratories Ltd. (DRL), started in 1984, exported bulk drugs and formulations to over 60 countries, with the US, the UK, Russia and China as its main markets. They were proficient in basic research, finished dosages, generics, bulk actives, biotechnology and diagnostics. Dr. Reddy's had filed for

64 patents and was the first Indian company to out-license a molecule for clinical trials to Novo Nordisk (the world leader in diabetes) and it had out-licensed two more molecules, one to Novo Nordisk and the other to Novartis. DRL's main focus segments were – diabetes, cardiovascular, anti-infective, cancer and inflammation.

DRL had planned to launch two new products – ciprofloxacin and isotretinoin and had a target of 15 ANDAs (Abbreviated New Drug Applications)[63] and DMFs in 2003, and was planning to launch 4-6 new products in 2004[64]. The challenges of Patent law implementation in 2005 had led the company to undertake NDDR; it had seven NCE in the process, out of which four were in the pre-clinical stage and three in clinical stage. DRL had achieved an increase in its turnover to Rs.18,070 million in the year 2002-2003 as compared to Rs.16,623 million in 2001-2002.

GlaxoSmithKline Pharmaceutical Ltd.

GlaxoSmithKline (GSK) was incorporated in 1924 as H.J Foster & Co., an agency house, to distribute Glaxo baby food. In December 2000, Glaxo Wellcome and SmithKline pharmaceuticals merged to form GlaxoSmithKline Pharmaceuticals Ltd., which became one of the industry leaders with an estimated 7% of the world's pharmaceutical market. GSK was a leader in four major therapeutic areas—anti-infectives, central nervous system (CNS) conditions, respiratory diseases and gastro-intestinal/metabolic disorders, apart from being the leader in the important area of vaccines and had a growing portfolio of oncology products. GSK had a strong product line with a few brands constituting the top 250 brands of the country. GSK included a Consumer Healthcare portfolio, comprising OTC medicines, oral care products and nutritional healthcare drinks. In India, it was the biggest pharmaceutical company in terms of market share, accounting for 5.6%[65] in 2003. GSK commanded the number one position in six of the 10 therapeutic categories in which it operated.

The net sale of GSK in 2003 was Rs.11.91 billion. The company registered a 5.8% growth in 2003. GSK planned to widen its product portfolio by introducing NCEs to cope with the 2005 product patent regime. The total R&D expenditure of GSK in India was Rs.35.4 million constituting 0.30% of its turnover in 2003.

Cipla Ltd.

The Chemical, Industrial & Pharmaceutical Laboratories (Cipla) was setup in 1935 and had made its presence felt in the fields of antibiotics, anti-bacterials, anti-asthmatics, anthelmintics, anti-ulcerants, oncology, corticosteroids, nutritional supplements and cardiovascular drugs. The company had achieved the tag of being the lowest cost manufacturer of anti-HIV drugs in the world. Formulations formed the major sales area for the company, contributing about 85%, and its exports contributed nearly 35% of its total turnover. The company already had filed 11 NDAs in the US and had planned to file few more in 2004. It also had 185 applications for bulk drugs, in various parts of Europe, to its credit.

Cipla, in 1998, was one of the few companies to become a provider of all three components (lamivudine, zidovudine and stavudine) of retroviral[66] combination therapy. It had also launched Nevirapine, antiretroviral drug; used to prevent the transmission of AIDS from mother to child in 1999. The R&D focus of Cipla was on NCE in the areas of anti-fungals, antihistamines and anti-AIDS compounds. The company had net sales and income from operations of Rs.15 billion in 2003 compared to Rs.14.28 billion in 2002 and PAT was Rs.2,477.44 million in 2003. Cipla products were exported to more than 140 countries, with 32% alone to America and 23% to Europe. In the domestic market, Cipla had shown good performance in anti-asthmatics and CVS, while in the export sector, the anti-AIDS, anti-depressants, anti-asthmatics and CNS segments had outperformed.

Future Scope

The product patent era was fast approaching the Indian pharmaceutical industry and, hence, most companies were under tremendous pressure to explore avenues to reposition themselves. In the recent years, the industry had been taking full advantage of the benefits offered by the government, and had allocated sufficient capital to R&D activities such as drug discovery, development of drug delivery systems, biotechnology and bioinformatics. Companies like Ranbaxy and Dr. Reddy's were focused on developing new molecules. Even relatively smaller companies were joining the race and those that could not afford to invest high-end research right away were allocating funds to develop new drug delivery systems. There were few exceptions to this trend – Cipla had decided to remain a generic drug manufacturer. Going by the change in many companies, industry experts believed that the Indian pharmaceutical industry would, in the next two decades, become a 30% patented product market[67].

Some pharmaceutical companies had started emphasising on OTC product segments as well. Also, companies like NPIL, Dr. Reddy's, Sun Pharmaceuticals were increasingly focusing on brand/company acquisition to increase their reach and market penetration. Companies were entering into marketing arrangements with other manufacturers too.

All these new efforts meant that the competition would intensify by 2005. While NPIL strongly hoped that its efforts would help maintain a competitive position in the market place, so did its competitors.

(Senthil Ganesan and K Malini were associated with ICFAI Business School Case Development Centre.)

Annexure I: Balance Sheet of NPIL (1999-2003)

(Rupees in Million)

	2003	2002	2001	2000	1999
Sources of Funds					
Owner's Fund					
Equity Share Capital	380.00	380.03	348.53	348.53	277.08
Share Application Money	0.00	0.00	0.00	0.00	0.00
Preference Share Capital	150.00	0.00	0.00	0.00	0.00
Reserves & Surplus	3,257.80	2,465.63	3,752.59	3,356.83	2,812.27
Loan Funds					
Secured Loans	2,066.80	847.22	651.66	760.28	906.23
Unsecured Loans	776.70	2,521.86	417.85	334.75	255.97
Total	**6,631.30**	**6,214.74**	**5,170.63**	**4,800.39**	**4,251.55**
Uses of Funds					
Fixed Assets					
Gross Block	4,136.00	3,894.37	2,852.76	2,690.13	2,092.86
Less: Revaluation Reserve	0.00	0.00	0.00	0.00	0.00
Less: Accumulated Depreciation	1,067.90	972.34	748.95	615.82	514.43
Net Block	3,068.10	2,922.03	2,103.82	2,074.32	1,578.43
Capital Work-in-progress	85.80	43.26	172.28	64.22	69.68
Investments	534.60	861.06	1,023.17	981.92	915.68
Net Current Assets					
Current Assets, Loans & Advances	5,466.70	4,536.67	3,366.30	2,689.35	2,554.75
Less: Current Liabilities & Provisions	2,523.90	2,488.23	1,494.93	1,009.43	867.06
Total Net Current Assets	2,942.80	2,048.44	1,871.38	1,679.93	1,687.70
Miscellaneous expenses not written	0.00	339.95	0.00	0.00	0.08
Total	**6,631.30**	**6,214.74**	**5,170.65**	**4,800.39**	**4,251.57**
Note:					
Book Value of Unquoted Investments	534.30	860.81	1,016.84	980.59	913.56

Contd...

Contd...

Market Value of Quoted Investments	0.20	0.21	6.04	1.73	2.51
Contingent liabilities	1,076.80	462.10	611.02	203.47	123.88
Number of Equity shares outstanding	38,003,201	38,003,201	34,853,201	34,853,051	27,708,370

Source: www.indiainfoline.com

Annexure II: Profit and Loss Account of NPIL (1999-2003)

(Rupees in Million)

	2003	2002	2001	2000	1999
Income:					
Operating Income	10,575.30	8,749.92	5,142.69	4,365.67	3,942.84
Expenses					
Material Consumed	4,767.00	4,310.97	2,455.71	2,172.06	1,790.62
Manufacturing Expenses	292.30	249.73	164.70	122.13	134.74
Personnel Expenses	894.20	789.85	563.36	482.15	495.15
Selling Expenses	1,488.30	345.82	159.07	44.37	63.15
Administrative Expenses	1,367.90	1,911.39	875.16	842.66	779.20
Expenses Capitalised	0.00	0.00	0.00	0.00	0.00
Cost of Sales	8,809.70	7,607.76	4,218.00	3,663.37	3,262.86
Operating Profit	1,765.60	1,142.16	924.69	702.30	679.98
Other Recurring Income	532.30	480.65	261.61	337.41	254.77
Adjusted PBDIT	2,297.90	1,622.81	1,186.30	1,039.71	934.75
Financial Expenses	401.80	547.19	294.23	332.21	353.84
Depreciation	234.90	168.94	139.01	105.83	89.22
Other Write Offs	0.00	0.00	0.00	0.08	0.04
Adjusted PBT	1,661.20	906.69	753.06	601.60	491.65
Tax Charges	61.10	243.38	62.50	60.00	55.00
Adjusted PAT	1,600.10	663.31	690.56	541.60	436.65
Non-Recurring Items	-396.20	-179.15	-18.25	-71.81	3.10

Contd...

Contd...					
Other Non Cash Adjustments	-22.80	-1.78	-7.70	0.00	0.00
Reported Net Profit	1,181.10	482.30	737.37	569.50	453.45
Earnings before Appropriation	2,246.70	1,436.91	1,346.02	939.42	682.76
Equity Dividend	399.00	323.03	243.97	190.11	152.40
Preference Dividend	2.30	0.00	0.00	0.00	0.00
Retained Earnings	1,794.00	1,113.88	1,077.16	728.40	513.60

Source: www.indiainfoline.com

Annexure III: Temporal Progress of the Pharmaceutical Industry

Year	Status	
1950s	Formulations	Mostly imported, MNC dominance
1960s	Formulations	Domestic endeavor on imported bulk drugs
1970s	Formulations	Some imports
	Bulk drugs	Indigenous manufacture by domestic companies
1980s	Formulations	Marginal imports (<5%)
	Bulk drugs	Significant indigenous manufacture (based on domestic R&D)
1990s	Formulations	Significant exports, minimal imports (< 2%)
	Bulk drugs	Self reliant (exports > imports)

Source: Report of Pharmaceutical Research & Development Committee.

Annexure IV: Growth of Indian Pharmaceutical Industry

	1965-1966	1999-2000
Number of units	2,257*	20,053
		(Rupees in Million)
Capital Investment	1,400	25,000 (18 times)
Production	1,680	197370
Formulation	1,500	159,600 (106 times)
Bulk Drugs	180	37,770 (210 times)
Foreign Exchange		
Import	82	34,410 (420 times)
Export	30.5	66,310 (2175 times)
R&D Expenditure	30	3,200 (110 times)

Note: * Number of units is for 1969-1970.

Sources:

1. *Organization of the Pharmaceutical Producers of India (OPPI) Annual Report 1999-2000.*
2. *www.pharmaceutical-drug-manufacturers.com/pharma-industry-statistics.*

Annexure V: Indian Pharmaceutical Industry

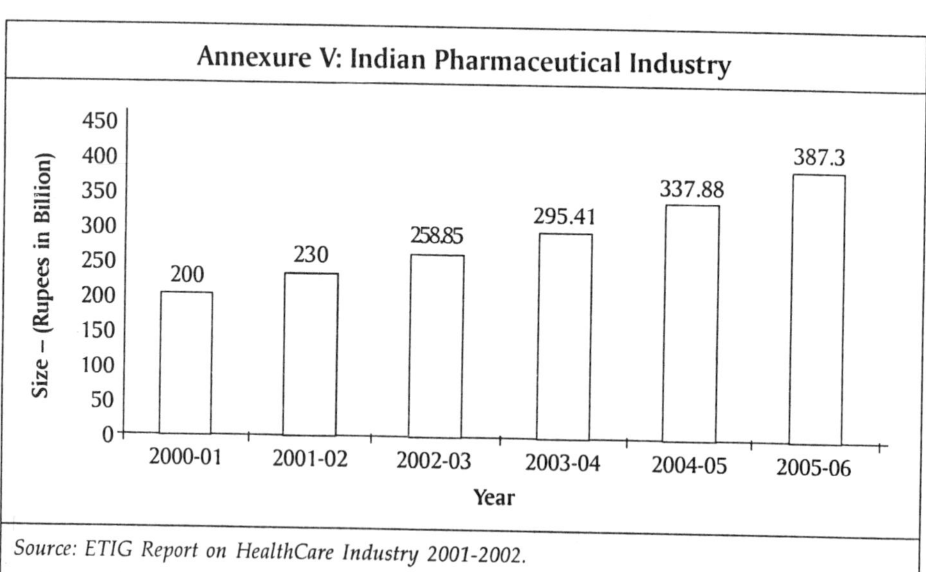

Source: ETIG Report on HealthCare Industry 2001-2002.

Annexure VI: Pharmaceutical Industry Employment

(Rupees in Million)

Direct	
Organised	0.29
Small-Scale units	0.17
Sub Total	**0.46**
Indirect	
Distribution Trade	1.65
Ancillary Industry	0.75
Sub Total	**2.40**
Total	**2.86**

Source: OPPI Annual Report 1999-2000.

Annexure VII: Contract Manufacturing Opportunities

Company	MNC	Drug
Ranbaxy	Eli Lilly	Cefaclor
Lupin	Cynamid	D2 amino butanol
Nicholas Piramal	Allergan Inc.	Allergan's products
	Siegfried of Switzerland	Four products that go off-patent in 2001
	Baker Norton of UK	Entire range of Norton's products
Wockhardt	Ferring BV of the Netherlands	Formulations
	Sidmak Labs of the US	Bulk drugs
IPCA	SmithKline Beecham	Formulations
	Merck	Bulk drugs
	Tillomed	Intermediates PHPA
	Zeneca	Intermediates PHPA
	Hoechst Celanese	Bulk drugs
Kopran	Synpac Labs	Penicillin-G bulk
Cadila Healthcare	Byk Gulden	Bulk drug for antiulcerant molecule

Source: The ET Intelligence Group – Report on HealthCare, 2000-2001.

Annexure VIII

(a) Total R&D Spend in Indian Pharmaceutical Business		(b) R&D Expenses as Percentage of Sales of Top Indian Pharmaceutical Companies	
Year	**Rupees in billion**	**Company**	**2003**
1993-94	1.25	Wockhardt	10.5%
1994-95	1.4	Ranbaxy	6%
1995-96	1.6	Cipla	4%
1996-97	1.85	Sun Pharma	4%
1997-98	2.2	Torrent	6.4%
1998-99	2.6	Dr. Reddy's	4.4%
1999-00	3.2	Nicholas Piramal	1.63%
		Lupin	1%
		Industry Average	2%

Annexure IX: R&D Initiatives by Major Indian Companies

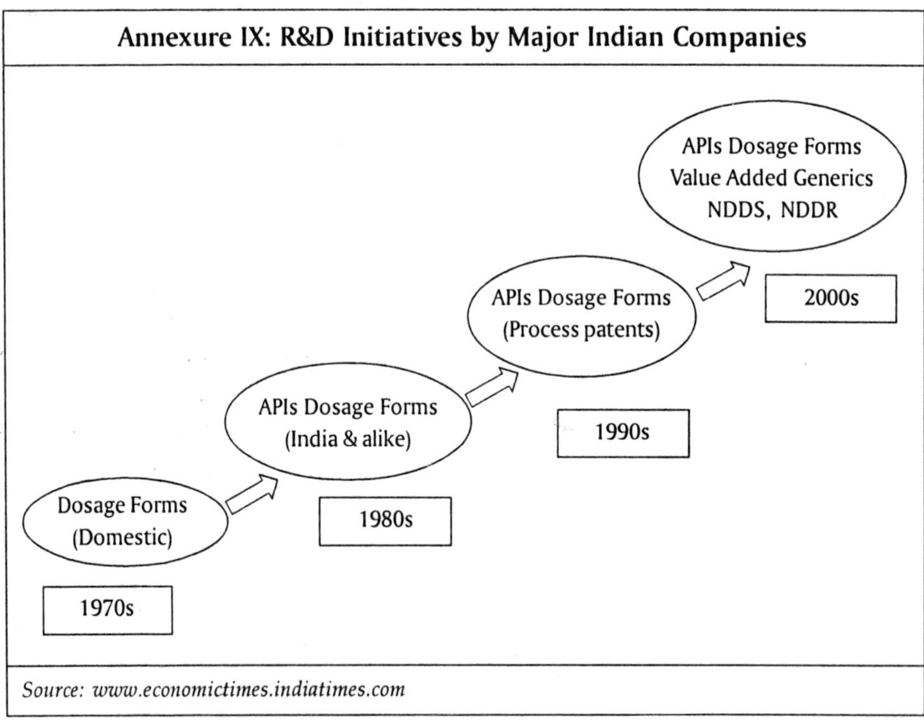

Source: www.economictimes.indiatimes.com

Annexure X: Therapeutic Categories and Different Brands Produced by NPIL

No.	Therapeutic Category	Brands
1	Anaesthetic Agents	Buprenorphine, Critifol, Entubate, Fluothane, Glutihyde, Isorane, Midaz, Midazolam, Pancuronium, Verunium
2	Analgesic/Anti-inflammatory	Coxegesic, Malidens, Orthobid, Orthobid Plus, Postadol, Rexib, Vah - P !, Vah !
3	Antibiotics	Amexel, Bactrim, Effimax, Gatri, Gatri IV 400, Genticyn, Gres, Gres IV 400, Maylox, Moxycarb, MoxycarbDT, Nivaquine – P, Omnatax, Omnatax – O, Paraxin, Paraxin Palmitate, Rovamycin, Zidime, Maxiguard
4	Anti Fungal	Not Available
5	Antihistamines	Xevor, Phenergan, Stemetil, Stemetil Inj.
6	Antiseptics	Aceptik HC, Aceptik LA, Cetrimide, Chlorhexidine Solution, Povidone Iodine
7	Cardiovascular	Acinopril, Bezalip, Bezalip Retard, Calaptin, Calaptin SR, Cardules, Cardules Plus, Cardules Retard, Carvetrend, Cytogard, Cytogard OD, Dopacard, Enace, Enace D, Fortius, Icidil CD, Icidob, Icikinase, Ismo 10, Ismo 20, Ismo Retard, Lerka, LMWX, Micropyrin, Monosorbitrate, Monosorbitrate CR, Nubeta, Sorbitrate, Stromix, Stromix A, Tenoclor, Tenormin, Tenormin Upbeat, X-Arb, X-Arb-H.
8	Central Nervous System	Gardenal, Garoin, Inderal, Librax, Librium, Madopar, Mysoline, Neostigmine Inj BP, Phenobarbitone inj, Reboot, Real One, Rivotril, Sizoquit, Szetalo, Valance, Valium, Zetalo
9	Diabetes	Diabetrol, Euglucon, Glimer, Gluformin, Gluformin G1, Gluformin G2, Gluformin XL, Gluspan, Nervup, Nervup INJ, Piozone, Piozone M, Piozone G, Semi-Euglucon
10	Dermatology	Ascabiol, Lobate, Lobate GM, Lobate M, Lobate G, Lobate S, Melagard, Melalite 15, Melalite Forte, Tetmosol Soap
11	Endocrinology	Aquaviron, Kidpred Oral Susp, Kidpred Forte Oral Susp., Neomercazole.

Contd...

Contd...

12	Gastroenteritis	Avomine, Essential – L, Famtac, Flagyl, Fybogel, Secnil Forte
13	Gynaecology	Mefipil, Rovamycin
14	Multivitamins/Nutraceuticals	A0-7, Becozym C Forte, Becozym Syrup, Benadon, Exerge, Osteospan, Supractiv, Supradyn, Vitamin A
15	Oncology	Bondronate, Cymevene, Herceptin, Mabthera, Neupogen, Recormon 1000, Recormon 2000, Recormon 5000, Roferon –A, Vesanoid, Xeloda
16	Pulmonary/Respiratory	Airitis, Deletus, Deletus BX, Deletus D, Deletus P, Monti Phensedyl Cough Linctus, Tixylix, Trustyl
17	Trauma/Emergency	Not Available

Source: www.nicholaspiramal.com

Annexure XI: Therapeutic Segment-wise Turnover

(Rupees in Million)

No.	Therapeutic Category	Sales %	FY2004 Half-Year	FY2003 Half-Year	Growth %	Market Growth %
1	Respiratory	19.8	824.9	744.8	10.8	4.6
2	Anti-Infective	10.4	433.5	447.2	(3.1)	(0.7)
3	Cardiovascular (CVS)	9.9	413.1	321.0	28.7	13.8
4	Central Nervous System (CNS)	9.5	396.2	336.0	17.9	9.4
5	Nutritionals	9.3	388.1	325.4	19.3	0.7
6	Biotek	8.2	342.4	315.1	8.7	–
7	Anti-Diabetic	4.6	192.6	122.6	57.2	15.6
8	Gastro-intestinal	4.3	181.0	196.7	(8.0)	6.4
9	Dermatology	4.0	168.4	142.2	18.4	1.7
10	NSAIDs	2.8	114.5	89.4	28.0	3.5
11	Others	17.0	709.4	645.8	9.8	–
	Total	**100.0**	**4,164.0**	**3,686.1**	**13.0**	4.4

Note: Market growth is as per CAN-ORG_MARG MAT-Aug-03. Market Growth figures not available for Biotek and Others.

Source: www.nicholaspiramal.com

Endnotes

1 Das, Nisha, "Nicholas Piramal-Rhone merger over," *www.domain-b.com,* October 10th 2001.

2 NPIL was a part of the Rs.2.5 billion (US$550 million) Piramal Enterprise Limited (PEL), one of India's largest diversified business groups.

3 Bulk Drugs – Chemicals used for production of pharmaceutical formulations.

4 Formulations are drugs in final dosage form.

5 Active Pharmaceutical Ingredients or Bulk Drugs are either produced by chemical synthesis or are of plant, animal, or biological origin.

6 *www.indiainfoline.com.*

7 Patents, in the case of drugs, allowed the drug to be made, used, imported/exported or sold by the patent holder, i.e., the initial developer only. A patented drug was usually marketed under a proprietary or brand name reserved exclusively to its owner, i.e., the individual or firm granted a patent on that invention.

8 The Indian Patents Act, 1970 allowed Indian companies to reverse engineer patented molecules and launch them in the domestic markets. IPA allowed only process patent, not product patent, so manufacturers were permitted to copy foreign drugs and, with a minor change in the process they could make them available to the common man at an affordable price.

9 *www.pharmaceutical-drug-manufacturers.com,* Exchange rate $1 = Rs.45.50.

10 HealthCare – An ETIG Presentation, 2001-2002.

11 *www.public.asu.edu*

12 TRIPS was one of a series of trade agreements administered by the WTO.

13 A generic drug was usually intended to be interchangeable with the original patented drug ("bioequivalent") as it did the same thing. Unless there was a prior agreement with the patent owner, a generic drug was usually made and marketed after the expiry of patent rights held by the patentee.

14 Analogue Research – a process that involved modifying an existing molecule or a new one that had not been commercialised after accessing international patent databases, to arrive at a new molecule.

15 "I expect a shakeout in Indian Healthcare Industry," *www.indiamarkets.com,* December 5th 2000.

16 A Drug Delivery System ensures that drugs are released slowly in the body once they're ingested; they also include tablets that have to be swallowed, say, once a day instead of thrice.

17 USFDA – United States Food and Drug Administration.

18 Since 1957, the principal owners of the Indian Schering Ltd, were Nicholas International Ltd., Melbourne, Australia, a pharmaceutical company well known for their registered trade marks – "Aspro", "Asmapax", "Albucid", "Olycrol", etc.

19 Ophthalmic – of or related to the eye.

20 NPIL and Reckitt & Coleman Plc held 40% each of the Rs.10-crore equity of Reckitt Piramal, & RCI held 20%.

21 NPIL pulled out of the JVs with Scholl (UK), Reckitt Piramal Pvt. Ltd, Stryker and US Surgicals in 2001.

22 Cosmoceuticals – A cosmetic with active pharmaceutical ingredients. Example: Fair and Lovely Anti-marks cream.

23 CSIR – The Council of Scientific and Industrial Research.

24 *www.nicholaspiramal.com,* Rig Veda is the most ancient collection of Hindu sacred verses, consisting principally of hymns to various deities.

25 Piramal Enterprises had taken over GGPL in 1984.

26 *www.indiainfoline.com*

27 Iyer, Ananth, "Hoechst, Nicholas Piramal to Co-market two Products," *www.domain-b.com,* July 1st 1999.

28 Therapeutic – Something that treats disease or injury. Therapeutic viruses, unlike wild-type viruses are helpful (www.onyx-pharm.com). Therapeutic means having healing or curative powers (neurolab.nasa.gov).

29 Mathew, James, "Nicholas Piramal to merge SPPL," *www.economictimes.indiatimes.com,* December 31st 2003.

30 The brands of BPHL included Strepsils (medicated sore throat lozenge), Ultra Clearasil (acne treatment cream), Icy (throat lozenge) and Sweetex (artificial sweeteners), Aspro (an analgesic), Lacto Calamine (a skincare lotion) and Polycrol (an antacid).

31 Maltols are artificial sweeteners.

32 "Nicholas Piramal to focus on Biotech," *www.domain-b.com,* November 13th 2001.

33 CFA – clearing and forwarding agents

34 *www.org-marg.com*

35 "After Avonex, NPIL-Biogen Tie-up to Market Amevive," *www.financialexpress.com,* November 28th 2003.

36 "Nicholas Piramal merges Hyderabad based Canere Actives and Fine Chemicals Pvt. Ltd," *www.prweb.com,* February 1st 2004.

37 A Drug Master File (DMF) is a submission to the Food and Drug Administration (FDA) that may be used to provide confidential detailed information about facilities, processes, or articles used in the manufacturing, processing, packaging, and storing of one or more human drugs.

38 "Nicholas' Take on Takeovers," *The Economic Times – Investors Guide*, March 13th 2003.

39 *www.ciionline.com*

40 ibid.

41 *www.sharekhan.com*

42 A generic drug product is one that is comparable to an innovator drug product in dosage form, strength, route of administration, quality, performance characteristics and intended use.

43 "Nicholas Piramal net leaps 77% year on year," *www.indiainfoline.com,* January 28th 2004.

44 "Nicholas Piramal rolls out growth plan; Maini, Choudhari on board," *www.domain-b.com,* October 3rd 2003.

45 Verma, Prachi "Nicholas Piramal plans to set up 2 R&D Centers for Clinical Trials," *www.financialexpress.com,* October 17th 2003.

46 *www.whartonglobalforum.com*

47 "Nicholas Piramal lays new thrust on R&D," *www.economictimes.indiatimes.com,* October 5th 2003.

48 Anti-oxidants – prolong the induction period of base oil in the presence of oxidizing conditions and catalyst metals at elevated temperatures. The additive is consumed and degradation products increase not only with increasing and sustained temperature, but also with increases in mechanical agitation or turbulence and contamination. Anti-oxidants increase the life span of the substance.

49 Praveen Chandran, "Nicholas Piramal's New Business Strategy," *www.domain-b.com,* March 4th 2004.

50 Ibid.

51 Vijay Shah, "Interview: We are Focused on Building Brands," *www.financialexpress.com,* September 7th 2003.

52 Shehla Hasan Raza, "Nicholas Piramal to focus on mega brands," *www.domain-b.com,* June 18th 2002.

53 Osteoarthritis – A degenerative joint disease affecting 65 years or above people, with over 75% being women. Here, the cartilage of the affected joint roughens and becomes worn out.

54 Writankar Mukherjee, "NPIL wants a larger pie of antioxidant market," *www.economictimes.indiatimes.com,* October 28th 2003.

55 "Nicholas Piramal launches new anti-allergic drug," *www.thehindubusinessline.com,* January 3rd 2003.

56 Op.cit, "Interview: We are Focused on Building Brands."

57 ACTIS is the respiratory division which markets NPIL's biggest brand – the Rs.1200 million Phensedyl cough syrup.

58 Kamath Gauri "Nicholas Piramal – A Different Tack," *www.businessworldindia.com,* December 22nd 2003.

59 Op.cit, "Nicholas Piramal Plans to set up 2 R&D centres for Clinical Trials."

60 Lasker Awards for basic clinical and medical research is also known as 'America's Nobels'. They were first awarded in 1946.

61 Op.cit, "Nicholas Piramal rolls out growth plan; Maini, Choudhari on board".

62 Benign Prostatic Hyperplasia – A nonmalignant enlargement of the prostate gland commonly occurring in men after the age of 50, and sometimes leading to compression of the urethra and obstruction of the flow of urine.

63 An Abbreviated New Drug Application (ANDA) contains data which when submitted to USFDA's Center for Drug Evaluation and Research, Office of Generic Drugs, provides for the review and ultimate approval of a generic drug product. Once approved, an applicant may manufacture and market the generic drug product to provide a safe, effective, low-cost alternative to the American public.

64 Rao, Harish "Top Indian Drug Companies," *www.pharmabiz.com,* October 23rd 2003.

65 ORG MAT, December 2003, *www.gsk-india.com*

66 Retrovial – Any of a group of viruses, many of which produce tumors, that contain RNA and reverse transcriptase, including the virus that causes AIDS.

67 Mathail Palakunnathu G and Surendar, "Pharma Drama," *www.businessworldindia.com,* April 7th 1999.

References

1. "Laporte and Piramal form JV in India," *www.findarticles.com, Chemical Market Reporter,* August 17, 1998.

2. Palakunnathu G. Mathail and Surendar, T, "Pharma Drama," *www.businessworldindia.com,* April 7th 1999.

3. Iyer, Ananth "Hoechst, Nicholas Piramal to Co-market Two Products," *www.domain-b.com,* July 1st 1999.

4. Landau, Peter "Danisco Cultor Licenses Maltol In India to Stay Competitive," *www.findarticles.com, Chemical Market Reporter,* September 20th 1999.

5. "I expect a Shakeout in Indian Healthcare Industry," *www.indiamarkets.com,* December 5th 2000.

6. Das, Nisha "Nicholas Piramal-Rhone Merger Over," *www.domain-b.com,* October 10th 2001.

7. "Nicholas Piramal to Focus on Biotech", *www.domain-b.com,* November 13th 2001.

8. Chandran, Praveen "NPIL ropes in McKinsey for Total Integration," *www.domain-b.com,* May 27th 2002.

9. Raza, Shehla Hasan "Nicholas Piramal to focus on mega brands," *www.domain-b.com,* June 18th 2002.

10. Chandran, Praveen "Nicholas Piramal Hikes its Stake in JV by 9%," *www.domain-b.com,* September 9th 2002.

11. "Nicholas Piramal launches new Anti-allergic Drug," *www.thehindubusinessline.com,* January 3rd 2003.

12. Joshi, Hemant "Analysis of Indian Pharmaceutical Industry," *www.pharmtech.com,* January 2003.

13. "Nicholas' Take on Takeovers," *The Economic Times – Investors Guide,* March 13th 2003.

14. "A Pure Pharma Play", *www.sharekhan.com,* June 14th 2003.

15. Shah, Vijay "Interview: We are focused on Building Brands," *www.financialexpress.com,* September 7th 2003.

16. "Nicholas Piramal Rolls out Growth Plan; Maini, Choudhari on Board," *www.domain-b.com,* October 3rd 2003.

17. Rane, Pradeep "Nicholas Piramal follows MNC Pharma Companies' Strategy," *www.domain-b.com,* October 3rd 2003.

18. "Nicholas Piramal lays new Thrust on R&D," *www.economictimes.indiatimes.com,* October 5th 2003.

19. Narendranath K G "Nicholas Piramal looks for Global Partnership in Therapeutic R&D," *www.economictimes.indiatimes.com,* October 8th 2003.

20. Verma, Prachi "Nicholas Piramal plans to set up 2 R&D Centers for Clinical Trials", *www.financialexpress.com,* October 17th 2003.

21. Rao, Harish "Top Indian Drug Companies," *www.pharmabiz.com,* October 23rd 2003.

22. Mukherjee, Writankar "NPIL wants a Larger Pie of Antioxidant Market," *www.economictimes.indiatimes.com,* October 28th 2003.

23. "After Avonex, NPIL-Biogen Tie-up to Market Amevive," *www.financialexpress.com,* November 28th 2003.

24. Ghaswalla, Nair Amrita "Nicholas Piramal takes Cancer Drug to Clinical Trial Stage," *www.economictimes.indiatimes.com,* December 2nd 2003.

25. Datta P, Jyothi T and Srivats, K T "Nicholas Piramal looking for Brands for Tail-brands: Ajay," *www.thehindubusinessline.com,* December 10th 2003.

26. Kamath, Gauri, "Nicholas Piramal – A Different Tack", *www.businessworldindia.com,* December 22nd 2003.

27. Mathew, James "Nicholas Piramal to Merge SPPL," *www.economictimes.indiatimes.com,* December 31st 2003.

28. Gupta, Shubra "The Pharmaceutical Market in India," *www.public.asu.edu,* 2003.

29. "Nicholas Piramal Net Leaps 77% Year on Year," *www.indiainfoline.com,* January 28th 2004.

30. "Nicholas Piramal: Focus Pays Off," *www.equitymaster.com,* January 29th 2004.

31. "Nicholas Piramal Merges Hyderabad based Canere Actives and Fine Chemicals Pvt. Ltd.," *www.prweb.com,* February 1st 2004.

32. "Nicholas Piramal to set up US Subsidiary," *www.economictimes.indiatimes.com,* February 11th 2004.

33. Chandran Praveen "Nicholas Piramal's New Business Strategy," *www.domain-b.com,* March 4th 2004.

34. Israni Jaya, "Indian Pharma: The Road Ahead," *ICFAI University Press,* 2004.

35. Srikanth Gandlur, "The Indian Pharmaceutical Industry: Opportunities and Challenges," ICFAI Business School Case Development Centre, 2004.

36. "Nicholas Piramal India – Contract Manufacturing of Active Pharmaceutical Ingredients, Key Intermediates and Formulations," *www.pharmaceutical-technology.com*

37. "Pharmaceuticals Market in India," *www.tradepartners.gov*

38. "About Pharmaceutical Industries in India," *www.medindia.net*

39. HealthCare – An ETIG Presentation, 2001-2002.

40. "Indian Pharmaceutical Industry: An Overview," *www.pharmaceutical-drug-manufacturers.com*

Section II

IPR: Indian Perspectives

6

IPRs in India

India has a well established statutory, administrative and judicial framework to safeguard intellectual property rights. Intellectual property laws in India are governed by the following statutes:

1. ***The Trade Marks Act, 1958***
2. ***The Patents Act, 1970***
3. ***The Copyright Act, 1957***
4. ***The Designs Act, 2000***
5. ***The Geographical Indication of Goods Act, 1999.***

The article gives a systematic explanation about the legislation, administration, events coming under the purview of the acts, rights and liabilities, people who could apply the related measures of all the above said Acts.

Intellectual Property

Intellectual property laws protect such ideas/information, which are of commercial value by preventing competitors from commercially exploiting the respective rights to the detriment of the owner of that property. Such laws are vital for obtaining and maintaining an advantage over competitors in any

Source: www.dubeypartners.com.

industrial and commercial activity. The right to prevent others from using ideas or information to their own commercial advantage is necessary to secure and retain share of the market.

In today's competitive world, the business houses world over invest huge amount of money and effort for invention and development of new products and ideas. In order to protect and capitalize on their investments, they need to ensure that they own the intellectual property rights over such innovation or development. Hence, it is crucial that companies understand how to protect their intellectual property rights as any negligence caused by them in doing so may altogether threaten their very existence in the market.

Protection of Intellectual Property in India

Generally speaking the intellectual property laws prevailing in India are commensurate to international standards, so as to attract investment and world-class technologies to Indian shores.

India has a well-established statutory, administrative and judicial framework to safeguard intellectual property rights (IPR) be it patents, trademarks, copyright or industrial designs. Recently, India has incorporated several changes in its IPR laws to make it more compatible with the WTO regime, notable among them being the extension of trademark laws to service sector in addition to trademarks for goods. Computer software companies have successfully curtailed piracy through court orders. Computer databases have been protected. Courts have, under the doctrine of breach of confidentiality, accorded an extensive protection of trade secrets. Right to privacy, which is not protected even in some developed countries, has been recognized in India.

Legal Framework

Intellectual property laws in India are governed by the following statutes:

- The Trademarks Act 1958
- The Patents Act 1970
- The Copyright Act, 1957

- The Designs Act 2000
- The Geographical Indications of Goods (Registration and Protection) Act, 1999.

India, in pursuance to its effort to comply with the international treaties, has a long history of protecting intellectual property rights through continuously upgrading the legislative enactments and the judiciary in India is supplementing it with its effort in extending the protection to the gray areas of the legislation.

Administrative Framework

In addition to the above legislative changes, the Government of India has taken several measures to streamline and strengthen the intellectual property administration system in the country. Projects relating to the modernization of patent information services and trademarks registry have been implemented with help from World Intellectual Property Organization (WIPO)/United Nations Development Programme (UNDP). The Government of India is implementing a project for modernization of patent offices incorporating several aspects such as human resource development, recruiting additional examiners, developing infrastructure support by way of computerization and re-engineering work practices, and elimination of backlog of patent applications in an expeditious manner etc. An amendment to the Patent Rules was notified on May 2, 2003 to simplify the procedural aspects in this regard.

As regards the aspect of enforcing IPR rights, Indian enforcement agencies are now working very effectively and there has been a notable decline in the levels of piracy in India. In addition to intensifying raids against copyright infringers, the Government has also taken a number of measures to strengthen the enforcement of copyright law. Special cells for copyright enforcement have been set up in 23 States and Union Territories. In addition to that, copyright societies have been set up for collective administration of copyright in, different classes of works.

Compliance to International Standards

In terms of Section 5 of the Patents Act, the patents are presently restricted to the methods or process of manufacture and not extended to the substances/products themselves. In terms of the Trade Related Intellectual Property Rights (TRIPS)

Agreement, India has time till January 1, 2005 to extend patent protection to this area.

However, to meet its current obligations required under Articles 70.8 and 70.9 of the TRIPS Agreement. the Government of India has taken the following steps:

1. It has promulgated an Ordinance to provide a means to receive product patent applications in the fields of pharmaceutical and agricultural chemical products and also for grant of exclusive marketing rights. Pursuant to this measure the Indian Patent Offices have been receiving product patent applications in those fields.
2. It has established a mailbox system through administrative instructions. Numerous applications have already been received by this mailbox system.

In August 1998 India joined the Patent Cooperation Treaty (PCT) by acceding to the Paris Convention on Intellectual Property.

Patents

The Legislation

The laws pertaining to Patent in India is governed by the Patents Act, 1970 which has been amended twice by The Patents (Amendment) Act, 1999 and The Patents (Amendment) Act, 2002. Although the New Patent Act, 2002 has been notified on June 25th 2002, only limited sections of it has been made applicable currently vide Gazette Notification from Government of India, dated May 20, 2003, Although, it is being implemented in phased manner, its only a matter of time that the new Act shall be applicable in completion.

Therefore, as of now, the old Acts i.e., The Patent Act, 1970 and The Patent Rules 1972 are applicable except for the sections made applicable through the Gazette Notification, as stated above.

The Administration

The Patent Office, under the Ministry of Commerce & Industry, Department of Industrial Policy & Promotion, administers the various provisions of the Patent and Design Laws relating to the grant of Patents and registration of Industrial Designs. As regards applicability of Indian patent provisions worldwide is concerned, India is a member of the following international treaties and the said provisions are applicable on the member countries on a reciprocal basis.

- Convention establishing World Intellectual Property Organization.
- TRIPS Agreement under the World Trade Organization which is being implemented in a phased manner.
- Paris Convention for the protection of Industrial Property with effect from Dec. 7, 1998.
- Patent Cooperation Treaty (PCT) with effect from Dec. 7, 1998.

What is Patentable

Patents are granted in respect of any invention in goods. An invention means any new and useful art, process, method or manner of manufacture, machine, apparatus or other article, or substance produced by manufacture, and includes any new and useful improvement in any of them. No patent is granted in respect of claims for the substances themselves, however, claims for the methods or processes of manufacture is patentable. However, in compliance with its commitment under the TRIPS agreement, India has been given time to introduce product patent by the year 2005.

Exclusive Marketing Rights

The Indian Patent Act does not recognize product patent for medicines and agro chemicals. However, in conformity with WTO norms it recognizes grant of Exclusive Marketing rights (EMR) in respect of above products. India offers EMR as an interim measure i.e before granting product patents for drugs with effect from 1.1.2005. Hence EMR shall be offered during the interregnum. To be eligible for EMR the applicant should have applied for and got patent in another country which is a signatory to the TRIPS agreement on or after 1.1.1995. The objective of the right is to have the exclusive right to sell or distribute in India either by himself or his agents or licensees, the product for a period of five years, or till the grant, or the date of rejection of application for the grant of patent, whichever is earlier.

Who Can Apply

Application for patents can be made by any person claiming to be the true and first inventor of the invention or by his assignee or legal representative. An application for patent can be made by any of these persons either alone or jointly with any other person. Two or more companies as assignees may also make an application jointly.

Steps Involved in Grant of Patent:

1. Filing of an application for grant of a patent accompanied by either a provisional specification or a complete specification before any public disclosure of the invention.
2. In case provisional specification accompanied the original application, then filing of the complete specification within 12 months of filing the provisional specification. The said period may be extended by a further period of 3 months by paying appropriate fee for extension.
3. Technical examination of the application by the patent office.
4. Acceptance of the application and advertisement of such acceptance in the official gazette.
5. Overcoming opposition, if any, to the grant of a patent.
6. Grant and sealing of the patent.
7. Maintenance of patent by payment of renewal fee.
8. Enforcement/revocation.

Patent Cooperation Treaty – PCT

PCT is the acronym of Patent Cooperation Treaty. It is a sister Treaty of the Paris Convention administered by the World Intellectual Property Organization (WIPO). The PCT which is more than 100 years old treaty facilitates filing of patent applications under a single umbrella and provides for simplified procedure for the search and examination of such applications.

The Paris Convention, offers a 12-month grace period for an inventor to file a patent application in other member countries after filing in the home country.

The PCT extends the benefits of the Paris Convention by allowing an inventor to file an international patent application, which has the effect of filing a separate patent application in each of the PCT member countries designated by the inventor. This application does not mature into an international patent but rather extends the grace period up to 30 months for an inventor to take further action to obtain a patent in each PCT member country where one is desired. The PCT serves to simplify and make more economical the patenting process in the member countries and facilitates the availability of technical information amidst member countries.

PCT – The Filing Procedure

1. International Phase

India being one of the contracting state in the PCT, any Indian applicant may file an international application in the standard format [Form PCT/RO/101] through any of the Indian Patent Offices as the Receiving Office i.e., The Patent Office, Kolkata, and its branch Offices at New Delhi, Mumbai, Chennai (RO/IN) along with the copy of Specification and Statutory Fees. Language of filing may be either in English or Hindi.

At the time of filing the said application the applicant is also required to mention the number of countries wherein eventually registration of patent is desired to be sought and also has to specify the name of the International Search Authority and the International Preliminary Examination Authority.

The following are the documents that must accompany a PCT Application filed through an Indian Patent office as the receiving office:

1. PCT Request (Form PCT/RO/101).
2. The complete specification in triplicate.
3. Power of Attorney
4. Certified priority document.

On the receipt of the application, the patent office shall prepare a certified copy of the priority documents and transmit the same to the International Bureau and the International Search Authority with intimation to the applicant. Thereafter, the international search is conducted and the copy of the search report is also forwarded to the applicant.

2. The National Phase

Once the formalities under step one are duly complied and the applicant receives the International Search Report or once the Final International Preliminary Examination Report, is complete and issued, the application enters the National Phase.

Filing of National Phase Application in India requires the request for the grant of patent to be made to the competent Receiving Office i.e., the Patent Office, Kolkata, and its branch Offices at New Delhi, Mumbai, Chennai in the prescribed form i.e., Form 1A. Language of filing may be either in English or Hindi.

Further the following information/documents are also required to be submitted along with the necessary fees with the Patent office:

1. Request (PCT/RO/101).
2. Description of Invention.
3. Abstract.
4. Drawings (where applicable).
5. P.A./G.P.A. (where applicable).
6. The Specification including drawing figures as published in the PCT Gazette.
7. Verified English translation of international application, if not in English.
8. International Search Report.
9. International Preliminary Examination Report (if India is elected for using the IPE results).
10. Certified Copies of the Priority Documents.
11. Particulars of amendments made to the specification/claims during the PCT International Phase.

12. Verified English translation of amendments filed during the international phase.
13. All the physical requirements of PCT, presentation style, paper size, print front etc., have also to be met, and such other information and documents that the patent office may require to be submitted.

Protection available to Patentee

Once the patent is granted, the patentee has the exclusive right to make, use, exercise, sell or distribute the patented article or substance in India or to use or exercise the method or process. He can prevent all others from making or using the patented process. A patentee has also the right to assign the patent, grant licenses under, or otherwise deal with it for any consideration. These rights created by statute can be exercised either by the patentee himself or by his agents or licensees during the term of patent.

Duration of Patents

The term of every patent granted shall be twenty years from the date of filing of the application with complete specification as per the Patents (Amendment) Act, 2000.

Renewal

Renewal fees are payable every year. The first renewal fee is payable for third year of the patent's life, and must be paid before the patent's second anniversary. If the patent has not been issued within that period, renewal fees may be accumulated and paid immediately after the patent is sealed, or within three months of its recording in the Register of the Patents.

Date of payment of Renewal fees is measured from the date of the patent. Six months grace period is available with extension fee. No renewal fees are payable on patents of addition, unless the original patent is revoked and the patent of addition is converted into an independent patent; renewal fees then become payable for the remainder of the term of the patent.

Statutory Requirements

Preparation of Annual reports as to the extent of working, by every patentee and licensee, are a statutory requirement and the same must be submitted by March, 31 each year for the previous year ending December, 31.

Compulsory Licence and Licence of Right

On failure to work a patent within three years from the date of its sealing, an interested party may file petition for grant of a compulsory license.

Every patent for an invention relating to a method or process for manufacture of substances intended for use, or capable of being used, as food, medicines, or drugs, or relating to substances prepared or produced by chemical process (including alloys, optical glass, semi-conductors and inter-metallic compounds) shall be deemed to be endorsed Licenses of Right from the date of expiry of three years from the date of sealing the patent.

Assignment

Applications must be filed in the prescribed form with the Controller for the registration of assignments. Any other document creating an interest in a patent must also be filed with the Controller in order for them to be valid. In order to be valid, an assignment must be recorded within six months from the date of the document. However, in case of delay, an extension of six months may be obtained.

License

Applications must be filed in the prescribed form with the Controller for the registration of licenses. Any other document creating an interest in a patent must also be filed with the Controller in order for them to be valid. A license must be recorded within six months from the date of the document.

Protection available against Infringement of Patent

The rights conferred by a patent are exclusive rights to make, use or sell or distribute the invention in India. Violation consists in misappropriation of any of these rights without the authorization of the registered owner. The onus is on the plaintiff that is the patentee to prove infringement. However, where the subject matter of patent is a process for obtaining a product, the court may direct the defendant to prove that the process used by him to obtain the product, identical to the product of the patented is different from the patented process.

Unlike in cases of Trademark or Copyrights, violation of patent does not entail any criminal proceedings. The remedies available are essentially of civil nature and includes following: (a) Injunction; (b) Damages or account of profit; (c) Seizure, forfeiture or destruction of infringing material.

Trademark

The Legislation

The provisions pertaining to Trademarks is governed by the Trade & Merchandise Act, 1958. Although the Trademark (Amendment) Act, 1999 has been notified, however, it has not yet been implemented and a Gazette Notification for its implementation date as well as that of its Rules are awaited. Accordingly, the new Act and rules thereof are yet to become effective.

The Trade & Merchandise Act, 1958 defines a trademark as a mark used in relation to goods so as to indicate a connection in the course of trade between the goods and the proprietor. At present, the protection of trademark is available on physical goods or commodities traded. But under the new Act, trademark registration would be extended to services also. However, presently marks used in connection with service sector are well protected by judicial decisions under the common law.

Trademark may be a letter mark or a Symbol mark. The symbol mark may be a brand name identifying the product or a Logo giving a visual depiction of the company and thereby identifying the company. Under the Act, a Mark includes a device, brand, heading, label, ticket, name, signature, word, letter or numeral or any combination thereof.

For the purposes of registration, a mark chosen should not be deceptively similar to an existing mark of another person and not the one expressly prohibited under the Act. The marks devoid of any distinctive character, or which are only indicative of the kind, quality, quantity, purpose, value or geographical origin of the goods, or which are marks already in vogue due to their customary use may not be registered. But these disqualifications do not apply to marks, which have already acquired distinction due to their popularity and consistent use. The new Act also seeks to make internationally acclaimed brand names freely available for use in India.

Who Can Apply

Any person intending to register a trademark in its name may apply for registration of such a trademark to the Trademark office under whose jurisdiction the principal place of the business of the applicant in India falls. In case of a company about to be formed, anyone may apply in its name for subsequent assignment of the registration in the company's favor.

Registration of the trademark can be only in respect of any or all goods comprised in a prescribed class of goods. Before making an application for registration it is recommended to conduct a search of the already registered trademarks to ensure that registration may not be denied due to resemblance of the proposed mark to an existing one or prohibited one.

Steps Involved in Registration

1. An application is filed with the office of the Trademarks registry in Form TM-1 along with the specified statutory fee. Goods for which registration is sought must also be stated. Suitable representation of trademark should be filed. It should be ensured that there is no prohibition on registering the particular Trademark.

2. Once an application is filed the Registrar will cause a search to be carried out among the registered trademarks and trademarks pending registration. An Examination report seeking clarifications and suggesting modifications may be forwarded to the Applicant.

3. The applicant is required to reply to the Examination Report within 3 months. Application could be suitably amended or hearing may also be asked.

4. Registrar may accept the trademark with or without modifications, and with limitations or conditions.

5. If the Registrar refuses to register a trademark, or the conditions or limitations imposed by him are not acceptable, an appeal against his decision may be made within a period of 1 month.

6. After a trademark is finally accepted, it is published in *Trade Marks Journal* to give to third parties an opportunity for opposition within 3 months. Opposition has to be filed in TM-5 in triplicate with prescribed fees. The

counter statement has to be filed in Form TM-6 in triplicate within 2 months. After that, there will be filing of evidence and hearing, and final order will be issued.

7. After the acceptance of the trademark, it will be registered on payment of prescribed fees and the Registrar issues certificate.

Protection available to Registered Trademarks

After registration of a trademark in the name of a person, such person gets a right over that trademark. Such right can only be acquired by user, or any other person by assignment or grant of license by the user.

Assignment and Transmission

A registered trademark is assignable and transmissible, whether with or without the goodwill of the business concerned and in respect of any or all the goods in respect of which it is registered. However, an unregistered trademark can be assigned or transmitted only with the good will of the business concerned. Assignment of trademark should also be registered.

Licensing of a Trademark

The Trade Marks Act contains provisions for registration of a licensee of a registered trade mark as its registered user. The advantage of such registration is that the use of the trademark by the licensee shall be deemed to be in use by the owner himself and can not be cancelled for non-use.

Procedures for Registration of Licence:

i. The application for the same is made jointly by the licensor and the licensee to the Registrar of Trademarks.

ii. The application is accompanied by the Registered User Agreement and other prescribed documents including an affidavit by the licensor or by some other person authorized by him to act on his behalf testifying to the genuineness of the documents accompanying the application and containing the prescribed particulars.

iii. The application shall be filed within 18 months from the date of the agreement between the parties.

Duration of a Trademark

Unlike other intellectual property rights, a trademark has a perpetual time period subject to its renewal from time to time. At present the initial term of registration of a trademark is seven years, after which it could be renewed for further periods of seven years each on payment of prescribed renewal fee. Under the new Act, the initial term of registration would be extended to ten years and after that it could be renewed for another 10 years and so on.

Convention Application and International Treaties

India has declared certain countries as convention countries, which grant similar privileges to Indians as granted to its own citizens. A person from a convention country, may within six months of making an application in his or her home country, apply for registration of the same trademark in India. If such a trademark is accepted for registration, such foreign national shall be deemed to have registered his or her trademark in India as well, from the same date on which he or she made application in his or her home country.

In other words, where applications have been made for the registration of trademark in two or more convention countries, the period of six months would be reckoned from the date on which the earliest of those applications was made.

Although the recovery of damages for infringement of a trademark is possible only if the infringement takes place after the date of filing application for registration with the concerned trademark office in India, yet the deemed seniority in making application in home country may entitle the applicant to initiate an action in India for injunction etc.

Same Privileges to Indians as well as to Foreigners

The Trade and Merchandise Act, 1958 makes no distinction between Indians and foreigners in the matter of registration of trademarks, registration of assignment of registered trademarks, or in applying for registration as registered user of trademarks. Likewise, common law also does not make any distinction on the ground of nationality. Therefore, in India except in case of nationals of countries, which do not give reciprocal protection to Indian goods, same treatment is accorded to Indians as well as foreigners in respect of protection of trademarks both under the statute and common law.

Protection available against Infringement and Passing-Off

Two types of remedies are available to the owner of a trademark for unauthorized use of his or her mark or its imitation by a third party. These remedies are:—'an action for infringement' in case of a registered trademark and an action for passing off in the case of an unregistered trademark. While former is a statutory remedy, the latter is a common law remedy. In a suit for infringement or for passing off, the relief that the court may grant includes injunction, damages or an account for profits with or without any order for delivery of the infringing labels and marks for destruction.

High courts in India have held that passing off action is maintainable in case of internationally recognised foreign trademarks even if they do not have any presence in India. Therefore, a foreign trademark which has gained international recognition by advertisements and information explosion can get protection in India under passing off action, even if such a trademark is not registered in India.

Copyright

The Legislation

The provisions pertaining to Copyrights and their protection in India are governed by the Copyright Act, 1957. Copyright exists in expression of an idea and it is not a right in the novelty of an idea. Copyright protects skill, labour and capital employed by the author. Its object is to protect the writer and author from the unlawful reproduction, plagiarism, piracy, copying and imitation. Violation of the copyright is confined to the form, manner, arrangement and expression of the idea by the author. Copyright is defined to mean the exclusive right to do or authorise other(s) to do certain acts in relation to literary, dramatic or musical works, artistic works, cinematograph film and sound recording.

Works in which Copyright Subsists

Copyright subsists throughout India in the following classes of works:

- original literary, dramatic, musical and artistic works;
- cinematograph film; and
- sound recording.

In respect of copyright, the word original does not mean that the work must be the expression of the original or inventive thought. The Act does not require that the expression must be in an original or novel form, but the work must not be copied from another work and it should originate from the author. The expenditure of original skill or labour is required in executing a work and not in the originality of thought. The term literary work includes computer programmes, tables and compilations including computer databases.

Computer Programmes – Patent or Copyright

Presently, computer softwares are protected under Copyrights Act, 1957, in India. This is confined only to its form and expression. The Present Copyright Act provides protection against piracy of softwares. Patent gives much better protection to an invention or new idea. Many leading companies file for patent application in addition to filing for copyright protection on the same work.

Steps Involved in Registration

Registration is prima facie evidence in favour of a person claiming copyright. Though this can be challenged, but if the stakes are high, it is always advisable to register a copyright for better protection.

Steps for Registering a Copyright in India:

i. Application for registration is made in Form IV in triplicate to the Registrar of Copyright.

ii. In respect of artistic work which is used or is capable of being used in relation to any goods, the application should include a statement to that effect and should be accompanied by a certificate from the Registrar of Trademarks to the effect that no trademark identical with or deceptively similar to such artistic work has been registered or application for registration has been made for such a mark.

iii. There should be one application for one work only and should be accompanied with fees prescribed as per Copyright Rules, 1958. The fees vary depending on the work.

iv. Applicant shall simultaneously send copy of the application to every person interested in the copyright of the work (e.g. publisher, co-author etc.)

v. If the Registrar of Copyrights receives no objection to such registration within 30 days of the receipt of the application by him, he shall, if satisfied about the correctness of the particulars given in the application, enter such particulars in the Register of Copyrights.

vi. After receipt of the objections and if not satisfied with the correctness of the particulars given in the application, if any, Registrar may make such enquiry as he may deem fit. After the Registrar is satisfied, entry will be made by him in the Register of Copyright and copies of the same shall be sent to all the concerned parties.

Duration of Copyright

The term of copyright in published literary, dramatic, musical or artistic work (other than a photograph) is the life time of the author plus sixty years from the beginning of the calendar year next following the year in which the author dies. In case of joint authorship, the period of sixty years shall commence after the death of the author who dies last.

Protection available to the Copyright Owners

A copyright owner has the exclusive right to do or authorize any other person to do the following:

(a) **In case of literary, dramatic or musical work, not being a computer program:** to reproduce the work in any material form including the storing of it in any medium by electronic means; to issue copies of the work to the public not being copies already in circulation; to perform the work in public or communicate it to the public; to make any cinematograph film or sound recording in respect of the work; to make any translation and adaptation of the work; to do, in relation to a translation or an adaptation of the work any of the aforesaid acts.

(b) **In case of computer program:** to do any of the acts mentioned in clause (a); to sell or give on hire, or offer for sale or hire any copy of the computer program, regardless of whether such copy has been sold or given on hire on earlier occasions.

(c) **In case of artistic work:** to reproduce the work in any material form to communicate the work to the public; to issue copies of the work to the public not being copies already in circulation; to include the work in any cinematograph film; to make any adaptation of the work; to do in relation to the adaptation of the work any of the aforesaid acts.

(d) **In respect of cinematograph film:** to make copy of the film including a photograph of any image forming part thereof; to sell or giving it on hire, or offer for sale or hire of any copy of the film, regardless of whether such copy has already been sold or given on hire on earlier occasion and to communicate the film to the public.

(e) **In respect of sound recording:** to make any other sound recording embodying it; to sell or give on hire, or offer for sale or hire any copy of the sound recording regardless of whether such copy has been sold or given on hire on earlier occasion and to communicate the sound recording to the public.

Assignment of Copyright

The owner of a copyright can assign the copyright to a work. Such assignment can be absolute or partial subject to limitations and either for a limited period or for the full term of the copyright.

Even the rights of future works could be assigned by a prospective owner, but the assignment in that case shall become effective only when the work comes into existence. However:

1. there is no prescribed form for assignment of copyright;
2. assignment must be in writing duly signed by the assignor or his authorised agent;
3. the assignment must specify details of the work being assigned, rights assigned, duration and territorial extent of assignment;
4. if the period of assignment is not specified, it is presumed to be 5 years. If territorial extent is not specified, it is presumed to extend to throughout India;
5. amount of royalty payable to assignor or his heirs should also be specified.

If the assignee does not make use of the rights assigned to him within a period of one year from the date of assignment, the assignment will be deemed to have lapsed, unless otherwise specified in the agreement.

Licensing of Copyrights

Owner of a copyright can grant interest in his right by licence in writing to another person. Licence relating to future work can also be granted, but in that case the licence takes effect only when the work comes into existence. The license must be in writing and should be signed either by the owner himself or by his authorised agent.

A licence deed in relation to work should contain the following particulars:

i. identification of work;

ii. duration of licence;

iii. the right licenced;

iv. territorial extent of licence;

v. quantum of royalty payable; and

vi. the terms regarding revision, extension and termination.

Provisions as applicable to assignment i.e., period, territorial assignment, resolution of dispute by Copyright Board are also applicable to license.

There are different kinds of licenses. A license may be exclusive or non-exclusive, it may be granted by the Copyright Board as a compulsory licence and may be limited to a specified period of time.

Copyright Rules, 1958 prescribe the procedure for making an application to the Copyright Board for obtaining licences and the manner of determining royalties under the following provisions of the Copyright Act, 1957 in India:

i. Compulsory licence in works withheld from public (Section 31): If the owner does not grant permission for republication, performance or communication to public, Copyright Board can direct Registrar of Copyrights to grant compulsory licence to complainant on such terms and conditions as it deems fit.

ii. Compulsory licence in unpublished Indian works (Section 31A).

iii. Licence to produce and publish translations (Section 32).

iv. Licence to reproduce and publish works for certain purposes (Section 32A): This is a licence to reproduce cheap edition or out of print work.

Provision with Respect to Foreign Work

Provisions in respect of licence to produce and publish translation of a literary work for educational purposes are available for both Indian and foreign work, as the Act does not make any distinction between Indian work and foreign work. The only differences are as follows:

(a) Permission for translation is normally available for educational purposes after a period of three years. However, if the work is in language other than the language of developed countries i.e., in other than English, French, German, Japanese, Spanish etc., the permission can be granted after one year.

(b) If the licence to produce translation is in respect of foreign work, it shall be subject to condition that the copy is available for distribution in India and cannot be exported outside India.

(c) Government or any of its authority can however export such translation of foreign work, if it is in a language other than English, French or Spanish. Such export can be for use of citizens of India residing out of India or for educational or research work.

Further, central government, by notification, can extend provisions of the Act to work published out of India or to unpublished work made out of India or work of a foreign author who has died. Such extension can be made only in respect of countries, which grant similar protection to work made in India. The order of Central Government can provide extension of Act to only specified class of works or restricts terms of copyright, conditions of enjoying the right etc.

Protection available from Infringement

Following amounts to infringement of a copyright:

i. doing anything without licence for which the owner of copyright has exclusive rights;

ii. permitting for profit without licence any place to be used for the communication of the work to the public where such communication constitutes an infringement of the copyright in the work (unless he was aware that there is any infringement of the right—the burden of proof is on him);

iii. making for sale or hire, selling or offering for sale or hire, distributing, exhibiting in public or importing into India any infringing copy of the work.

In case of infringement, the Copyright Act, 1957 provides for both civil as well as criminal remedies. Civil remedies available to the owner of a copyright against infringement include injunction, damages or share of profits, delivery of infringing copies and damages for conversion. The Act also provides for punishment by criminal courts for criminal offences. Further, police officers are empowered to seize all copies of the work and all plates used for making infringing copies of work without warrant.

Designs

The Legislation

The provisions with respect to designs were contained in the Designs Act, 1911, which are now repealed with the passing of the Designs Act 2000. The new Act contains substantially the same provisions as were contained in Designs Act, 1911 except some minor changes in the definitions of article, design. It has introduced the definition of the word original. The new Act has also enhanced the amount of penalty in case of infringement of registered design. The objective of the law governing the Designs is to protect novel designs, which are applied to particular articles, which are commercially manufactured and marketed. The objective is to encourage competition and industrial progress.

The highlights of the definition of design mentioned in the Designs Act, 2000 are:

- Design deals with external appearance only. It has to be judged by naked eye only.
- It relates to features of shape, configuration, pattern or ornamental decoration or composition of lines or colours applied to any article.

- Application of shape, configuration etc., to an article should be by an industrial process or means.
- In the finished article, it should appeal to and be judged solely by the eye.
- It does not include any trademark or property mark or any artistic work as defined in the Copyright Act, 1957.

Therefore, the Act covers only the artistic designs and not engineering designs. Design cannot be registered under the Trademarks Act as well as under the Designs Act. Design is different from a trademark. Design is necessarily part and parcel of the article manufactured while a trademark is not necessarily so.

Design induces a favourable impression on the consumer which induces him to buy the goods. Design covers the whole body of goods and must be novel and original. Design registration is obtained for novelty in the external appearance only. The registrable design is not the article itself, but a feature, an idea or characteristic look applied to an article e.g., novel shape of a cellular phone or a pager, wash basin, motor car, a locomotive engine etc. The design can be registered only with respect to an article or set of articles. The registrable design must be capable of being applied to an article by an industrial process or means. The article must be movable. Thus, design of buildings, permanent structures and naturally occurring unprocessed objects are not registrable.

The Act specifically prohibits registration of a design which: (a) is not new or original; or (b) has been disclosed to the public anywhere in India or in any other country by publication in tangible form or by use or in any other way; or (c) is not significantly distinguishable from known designs; or (d) comprises or contains scandalous or obscene matter.

Steps Involved in Registration

1. An application for the registration of design shall be made in the prescribed form and shall be filed in the patent office along with the prescribed fee.

2. Four copies of the representation of the design shall accompany such an application.

3. The application shall state the class in which the design is to be registered and the article or the articles to which the design is to be applied. Separate applications are required to be filed for each class of article.

4. Where words, letters or numerals are not the essence of the design, they shall be removed from the representations or specimens and where they are the essence of the design, the Controller may require the insertion of a disclaimer of any right to their exclusive use.

5. The Controller shall refer the application for examination to the examiner to know whether such design is capable of being registered under the Act and rules made there under.

6. The Controller may accept the application for registration, if he finds that there is no lawful objection in the report of the examiner to the design being registered.

7. However, if on consideration of the report of the examiner, any objection contained therein appears to the Controller as adverse to the applicant or if the controller requires any amendment to the application, a statement of such objections or amendments is sent to the applicant or his authorized agent in writing.

8. If the applicant or his agent does not remove the objections or apply for hearing within 3 months, his application is deemed to have been withdrawn, provided that the period for removal of objection shall not exceed 6 months from the date of filing.

9. After giving the applicant an opportunity of being heard or otherwise if the applicant has not attended to the hearing or has notified that he does not desire to be heard, the Controller may register or refuse to register the design as he thinks fit.

10. The Controller shall grant a Certificate of Registration to the proprietor of the design when registered.

11. An application which owing to any neglect or default of the applicant, has not been completed so as to enable registration to be effected within 6 months from the date of application, shall be deemed to be abandoned.
12. On acceptance of the design filed in respect of the application, the Controller shall direct the registration and publication of the particulars of the application and the representation of the article to which the design has been applied in the Official Gazette.

Copyright in Registered Design

Once the design is registered, the registered proprietor of the design acquires copyright in the design for 10 years from the date of registration. The same could be extended for a further period of 5 years on payment of the prescribed fee. After the expiry of the period of 15 years, the design is available for public use.

Geographical Indication

Introduction

India has a rich heritage of products originating from specific regions that are nurtured by knowledge and tradition built up by communities over the years.

International Framework

A number of treaties administered by the WIPO provide for the protection of geographical indications, most notably the Paris Convention for the Protection of Industrial Property of 1883, and the Lisbon Agreement for the Protection of Appellations of Origin and their International Registration. In addition, Articles 22 to 24 of the Agreement on Trade-Related Aspects of Intellectual Property Rights deal with the international protection of geographical indications within the framework of the World Trade Organization.

The Legislative Framework

The Geographical Indication Act 2001, in India, defines a geographical indication as: an indication which identifies such goods as agricultural goods, natural goods or manufactured goods as originating, or manufactured in the territory of a country, or a region or locality in that territory, where a given quality, reputation or other characteristic of such goods is essentially attributable to its geographical origin and in case where such goods are manufactured goods one of the activities of either the production or of processing or preparation of the goods concerned takes place in such territory, region or locality, as the case may be.

Who Can Apply

Any association of persons, producers, organisation or authority established by or under the law could apply for an geographical indication provided that: (a) the application should be in writing in the prescribed form along with the prescribed fee and (b) the applicant must represent the interest of the producers.

Steps Involved in Registration

An application for registration of a geographical indication is to be made in writing using a replica of the official application Form GI-1 for the registration of a Geographical Indication in Part A of the Register by an Indian applicant; Form GI-2 for a convention application; an application for goods falling in different classes by an Indian applicant in Form GI-3 and an application for registration of goods falling in different classes from a convention country in Form GI-4 along with prescribed fee and should be addressed to the Registrar of Geographical Indications. The application should include the various requirements and criteria for processing a geographical application as specified in Rule 32(1) which details *interalia:*

i. How the indication serves to designate the goods as a Geographical Indication?

ii. The Class of goods;

iii. The territory;

iv. The particulars of appearance;

v. Particulars of producers;

vi. An affidavit of how the applicant claims to represent the interest;

vii. The standard benchmark or other characteristics of the geographical indication;

viii. The particulars of special characteristics;

ix. Textual description of the proposed boundary;

x. The growth attributes in relation to the GI pertinent to the application;

xi. Certified copies of the map of the territory;

xii. Special human skill involved, if any;

xiii. Number of producers; and

xiv. Particulars of inspection structures, if any, to regulate the use of geographical indication.

On receipt of the application, a number will be allotted by the Registrar. Thereafter, the application would be examined to check whether it meets the requirements of the Act and Rules. For this purpose the Registrar shall ordinarily constitute a Consultative Group of experts to ascertain the correctness of the particulars furnished. Thereafter, an Examination Report is issued by the Registrar to the applicant. The applicant is then required to submit the reply to the Examination Report and the clarifications provided therein is considered by the Registrar. If no objections is raised it would be accepted and would be advertised in the *Geographical Indications Journal.* An opposition could be lodged within a maximum period of four months.

After a geographical indication is registered any person claiming to be the producer of the registered geographical indication can file an application for registration as an authorised user in Part B of the Register. The procedure for registration as an authorised user is similar to that for the registration of a geographical indication.

Protection available to registered Geographical Indication

Geographical indications are protected in accordance with national laws and under a wide range of concepts, such as laws against unfair competition, consumer protection laws, laws for the protection of certification marks or special laws for the protection of geographical indications or appellations of origin. In essence, unauthorized parties may not use geographical indications if such use is likely to mislead the public as to the true origin of the product. Applicable sanctions range from court injunctions preventing the unauthorized use to the payment of damages and fines or, in serious cases, imprisonment.

Further,

- It confers legal protection to Geographical Indications in India.
- Prevents unauthorised use of a Registered Geographical Indication by others.
- It provides legal protection to Indian Geographical Indications which in turn boost exports.
- It promotes economic prosperity of producers of goods produced in a geographical territory.

Assignment and Transmission

A geographical indication is a public property belonging to the producers of the concerned goods hence assignment, transmission, licensing, pledge or mortgage are not permissible.

Duration of a Geographical Indication

The registration of a geographical indication is valid for a period of 10 years and It can be renewed from time to time for a further period of 10 years each.

Confidental Information and Know-how

Confidential Information is generally information, which is the object of an obligation of confidence and is used to cover all information of a confidential character. This includes:

1. Trade secrets,
2. Literary and artistic secrets,
3. Personal secrets,
4. Public and Government Secrets.

In case of confidential information relating to trade secrets,

1. the information must be such that the owner must believe that the release of which would be injurious to the owner or advantageous to his rivals or others,

2. the owner must believe that the information is confidential and secret,
3. the owner's belief on the above points must be reasonable,
4. the information must be judged in the light of the usage and practices of the particular industry or trade concerned.

Know-how generally indicates something essentially different from secret and confidential information. It indicates the way in which a skilled man does his job, and is an expression of his skill and experience.

Generally breach of confidence is not applicable in case of know-how, however it is applicable in case of trade secrets.

Three elements essential to a cause of action for breach of confidence are: a) that the information was of a confidential nature, b) that it was communicated in circumstances importing an obligation of confidence, and c) that there was an unauthorized use of the information. [1977 FSR 260]

How to Protect Confidential Information or Know How

Under Article 34 of the TRIPS agreement, every member country must enact legislation for the protection of confidential information. Though India is yet to enact any such legislation, Indian courts have protected misuse of confidential information either as a violation of contract or as a violation of intellectual property rights. Confidential information can be protected under common law by entering into oral as well as written agreements by the concerned parties. An oral agreement is enough to provide an obligation of confidence, however, it may be difficult to prove the existence of such an agreement in a court of law. Hence it is recommended that the Companies enter into following agreements with their employees and the outside consultants:

i. agreement assigning to the company any trademark, copyright or patentable invention which the employee develops or is involved in developing during the course of his employment;
ii. non-disclosure agreement regarding confidential information/know-how;

[Note: The content of this article shall not be taken as legal advice and is intended to provide a general guide to the subject matter.]

(Dubey & Partners – advocates, a Multidisciplinary Indian law firm having global practice base. They can be reached at Dubey & Partners – Advocates, 310, New Delhi House, 27 Borkhamba Road, New Delhi - 110 001, INDIA. Tel: +91-11-2332884/ 41511473, Fax: +91-11-23323890 and newdelhi@dubeypartners.com).

7

An Insight on Copyright, Geographical Indications and Confidential Information Laws in India

Rajkumar Dubey

The provisions pertaining to copyrights and their protection in India are governed by the Copyright Act, 1957. The article focuses on the protection available to the copyright owners, assignment and licensing of copyright and protection available from infringement. With respect to the geographical indication, the article describes the legislative framework, its registration process, benefits available due to registration and a brief on the international framework of the same.

The Copyright Legislation

The provisions pertaining to Copyrights and their protection in India are governed by the Copyright Act, 1957. Copyright exists in expression of an idea and it is not a right in the novelty of an idea. Copyright protects skill, labour and capital employed by the author. Its object is to protect the writer and author from the unlawful reproduction, plagiarism, piracy, copying and imitation. Violation of the copyright is confined to the form, manner, arrangement and expression of

Source: www.mondaq.com © Dubey & Partners – Advocates. Reprinted with permission.

the idea by the author. Copyright is defined to mean the exclusive right to do or authorise other(s) to do certain acts in relation to – literary, dramatic or musical works, artistic works, cinematograph film and sound recording.

Works in which Copyright Subsists

Copyright subsists throughout India in the following classes of works:

- original literary, dramatic, musical and artistic works;
- cinematograph film; and
- sound recording.

In respect of copyright, the word 'original' does not mean that the work must be the expression of the original or inventive thought. The Act does not require that the expression must be in an original or novel form, but the work must not be copied from another work and it should originate from the author. The expenditure of original skill or labour is required in executing a work and not in the originality of thought. The term 'literary work' includes computer programmes, tables and compilations including computer databases.

Computer Programmes – Patent or Copyright

Presently, computer softwares are protected under Copyrights Act, 1957, in India. This is confined only to its form and expression. The Present Copyright Act provides protection against piracy of softwares. Patent gives much better protection to an invention or new idea. Many leading companies file for patent application in addition to filing for copyright protection on the same work.

Steps Involved in Registration

Registration is prima facic evidence in favour of a person claiming copyright. Though this can be challenged, it is always advisable to register a copyright for better protection, if the stakes are high.

Steps for registering a copyright in India:

i. Application for registration is made in Form IV in triplicate to the Registrar of Copyright.

ii. In respect of artistic work which is used or is capable of being used in relation to any goods, the application should include a statement to that effect and should be accompanied by a certificate from the Registrar of Trademarks to the effect that no trademark identical with or deceptively similar to such artistic work has been registered or application for registration has been made for such a mark.

iii. There should be one application for one work only and should be accompanied with fees prescribed as per Copyright Rules, 1958. The fees vary depending on the work.

iv. Applicant shall simultaneously send copy of the application to every person interested in the copyright of the work (e.g. publisher, co-author etc.).

v. If the Registrar of Copyrights receives no objection to such registration within 30 days of the receipt of the application by him, he shall, if satisfied about the correctness of the particulars given in the application, enter such particulars in the Register of Copyrights.

-vi. After receipt of the objections and if not satisfied with the correctness of the particulars given in the application, if any, Registrar may make such enquiry as he may deem fit. After the Registrar is satisfied, entry will be made by him in the Register of Copyright and copies of the same shall be sent to all the concerned parties.

Duration of Copyright

The term of copyright in published literary, dramatic, musical or artistic work (other than a photograph) is the life time of the author plus sixty years from the beginning of the calendar year next following the year in which the author dies. In case of joint authorship, the period of sixty years shall commence after the death of the author who dies last.

Protection available to the Copyright Owners

A copyright owner has the exclusive right to do or authorize any other person to do the following:

a. **In case of literary, dramatic or musical work, not being a computer program:** to reproduce the work in any material form including the storing of it in any medium by electronic means; to issue copies of the work to the public not being copies already in circulation; to perform the work in public or communicate it to the public; to make any cinematograph film or sound recording in respect of the work; to make any translation and adaptation of the work; to do, in relation to a translation or an adaptation of the work any of the aforesaid acts.

b. **In case of computer program:** to do any of the acts mentioned in clause (a); to sell or give on hire, or offer for sale or hire any copy of the computer program, regardless of whether such copy has been sold or given on hire on earlier occasions.

c. **In case of artistic work:** to reproduce the work in any material form to communicate the work to the public; to issue copies of the work to the public not being copies already in circulation; to include the work in any cinematograph film; to make any adaptation of the work; to do in relation to the adaptation of the work any of the aforesaid acts.

d. **In respect of cinematograph film:** to make copy of the film including a photograph of any image forming part thereof; to sell or giving it on hire, or offer for sale or hire of any copy of the film, regardless of whether such copy has already been sold or given on hire on earlier occasion and to communicate the film to the public.

e. **In respect of sound recording:** to make any other sound recording embodying it; to sell or give on hire, or offer for sale or hire any copy of the sound recording regardless of whether such copy has been sold or given on hire on earlier occasion and to communicate the sound recording to the public.

Assignment of Copyright

The owner of a copyright can assign the copyright to a work. Such assignment can be absolute or partial, subject to limitations, and either for a limited period or for the full term of the copyright.

Even the rights of future works could be assigned by a prospective owner, but the assignment in that case shall become effective only when the work comes into existence. However,

1. there is no prescribed form for assignment of copyright;

2. assignment must be in writing duly signed by the assignor or his authorised agent;
3. the assignment must specify details of the work being assigned, rights assigned, duration and territorial extent of assignment;
4. if the period of assignment is not specified, it is presumed to be 5 years. If territorial extent is not specified, it is presumed to extend to throughout India;
5. amount of royalty payable to assignor or his heirs should also be specified.

If the assignee does not make use of the rights assigned to him within a period of one year from the date of assignment, the assignment will be deemed to have lapsed, unless otherwise specified in the agreement.

Licensing of Copyrights

Owner of a copyright can grant interest in his right by licence in writing to another person. Licence relating to future work can also be granted, but in that case the licence takes effect only when the work comes into existence. The license must be in writing and should be signed either by the owner himself or by his authorised agent.

A licence deed in relation to work should contain the following particulars:

i. identification of work;

ii. duration of licence;

iii. the right licenced;

iv. territorial extent of licence;

v. quantum of royalty payable; and

vi. the terms regarding revision, extension and termination.

Provisions as applicable to assignment i.e., period, territorial assignment, resolution of dispute by Copyright Board are also applicable to license.

There are different kinds of licenses. A license may be exclusive or non-exclusive, it may be granted by the Copyright Board as a compulsory licence and may be limited to a specified period of time.

Copyright Rules, 1958 prescribe the procedure for making an application to the Copyright Board for obtaining licences and the manner of determining royalties under the following provisions of the Copyright Act, 1957 in India:

i. Compulsory licence in works withheld from public (Section 31): If the owner does not grant permission for republication, performance or communication to public, Copyright Board can direct Registrar of Copyrights to grant compulsory licence to complainant on such terms and conditions as it deems fit.

ii. Compulsory licence in unpublished Indian works (Section 31A).

iii. Licence to produce and publish translations (Section 32).

iv. Licence to reproduce and publish works for certain purposes (Section 32A): This is a licence to reproduce cheap edition or out of print work.

Provision with Respect to Foreign Work

Provisions in respect of licence to produce and publish translation of a literary work for educational purposes are available for both Indian and foreign work, as the Act does not make any distinction between Indian work and foreign work. The only differences are as follows:

a. Permission for translation is normally available for educational purposes after a period of three years. However, if the work is in language other than language of developed countries i.e., in other than English, French, German, Japanese, Spanish etc., the permission can be granted after one year.

b. If the licence to produce translation is in respect of foreign work, it shall be subject to condition that the copy is available for distribution in India and cannot be exported outside India.

c. Government or any of its authority can however export such translation of foreign work, if it is in a language other than English, French or Spanish. Such export can be for use of citizen of India residing out of India or for educational or research work.

Further, central government, by notification, can extend provisions of the Act to work published out of India or to unpublished work made out of India or work of a foreign author who has died. Such extension can be made only in respect of countries, which grant similar protection to work made in India. The order of Central Government can provide extension of Act to only specified class of works or restricts terms of copyright, conditions of enjoying the right etc.

Protection available from Infringement

Following amounts to infringement of a copyright:

i. doing anything without licence for which the owner of copyright has exclusive rights;

ii. permitting for profit without licence any place to be used for the communication of the work to the public where such communication constitutes an infringement of the copyright in the work (unless he was aware that there is any infringement of the right – the burden of proof is on him);

iii. making for sale or hire, selling or offering for sale or hire, distributing, exhibiting in public or importing into India any infringing copy of the work.

In case of infringement, the Copyright Act, 1957 provides for both civil as well as criminal remedies. Civil remedies available to the owner of a copyright against infringement include injunction, damages or share of profits, delivery of infringing copies and damages for conversion. The Act also provides for punishment by criminal courts for criminal offences. Further, police officers are empowered to seize all copies of the work and all plates used for making infringing copies of work without warrant.

Geographical Indication

Introduction

India has a rich heritage of products originating from specific regions that are nurtured by knowledge and tradition built up by communities over the years.

International Framework

A number of treaties administered by the WIPO provide for the protection of geographical indications, most notably the Paris Convention for the Protection of Industrial Property of 1883, and the Lisbon Agreement for the Protection of Appellations of Origin and their International Registration. In addition, Articles 22 to 24 of the Agreement on Trade-Related Aspects of Intellectual Property Rights deal with the international protection of geographical indications within the framework of the World Trade Organization.

The Legislative Framework

The Geographical Indication Act 2001, in India defines a geographical indication as: "an indication which identifies such goods as agricultural goods, natural goods or manufactured goods as originating, or manufactured in the territory of a country, or a region or locality in that territory, where a given quality, reputation or other characteristic of such goods is essentially attributable to its geographical origin; and in case where such goods are manufactured, goods one of the activities of either the production or of processing or preparation of the goods concerned takes place in such territory, region or locality, as the case may be."

Who Can Apply

Any association of persons, producers, organisation or authority established by or under the law could apply for an geographical indication provided that:

a. the application should be in writing in the prescribed form along with the prescribed fee

b. the applicant must represent the interest of the producers.

Steps Involved in Registration

"An application for registration of a geographical indication is to be made in writing using a replica of the official application Form GI-1 for the registration of a Geographical Indication in Part A of the Register by an Indian applicant; Form GI-2 for a convention application; an application for goods falling in different classes by an Indian applicant in Form GI-3 and an application for registration of goods falling in different classes from a convention country in Form GI-4 along with prescribed fee and should be addressed to the "Registrar of Geographical Indications".

The application should include the various requirements and criteria for processing a geographical application as specified in Rule 32(1) which details interalia:

i. How the indication serves to designate the goods as a Geographical Indication?

ii. The class of goods;

iii. The territory;

iv. The particulars of appearance;

v. Particulars of producers;

vi. An affidavit of how the applicant claims to represent the interest;

vii. The standard benchmark or other characteristics of the geographical indication;

viii. The particulars of special characteristics;

ix. Textual description of the proposed boundary;

x. The growth attributes in relation to the GI pertinent to the application;

xi. Certified copies of the map of the territory;

xii. Special human skill involved, if any;

xiii. Number of producers; and

xiv. Particulars of inspection structures, if any, to regulate the use of geographical indication.

On receipt of the application, a number will be allotted by the Registrar. Thereafter, the application would be examined to check whether it meets the requirements of the Act and Rules. For this purpose the Registrar shall ordinarily constitute a Consultative Group of experts to ascertain the correctness of the particulars furnished. Thereafter, an Examination Report is issued by the Registrar to the applicant. The applicant is then required to submit the reply to the Examination Report and the clarifications provided therein is considered by the Registrar. If no objections is raised it would be accepted and would be advertised in the *Geographical Indications Journal.* An opposition could be lodged within a maximum period of four months.

After a geographical indication is registered any person claiming to be the producer of the registered geographical indication can file an application for registration as an authorised user in Part B of the Register. The procedure for registration as an authorised user is similar to that for the registration of a geographical indication.

Protection available to Registered Geographical Indication

Geographical indications are protected in accordance with national laws and under a wide range of concepts, such as laws against unfair competition, consumer protection laws, laws for the protection of certification marks or special laws for the protection of geographical indications or appellations of origin. In essence, unauthorized parties may not use geographical indications if such use is likely to mislead the public as to the true origin of the product. Applicable sanctions range from court injunctions preventing the unauthorized use to the payment of damages and fines or, in serious cases, imprisonment.

Further,

- It confers legal protection to Geographical Indications in India.
- Prevents unauthorised use of a Registered Geographical Indication by others.
- It provides legal protection to Indian Geographical Indications which in turn boost exports.
- It promotes economic prosperity of producers of goods produced in a geographical territory.

Assignment and Transmission

A geographical indication is a public property belonging to the producers of the concerned goods hence assignment, transmission, licensing, pledge or mortgage are not permissible.

Duration of a Geographical Indication

The registration of a geographical indication is valid for a period of 10 years and it can be renewed from time to time for a further period of 10 years each.

Confidential Information and Know-how

Confidential Information is generally information, which is the object of an obligation of confidence and is used to cover all information of a confidential character. This includes:

1. Trade secrets,
2. Literary and artistic secrets,
3. Personal secrets,
4. Public and Government secrets.

In case of confidential information relating to trade secrets,

1. the information must be such that the owner must believe that the release of which would be injurious to the owner or advantageous to his rivals or others,
2. the owner must believe that the information is confidential and secret,
3. the owner's belief on the above points must be reasonable,
4. the information must be judged in the light of the usage and practices of the particular industry or trade concerned.

Know-how generally indicates something essentially different from secret and confidential information. It indicates the way in which a skilled man does his job, and is an expression of his skill and experience.

Generally breach of confidence is not applicable in case of know-how, however it is applicable in case of trade secrets.

Three elements essential to a cause of action for breach of confidence are:

a. that the information was of a confidential nature,

b. that it was communicated in circumstances importing an obligation of confidence, and

c. that there was an unauthorized use of the information. [1977 FSR 260]

How to Protect Confidential Information

Under Article 34 of the TRIPS agreement, every member country must enact legislation for the protection of confidential information. Though India is yet to enact any such legislation, Indian courts have protected misuse of confidential information either as a violation of contract or as a violation of intellectual property rights. Confidential information can be protected under common law by entering into oral as well as written agreements by the concerned parties. An oral agreement is enough to provide an obligation of confidence, however, it may be difficult to prove the existence of such an agreement in a court of law. Hence, it is recommended that the Companies enter into following agreements with their employees and the outside consultants:

i. agreement assigning to the company any trademark, copyright or patentable invention which the employee develops or is involved in developing during the course of his employment;

ii. non-disclosure agreement regarding confidential information/know-how;

iii. a non-compete provision covering a specified period of time following the termination of employment;

iv. discourage solicitation of the clients and employees of the company by the former employees.

Note: The content of this article shall not be taken as legal advice and is intended to provide a general guide to the subject matter.

(Mr. Rajkumar Dubey, B.Com, ACS, LLB is a Managing Partner of Dubey & Partners – advocates, a Multidisciplinary Indian law firm having global practice base. Mr. Dubey is also a member of the International Bar Association, the American Bar Association, and the World Jurist Association. He has been taken on the board of the subsidiaries of several International Companies for his in-depth knowledge of Indian laws and practical approach. He can be contacted at Dubey & Partners – Advocates 310, New Delhi House, 27, Barakhamba Road, New Delhi – 110001, INDIA. Tel: +91-11-2332884/41511473, Fax: +91-11-23323890 and newdelhi@dubeypartners.com).

8

Intellectual Property Rights Protection in India: An Analysis

The major Indian intellectual property rights can be categorized into: copyright, patent, trademark, design. National agencies like national academy of custom, Department of Education, Copyright Enforcement Advisory Council etc, have come up with training programs, seminars and workshops. Protection of intellectual property is a critical element in the offshore business model. Therefore, commitment to protect the intellectual property of a company should be developed at all levels of the organization. The article focuses on the Indian Scenario with regards to IPRs, key intitatives taken by the Government in this direction and best practices followed by the companies in the field of IPR.

1.0 Introduction

"How are we going to ensure that our Intellectual property is protected at an offshore location?" is a question often asked in board meetings of companies that are planning their offshore initiatives in India. The importance of IP exponentially increases in companies that are planning to execute some of their core projects offshore and in companies that need to provide access to classified company data to the offshore location for BPO/Call center initiatives. It is important for

Source: http://www.zinnov.com/research_ip.html.

companies to understand IP rights in India and the best practices that can be followed to protect the IP.

In this paper, Indian Intellectual Properties Rights, key initiatives taken by the Indian government to protect the Intellectual Properties, best practices that companies can follow to protect their Intellectual property, case studies related to Indian IP Protection are described.

2.0 Indian Software Intellectual Properties Rights

World Intellectual Property Organization defines Intellectual Property as legal rights that result from intellectual activity. The intellectual activity may include any activity in the industrial, scientific, literary and artistic fields. According to the Center for Intellectual Property Rights in India, the major Indian Intellectual properties typically fall into 4 major buckets: Copyright, Patent, Trademark and Design Protection.

In India, the Intellectual Property Rights (IPR) of computer software is covered under the Copyright Law. Accordingly, the copyright of computer software is protected under the provisions of Indian Copyright Act 1957. Major changes to Indian Copyright Law were introduced in 1994 and came into effect from 10 May 1995. These changes or amendments made the Indian Copyright law one of the toughest in the world. The amendments to the Copyright Act introduced in June 1994 were, in themselves, a landmark in the India's copyright arena. For the first time in India, the Copyright Law clearly explained:

- The rights of a copyright holder
- Position on rentals of software
- The rights of the user to make backup copies.

Since most software is easy to duplicate, and the copy is usually as good as original, the Copyright Act was needed. Some of the key aspects of the law are: According to section 14 of this Act, it is illegal to make or distribute copies of copyrighted software without proper or specific authorization. The violator can be tried under both civil and criminal law. A civil and criminal action may be instituted for injunction, actual damages (including violator's profits) or statutory damages per infringement etc. Heavy punishment and fines are there for infringement of software copyright. Section 63 B stipulates a minimum jail term of 7 days, which can be extended up to 3 years.

3.0 Summary of Indian Government Initiatives to Protect IPR

The Indian government has initiated various steps towards Intellectual Properties Rights Protection.

Indian enforcement agencies are working effectively and there is a decline in the levels of piracy in India. In addition to intensifying raids against copyright violators, the Government has taken a number of measures to strengthen the enforcement of copyright law. A summary of these measures is given below:

1. The Government has brought out *A Handbook of Copyright Law* to create awareness of copyright laws amongst the stakeholders, enforcement agencies, professional users like the scientific and academic communities and members of the public. Copies of the Handbook have been circulated free-of-cost to the state and central government officials, police personnel and to participants in various seminars and workshops on IPR.
2. National Police Academy, Hyderabad and National Academy of Customs, Excise and Narcotics conducted several training programs on copyright laws for the police and customs officers. Modules on copyright infringement have been included in their regular training programs.
3. The Department of Education, Ministry of Human Resource Development, Government of India has initiated several measures in the past for strengthening the enforcement of copyrights that include constitution of a Copyright Enforcement Advisory Council (CEAC), creation of separate cells in state police headquarters, encouraging setting up of collective administration societies and organization of seminars and workshops to create greater awareness of copyright laws among the enforcement personnel and the general public.
4. Special cells for copyright enforcement have so far been set up in 23 States and Union Territories, i.e., Andhra Pradesh, Assam, Andaman & Nicobar Islands, Chandigarh, Dadra & Nagar Haveli, Daman & Diu, Delhi, Goa, Gujarat, Haryana, Himachal Pradesh, Jammu & Kashmir, Karnataka,

Kerala, Madhya Pradesh, Meghalaya, Orissa, Pondicherry, Punjab, Sikkim, Tamil Nadu, Tripura and West Bengal.

5. The Government also initiates a number of seminars/workshops on copyright issues. The participants in these seminars include enforcement personnel as well as representatives of industry organizations.

As a consequence of the number of measures initiated by the government, there has been more activity in the enforcement of copyright laws in the country. Over the last few years, the number of cases registered has gone up consistently.

4.0 Best Practices to Minimize the Risk of Offshore Intellectual Property Loss

The following Best Practices will help minimize the risk of losing Intellectual Property in conducting business offshore.

1. **Understand the Intellectual Property rights:** The first and foremost step is to get an overview of the different initiatives and laws undertaken by the offshore country to protect the Intellectual Property.
2. **Set up an Internal Intellectual Property protection team:** Intellectual property protection is an ongoing business responsibility and not a one-time act. This makes it very critical to have a team in the company that is responsible for monitoring their Intellectual properties, violations etc.
3. **Examine the work entities that can be copyrighted/patented:** An ongoing evaluation of the company's work entities to identify copyright protection/ patents is very critical. While copyrighting, it is important to make sure that such a protection will be valid in the country of offshore activity/ development.
4. **Offshore vendor history:** If the company is planning to enter into a vendor relationship with an offshore entity, extreme caution has to be exercised in understanding the vendor's history with respect to any Intellectual property violations.
5. **Define IP violation clause:** In executing a contract with the offshore vendor, define a separate Intellectual Property Violation clause and define the consequences of Intellectual property violation (Some companies sign

the contract with the onsite entity of the offshore vendor as it gives them more leverage to take any legal action if they have to).

6. **Seek a reference check for all the team members:** It is not only important to look at the resumes of the offshore team but also very important to seek the appropriate references to make sure there is no IP violation case history behind the individual.

7. **Pay Attention to use of unauthorized software/third party products:** As the saying goes, "Practice what you Preach". Heavily discourage the use of unlicensed software or products both by the onsite and the offshore team.

8. **Enforce Central Repository:** Enforcing a central repository for all the code and documents can not only improve the overall efficiency, and will also avoid numerous placeholders for critical documents and code.

9. **Perform Periodic IP Audit:** Perform a periodic IP audit and examine any new work that can be copyrighted, remove all the unauthorized software/product, reiterate the importance of IP, look into all the place holders of the code/documents, assign appropriate ownership to the critical documents and update any change of ownership to patents.

10. **Enforce the use of References:** In all the company meetings/presentations make sure the appropriate references and credits are given to the owner of the work (be it internal or external). Making this practice a habit will raise the standards of the employees to acknowledge and respect and protect other people's work.

11. **Develop Awareness:** Protecting the Intellectual property can be greatly enhanced if all the employees of the company and the offshore team are on the same page as to how much attention the company pays to protect Intellectual Properties. In some companies IP protection is made as a part of the performance plan for each employee and reviewed periodically.

5.0 Case Studies Related to Indian IPR Protection

Bangalore, Aug 10, 2003. Banashankari police arrested three software engineers for illegally copying software from a company they were working for. The accused engineers, who were working with the Ishoni Networks India Private Limited, had started a new company called Ample Wave Communication Network in Koramangala. They had illegally copied code of the company's software and were using at their company, police said. Ishoni Director, Antonio Mario Alvares had lodged the complaint with Banashankari police. Police have seized four computers, four CPUs, four keyboards, one server and one laptop from the accused. (Source: DH News Service, Bangalore)

New Delhi, Aug 28, 2002. Central Bureau of Investigation officials in New Delhi nabbed Shekhar Verma, a former employee of Mumbai-based Geometric Software Solutions Company and a computer engineer from the Indian Institute of Technology, Kharagpur. It turned out that Verma was accused of stealing $60 million worth of source code of a software product of Geometric Software's US-based client, SolidWorks, and trying to sell them to other companies for a fortune. The American firm has the exclusive rights over the software. (Source Rediff.com)

Results of Nasscom Initiatives

Calcutta, 7 April 2000: The Enforcement Branch, Calcutta police with the assistance from Nasscom and BSA, seized pirated software worth of Rs.2.61 crore (US$6,08,000) from companies while conducting raids in the city. 4 persons, including owners, partners and senior level employees of the companies, were arrested for this offence. The police recovered around 636 CDs, and 2 computers loaded with pirated software.

Hyderabad, March 2000: Hyderabad Police, with assistance from Nasscom and BSA, seized pirated software worth of Rs.75,16,400 (US$174,800) from 7 companies at a conducted raid. 13 people, including senior level employees of the companies, were arrested in this regard. The Police recovered around 293 CDs, 5 hard disks and 7 computers loaded with pirated software. The estimated value of the pirated software was worth Rs.77 lakh.

Chennai, February 2000: Pirated software worth Rs.1.11 crore (US$253,200) was seized by the Chennai police at a raid conducted at the premises of four outlets. A total of 6 employees were arrested which included the Managing Director of one outlet and proprietors of each of the outlets.

New Delhi, 1st December 2000: Nasscom and BSA launched a new anti-piracy initiative—The Reward Programme to make India's business community take note of the dangers of software piracy. The reward offered, an amount up to Rs.50,000 is for information leading to successful legal action against companies using unlicensed software. The reward program was aimed to encourage people to support the fight against piracy and to report software piracy to the NASSCOM-BSA Anti-Piracy Software Hotline on 1600 334455 to help Nasscom and the BSA remedy the illegal activity.

6.0 Conclusion

Protection of Intellectual Properties is a very critical element in the offshore business model. There have been many cases where companies have lost their position in the market due to the loss of intellectual property. Understanding the country's IP Rights and following the best practices described in this paper can drastically reduce the risk of loosing the company's intellectual property. Commitment to protect the intellectual property of a company should be developed and nurtured at all levels of the organization.

9

Trade Secrets Law in India

Praveen Dalal

The aim and purpose of this article is to explore various possibilities, which can effectively be used to protect the trade secrets in India. The traditional methods of trade secrets protection, like Common law remedies of Torts, etc., have been deliberately not dealt with in detail, or have been simply ignored in this article so that the unexplored possibilities and remedies could be tested and tried in India, where the trade secret law is in its infancy. These possibilities can be considered by the Legislature while making a law on the subject, which will suit the socio-economic conditions prevailing in India.

Introduction

An Intellectual Property Right (IPR) has no value if it cannot be asserted and protected. If an individual cannot protect what he owns, he owns nothing. This is more so in case the right falls under the "Trade Secret" category. The trade secret presupposes the existence of valuable business information, which provides an additional benefit or competitive advantage over the competitors. The right in trade secret remains as long as the owner can prevent its disclosure. The moment it is disclosed or becomes public, the right in it ceases to exist. Thus, if properly

Source: ICFAI Journal of Intellectual Property Rights, November 2004. © Praveen Dalal. Reprinted with permission.

protected, trade secrets may last forever. It is believed that the formula for Coca-Cola is locked in a vault with no person having access to it. This shows that information, which provides a competitive edge over rivals, must be protected on a priority basis. Thus, recognizing the importance of this right, the countries all over the world provide protection to trade secrets. If trade secrets are not legally protected, the companies would lose incentive for investing time, money and labor in research and development, which is very important for the overall development of the country. Further, the existence of law also works as a deterrence for wrongdoers and discourages unfair conduct of the business.

Trade Secret and TRIPS Agreement

The agreement on Trade-Related Aspects of Intellectual Property Rights (TRIPS) desires to reduce distortions and impediments to international trade, and takes into account the need to promote effective and adequate protection of intellectual property rights. It also ensures that measures and procedures to enforce intellectual property rights do not themselves become barriers to legitimate trade. The agreement also requires the Members to give effect to the provisions of this agreement. The Members are, however, not required to implement in their laws more extensive protection than is required by this agreement. The protection given in municipal laws must not conflict with the provisions of this agreement.[1] The term "intellectual property" refers to all categories of intellectual property that are the subject of Sections 1 to 7 of Part II.[2] Thus, it is clear that trade secrets are protected as "undisclosed information".[3] The TRIPS requires the Members to protect undisclosed information in accordance with paragraph 2 and data submitted to governments or governmental agencies in accordance with paragraph 3.[4] According to the TRIPS, the natural and legal persons shall have the possibility of preventing information lawfully within their control from being disclosed to, acquired by, or used by others without their consent in a manner contrary to honest commercial practices so long as such information:

- Is secret in the sense that it is not, as a body or in the precise configuration and assembly of its components, generally known among or readily accessible to persons within the circles that normally deal with the kind of information in question;
- Has commercial value because it is secret; and
- Has been subject to reasonable steps under the circumstances, by the person lawfully in control of the information, to keep in secret.[5]

There are several factors, which determine whether particular information qualifies as a trade secret. These factors must be considered in totality and none of the factor alone is determinative. These factors are:

- The extent to which the information is known outside the company,
- The extent to which the information is known within the company,
- The extent of the measures taken by the company to maintain the secrecy of the information,
- The extent of the value of the information to the company and its competitors,
- The extent of the expenditure of time, effort, and money by the company in developing the information, and
- The extent of the ease or difficulty with which the information could be acquired or duplicated by others.

The agreement also provides that Members, when requiring, as a condition of approving the marketing of pharmaceutical or of agricultural chemical products, which utilize new chemical entities, the submission of undisclosed test or other data, the origination of which involves a considerable effort, shall protect such data against unfair commercial use. In addition, Members shall protect such data against disclosure, except where necessary to protect the public, or unless steps are taken to ensure that the data are protected against unfair commercial use.[6]

The following are the "Data Protection Principles" which must be kept in mind by the government or its agencies while receiving the data:

- The data should be processed fairly and lawfully,
- The data should be obtained for specific and lawful purpose,
- The data should be adequate, relevant and not excessive,
- The data should not be kept for longer than necessary,
- The data should be processed in accordance with the rights of data subjects, and
- Measures should be taken against unauthorized or unlawful processing.

Inter-relationship between Trade Secret, Copyright and Patent

There is an inherent conflict between copyright protection and trade secret rights. For instance, a person may be secretly developing new computer software. In that process, any material or document pertaining to it will be a trade secret. Once the software is developed it is automatically protected under the copyright law. Even if the software owner wishes to get it registered, the source code of the software will remain a trade secret though the documentary materials have to be submitted.

Similarly, regarding patents, the patent application remains confidential until a patent is granted. Thus, during the period of application and granting of the patent, the invention will be protected by trade secret law. The moment patent is granted, the invention is fully disclosed and it ceases to be a trade secret. The protection then is available under the patent law only and that also for limited period. On the other hand, information that is properly protected as a trade secret can be secret forever.

Trade Secret Law in India

In India, the trade secret protection is not expressly recognized as an intellectual property right. The same can, however, be inferred from the provisions of the Constitution of India and other statutes. The nature of protection available can be grouped under the following categories:

- Constitutional Rights, and
- Statutory Rights.

Constitutional Rights

A person owning a trade secret can seek the protection of the Fundamental Rights as available under Part III of the Constitution of India and other Constitutional rights. Some of them are available to all "persons", whether natural or artificial, while others are available only to the "citizens" and not to artificial persons like companies.

It must be noted that as a general rule the protection of fundamental rights is available against the might of the "State and its Instrumentalities". This, however, does not mean that the protection cannot be extended against "Private individuals" having no element and color of Statehood. There are instances where the Supreme

Court has extended the protection of fundamental rights against private individuals. For instance, a writ of *Habeas Corpus* can be issued, when a person complains of illegal custody or detention of an individual by a private person.[7] Similarly, the Supreme Court has the power to regulate private rights in public interest by legitimately exercising its powers.[8] In *Vishaka vs. State of Rajasthan*[9] the Supreme Court held that the protection against sexual harassment at workplace is available even against private employers and individuals. The court held that this protection originates from Articles 14,15,19(1)(g) and 21 of the Constitution of India. It is interesting to note that the decision was given even in the absence of any domestic law dealing with protection against sexual harassment. In fact, there have been some instances where no violation of any specified fundamental right was alleged and yet the Supreme Court entertained a petition under Article 32 of the Constitution of India and granted the relief.[10] Even the writ jurisdiction U/A 226 can be exercised against private individuals. This legal position has been clarified in *Federal Bank Limited vs. Sagar Thomas*[11] where the Supreme Court held that a writ petition U/A 226 of the Constitution of India might be maintainable against:

- The State,
- An authority,
- A statutory corporation,
- An instrumentality or agency of the State,
- A company which is financed or owned by the State,
- A private body run substantially on State funding,
- A person or a body under liability to discharge any function under the statute,
- A private body discharging public duty or positive obligation of public nature.

Thus, private individuals would normally not be amenable to the writ jurisdiction U/A 226 of the Constitution of India. But in certain circumstances, a writ may be issued to such private person, as there may be statutes, which need to be complied with by all concerned including the private individuals and companies.

As far as "Constitutional Rights" are concerned, they can be enforced against private individuals without any doubt or hesitation. If in a given cause of action both Fundamental Rights and the Constitutional rights are pleaded and proved to be violated, then they can be enforced under Part III of the Constitution of India.

The remedy for the violation of these Fundamental and Constitutional Rights can be claimed as "public law remedy" or "Private law remedy". Under the former category, the relief can be claimed only if the aggrieved person can show that there is a violation of his/her Fundamental Rights by the State or its instrumentalities. On the other hand, a private law remedy can be claimed by filing a civil suit for damages or other appropriate proceedings before the competent court. These two remedies are not mutually exclusive and the aggrieved person can combine both of them in an appropriate and deserving case.[12]

The following Articles of the Constitution are relevant for this purpose:

- Article 19(1)(g),
- Article 21,
- Article 300A, and
- Articles 301 to 305.

Article 19(1)(g): Article 19 of the Constitution guarantees to the "citizens" of India the six fundamental freedoms which are exercisable by them throughout and in all parts of the territory of India. Article 19(1)(g) guarantees that all citizens have the right to practice any profession or to carry on any occupation or trade or business. This freedom is, however, not absolute and is subject to Clause (6) of Article 19. Thus, reasonable restrictions can be imposed to curtail this right.

Since, trade secret is an integral and inseparable part of any trade, occupation or business, the same can safely be presumed to be a part of Article 19 (1)(g). Similarly, the reasonable restrictions are equally applicable to it. Further, the State can make any law relating to the carrying on by the State, or by a corporation owned or controlled by the State, of any trade, business, industry or service, whether to the exclusion, complete or partial, of citizens or otherwise.[13]

Article 21: Article 21 mandates that no person shall be deprived of his life and personal liberty except according to procedure established by law. It must be noted that Article 21 is available to all persons, whether natural or artificial. Further, right to life includes right to livelihood because no person can live without the means of living.[14] The question whether deprivation of property leading to "deprivation of life or liberty or livelihood" falls within the reach of Article 21 has been left open though where it does not result in such deprivation, Article 21 has no application.[15] It is submitted that the answer to this question should be in affirmative since if the means of livelihood are themselves taken away, then right to life is definitively violated. The Apex Court in *Kapila Hingorani vs. State of Bihar*[16] held that the term "life", as used in the Article 21, includes livelihood and facets thereof. Thus, it can be presumed that means of livelihood cannot be taken away except by a procedure established by law.

The relationship between trade secret and right to livelihood is apparent. The trade secret is an indispensable part of the livelihood since it is the trade secret, which distinguishes the goods or services of one person from another. The trade secret gives a commercial advantage over the products of the competitors and enhances the profit margin. Hence, protection of trade secret can be claimed as a fundamental Right.

Article 300A: Article 300A of the Constitution confers a right on all persons to hold and enjoy their properties. Thus, a person cannot be deprived of his property save by authority of law. Any violation of this right can be challenged in a court of law. In view of the interpretation given to the word "law" by the Supreme Court in *Maneka Gandhi vs. U.O.I*[17], a law depriving a person of his property must be fair, reasonable and just. An arbitrary and unreasonable law is vulnerable to attack U/A 14 of the Constitution and is liable to be struck down. In *Bhavnagar University vs. Palitana Sugar Mills Pvt Ltd.*[18] the Supreme Court held that an owner of a property, subject to reasonable restrictions, which may be imposed by the Legislature, is entitled to enjoy the property in any manner he likes. A right to use a property in a particular manner or in other words a restriction imposed on user thereof except in the mode or manner laid down under the statute would not be presumed. In *Dharam Dutt vs. U.O.I*[19] the Supreme Court held that the protection of Article 300A is available to any person, including legal or juristic person and is not confined only to a citizen. However, the same cannot be sought to be enforced by a petition U/A 32 of the Constitution, since it is not a fundamental right but merely a Constitutional Right.

The expression "property" is of wide amplitude and it includes tangible as well as intangible properties. It is difficult to accept the proposition that a trade secret is not a property falling within the scope of Article 300A of the Constitution of India. It is definitely a property within the meaning of this Article and deserves the Constitutional protection. Thus, Article 300A would be violated if the trade secrets of an individual is violated or misappropriated. The same can safely be invoked for protecting a trade secret.

Articles 301 to 305: Articles 301 to 305 of the Constitution confer on a person a right to have a free trade, commerce and intercourse throughout the territory of India. This right, however, is subject to the provisions of Articles 302 to 305 of the Constitution. Thus, so long as the individual is carrying on his business in accordance with the law, his business activities cannot be interfered with.

A free trade, commerce and intercourse cannot be visualized without protecting the trade secrets. Thus, these beneficial provisions can be effectively used to enhance trade secret protection in India.

It would be appropriate to refer Article 253 at this juncture. Article 253 provides that the Parliament has the power to make any law for the implementation of any treaty, agreement or convention with any other country or countries or any decision made at any international conference, association or other body. Since, India is a signatory to TRIPS Agreement, the Parliament can make a law covering the area of trade secrets rights.

Statutory Rights

The statutory provisions dealing with trade secret protection are not expressly brought on the statute book. The same is expected to be enacted very soon in the distant future. Till then the existing provisions of other statutes have to be considered to extend protection to the trade secrets. For instance, under Section 8 of The Freedom of Information Act, 2002, the Public Information Officer has the power to withhold any information pertaining to trade or commercial secrets protected by law or information, the disclosure of which would prejudicially affect the legitimate economic and commercial interests or the competitive position of a public authority; or would cause unfair gain or loss to any person. Similarly, the Securities Exchange Board of India (Prohibition of Insider Trading) Regulations, 1992 renders the use and disclosure of confidential information by an insider subject to prosecution under the Securities Exchange Board of India Act.

In *P.U.C.L. vs. U.O.I*[20] the Supreme Court specified the grounds on which the government can withhold information relating to various matters, including trade secrets. The Supreme Court observed: "Every right, legal or moral, carries with it a corresponding objection. It is subject to several exemptions/exceptions indicated in broad terms. Generally, the exemptions/exceptions under those laws entitle the government to withhold information relating to the following matters:

- International relations;
- National security (including defiance) and public safety;
- Investigation, detection and prevention of crime;
- Internal deliberations of the government;
- Information received in confidence from a source outside the government;
- Information, which, if disclosed, would violate the privacy of the individual;
- Information of an economic nature (including Trade Secrets) which, if disclosed, would confer an unfair advantage on some person or concern, or, subject some person or government, to an unfair disadvantage;
- Information, which is subject to a claim of legal professional privilege, e.g., communication between a legal adviser and the client; between a physician and the patient;
- Information about scientific discoveries.

Trade Secret and Information Technology

The interaction between trade secrets and information technology is inevitable in this modern era. The trade secret may be kept secret in an electronic form rather than in a paper form. If a trade secret is so kept, then tampering with or unauthorized access to the computer may result in the cessation of right in it the moment it is disclosed, either intentionally or unintentionally. Thus, a trade secret may be lost due to "cyber crime" or accidental disclosure. The term "cyber crime" refers to the use of a computer to facilitate or carry out a criminal offense. A computer can be electronically attacked and an unauthorized access to the trade secret can be obtained.

The solution to these problems lies in the provisions of the Information Technology Act, 2000. The relevant provisions are:

Penalty for damage to computer, computer system, etc: If any person without the permission of the owner or any other person who is in charge of a computer, computer system or computer network:

- Accesses or secures access to such computer, computer system or computer network or,
- Downloads, copies or extracts any data, computer data base or information from such computer, computer system or computer network including information or data held or stored in any removable storage medium, he shall be liable to pay damages by way of compensation not exceeding one crore rupees to the person so affected.[21] Thus, violating the trade secrets right by unauthorized access, downloading, copying, etc., would attract the stringent penalties in the form of damages up to the tune of rupees one crore.

Hacking with computer system: The Act provides that whoever with intent to cause or knowing that he is likely to cause wrongful loss or damage to the public, or any person destroys or deletes or alters any information residing in a computer resource or diminishes its value or utility or affects it injuriously by any means, commits hacking which is punishable with imprisonment up to three years, or with fine which may extend up to two lakh rupees, or with both.[22] The value of a trade secret is lost the moment it is made public even to a single person. A hacker thus, adversely affects the inherent value of the trade secret. In this sense he violates the same and can be made liable for his wrong under this provision.

Penalty for breach of confidentiality and privacy: If any person who, in pursuance of any of the powers conferred under this Act, rules or regulations made thereunder, has secured access to any electronic record, book, register, correspondence, information, document or other material without the consent of the person concerned and discloses the same to any other person, he shall be punished with imprisonment for a term which may extend to two years, or with fine which may extend to one lakh rupees, or with both.[23] Thus, the prohibition on the disclosure of trade secret applies equally to both individuals and the authorities having powers under the Act.

Penalties or confiscation not to interfere with other punishments: The Act makes it very clear that no penalty imposed or confiscation made under the Act shall prevent the imposition of any other punishment to which the person affected thereby is liable under any other law for the time being in force.[24] Thus, the punishment prescribed under the Act is in addition to and not in derogation of the provisions of any other statute prescribing a punishment for the violation of the trade secret rights.

Liability of network service providers: The Act provides that no person providing any service as a network service provider shall be liable under the Act, rules or regulations made thereunder for any third party information or data made available by him if he proves that the offense or contravention was committed without his knowledge or that he had exercised all due diligence to prevent the commission of such offense or contravention.[25] Thus, the network service provider is vulnerable to the stringent provisions of the Act if he intentionally or knowingly permits the display of the trade secrets on the network.

Offenses by companies: The Act not only fixes the liability for contraventions and offenses upon the individuals, but it equally makes artificial persons like companies liable for the same.[26] This provision is very important because it is the companies, which are more prone to commit the contravention or offenses in order to raise their profits and to gain competitive advantages. They are more interested in knowing the trade secrets of their competitors. Thus, if the company to violate the trade secrets of the competitors uses the medium of information technology, this provision can be invoked to protect the same.

Trade Secret Violation and the Possible Remedies: The discussion under this category can be grouped under the following categories:

- Liability for misappropriation of trade secrets, and
- Remedy for the misappropriation of a trade secret.

Liability for the Misappropriation of a Trade Secret

The misappropriation of a trade secret occurs when a person possesses, discloses, or uses a trade secret owned by another without express or implied consent. The misappropriation may occur either when a trade secret is lawfully acquired but then improperly used or when the trade secret is acquired by improper means. A trade secret is deemed to be unlawfully acquired when the person:

- Used improper means to gain knowledge of the trade secret;
- Knew or should have known that the trade secret was acquired by improper means; or
- Knew or should have known that the trade secret was acquired under circumstances giving rise to a duty to maintain its secrecy.

Remedies for the Violation of Trade Secrets

The liability for violation of a trade secret can arise in the following two situations:

- Where the medium of information technology is used for the violation, and
- Where a medium other than the information technology is used.

Violation through Information Technology

Where the violation of a trade secret occurred with the aid of information technology, then the provisions of the Information Technology Act, 2000 will apply. This is so because the provisions of the Act shall have effect notwithstanding anything inconsistent therewith contained in any other law for the time being in force.[27] Thus, the provisions as discussed above[28] would apply accordingly as per the facts and circumstances of the case.

Violation through means other than Information Technology

If the trade secret is violated through a non-information technology method, then the provisions of various independent statutes will govern the position. These remedies can be classified under the following two broad categories:

- Civil Remedies, and
- Criminal Remedies.

Civil Remedies: The remedies under this category can be further sub-divided under the following heads:

- Remedies under the Indian Contract Act, 1872,
- Remedies under the Code of Civil Procedure, 1908, and
- Remedies under the Law of Torts.

Remedies under the Indian Contract Act, 1872: The Act provides remedies for the violation or misappropriation of the trade secrets under two circumstances:

i. Where employer-employee relationship exists, and

ii. Where principal-agent relationship exists.

Employer-employee relationship: While a written contract prohibiting misappropriation of trade secrets can be enforced through an action for breach of contract, an employer's trade secrets can be protected against misappropriation even in the absence of any written contract between the employer and employee. The Contract Act provides that when a contract has been broken, the party who suffers by such breach is entitled to receive, from the party who has broken the contract, compensation for any loss or damage caused to him thereby, which naturally arose in the usual course of the things from such breach, or which the parties knew, when they made the contract, to be likely to result from the breach of it. Such compensation is, however, not to be given for any remote and indirect loss or damage sustained by reason of the breach.[29] Thus, an employee who reveals or discloses the trade secret of his employer is accountable under this provision.

Principal-agent relationship: The principal has a similar right against the agent. An agent is bound to conduct the business of his principal according to the directions given by the principal, or in the absence of any such directions according to the custom, which prevails in doing business of the same kind at the place where the agent conducts such business. When the agent acts otherwise, if any loss is sustained, he must make it good to his principal, and if any profit accrues, he must account for it.[30] Thus, an unlawful disclosure of the trade secret by the agent would make him liable under this provision.

The above provision's indicate the liability of the employee or the agent, as the case may. This does not mean that third parties are not accountable for the misappropriation of the trade secret. A number of other parties may also have liability for misappropriation of trade secrets if they knew or should have known they were receiving trade secrets. Further, a recipient of trade secrets may be liable for misappropriation even if modifications or workshop improvements are made to the original trade secret if the ultimate information is substantially derived from the owner's original trade secret.

Remedies under the Civil Procedure Code, 1908: A trade secret owner may request the following remedies from a civil court:

i. Injunctive relief,

ii. Monetary damages, and

iii. Costs of the proceedings.

Injunctive Relief: An injunction can be granted by the Civil Court under Order 39 of the Code to prohibit a party from violating or further using or disclosing the trade secret. A court may issue a preliminary injunction during the pendency of the action and if the plaintiff succeeds ultimately, the injunction may be made permanent. In *Colgate Palmolive (India) Ltd. vs. Hindustan Lever Ltd.*[31] the Supreme Court laid down the following considerations, which ought to weigh with the court hearing the application for the grant of injunctions:

- Extent of damages being an adequate remedy;
- Protect the plaintiff's interest for violation of his rights though, however, having regard to the injury that may be suffered by the defendants by reason thereof;
- The court while dealing with the matter ought not to ignore the factum of strength of one party's case being stronger than the other's;
- No fixed rules or notions ought to be had in the matter of grant of injunction but on the facts and circumstances of each case, the relief being kept flexible;
- The issue is to be looked at from the point of view as to whether on refusal of the injunction the plaintiff would suffer irreparable loss and injury keeping in view the strength of the parties' case;

- Balance of convenience or inconvenience ought to be considered as an important requirement even if there is a serious question or *prima facie* case in support of the grant;
- Whether the grant or refusal of injunction will adversely affect the interest of the general public, which can or cannot be compensated otherwise.

The court should not express any opinion as to the merits of the matter since the issue of grant of the injunction, usually, is at the earliest possible stage so far as the time frame is concerned.

Monetary Damages: The owner of a trade secret whose trade secret has been misappropriated may recover money damages from the wrongdoer. He may recover his lost profits as well as the profits made by the defendant. The owner may also recover, alternatively, royalty arising from wrongdoer's use of the trade secret.

Costs: If the competent court finds the wrongdoer guilty, the court can award appropriate costs, which have been incurred by the owner while defending his rights.[32]

Remedies under the Law of Torts: A party owning the trade secret can bring an action in tort for breach of the duty of confidentiality, which can arise even without an express agreement. Normally, the courts will impose a duty of confidentiality when parties stand in a special relationship with each other, such as an agent-principal relationship, employer-employee relationship or other fiduciary or good faith relationships such as relationships among partners. The other persons found to be subject to duty of confidentiality are customers, suppliers, trainees and students, licensees, and independent contractors.

Criminal Remedies: The owner of a trade secret can seek the remedy of criminal breach of trust against the person violating the same. It must be noted that the Indian Penal Code, 1860 contains provisions, which can safely be invoked against the person violating the trade secrets. For instance, Section 405 of the Code provides that whoever, being in any manner entrusted with property, or with any dominion over property, dishonestly misappropriates or converts to his own use that property, or dishonestly uses or disposes of that property in violation of any direction of law prescribing the mode in which such trust is to be discharged, or of any legal contract, express or implied, which he has made touching the discharge of such trust, or willfully suffers any other person so to do, commits "criminal breach of trust". Similarly, Section 408 of the Code considers the criminal breach of trust by a clerk or servant an aggravated form of such breach.

It must be noted that the definition of property is not restricted to moveables or immoveables alone. In *R K Dalmia vs. Delhi Administration*[33] the Supreme Court held that the word "property" is used in the Code in a much wider sense than the expression "movable property". There is no good reason to restrict the meaning of the word "property" to moveable property only, when it is used without any qualification in Section 405. Whether the offense defined in a particular section of IPC can be committed in respect of any particular kind of property, will depend not on the interpretation of the word "property" but on the fact whether that particular kind of property can be subject to the acts covered by that section. Chose in action will also amount to property under this section. A "chose or thing in action" refers to cases where the title to the money or property is in one person and the "possession is in another, which by contract he is bound to deliver to the owner".[34]

These provisions can be safely and legally invoked if the trade secret of a person is violated or misappropriated because the definition of "property" would include a trade secret as well, being an intellectual property.

Conclusion

The trade secret is an important and valuable "intellectual property right". Its importance is recognized all over the world. In the Indian context, however, it has not aroused a deeper interest. The Legislature has not shown its sensitivity and political will also seems to be deficient. In the absence of awareness, the right holders are also slow to react to the violation of trade secrets. It is high time that India should understand the need of the hour and enact a law specifically dealing with the protection of trade secrets. This is more so when India is a signatory to the TRIPS Agreement, which mandates the protection of trade secrets by the "Members" to the agreement. We cannot afford to be indifferent to this situation and realizing the importance of the subject, the legislature should act appropriately.

A law on trade secret should be formulated as soon as possible so that it can be protected properly. Till then, the owners of trade secrets for protecting their rights can effectively utilize the provisions mentioned above.

(Praveen Dalal is a Consultant and Advocate, Delhi High Court.)

Endnotes

1 Article 1(1)

2 Article 1(2). These include copyright and related rights, trademarks, geographical indications, industrial designs, patents, layout-designs (Topographies) of integrated circuits, protection of undisclosed information and control of anti-competitive practices in contractual licenses.

3 Section 7, Article 39

4 Article 39(1)

5 Article 39(2)

6 Article 39(3)

7 *Madhu Bala v. Narendra Kumar, AIR 1982 SC 938.*

8 *PD Shamdasani v. Central Bank of India Ltd, AIR1852 SC 59.*

9 (1997) 6 SCC 241.

10 *MC Mehta v. U.O.I, AIR 1988 SC 1115.*

11 2003 (8) SCALE 143.

12 *Chairman, Railway Board v. Chandrima Das, AIR 2000 SC 988.*

13 Article 19 (6).

14 *Olga Tellis v. Bombay Municioal Corporation, AIR 1986 SC 180.*

15 *State of Maharashtra v. Basantibai AIR 1986 SC 1466, 1486.*

16 2003 (4) SCALE 712.

17 AIR 1978 SC 597.

18 AIR 2003 SC 51.

19 2003 (10) SCALE 141.

20 AIR 2004 SC 1442.

21 Section 43.

22 Section 66.

23 Section 72.

24 Section 77.

25 Section 79.

26 Section 85.

27 By virtue of Section 81 of Information Technology Act, 2000.

28 Please refer to "Trade secret and Information Technology" portion of the present article.

29 Section 73.

30 Section 211.

31 (1999) 7 SCC 1.

32 Order XXA.

33 AIR 1962 SC 1821.

34 *Shivnarayan Joshi v. State of Maharashtra AIR 1980 SC 439.*

10

Reflections on the Amendments to the Patent Act of 1970

Bharti Thakar

A patent assigns exclusive rights to the inventor. India has been rich by way of traditional knowledge and research, however, due to the fact that it is mostly undocumented and the laws of patents are not very conducive, India has not been able to gain by way of intellectual property. The Patents Act 1970 where process patents were granted replaced the British regime act but was not successful in increasing the knowledge wealth of the nation. The various amendments of 1999, 2002 and 2005 have been able to remove some lacunae in our legislations. The Indian laws have been amended to comply with the provisions of the TRIPS agreement but have not been able to take advantage of its flexibility. The law could have been much better drafted to suit the national interest. With the passage of time and implementation of the Patent regime, India can therefore look forward to more litigations and consequent judicial pronouncements than the number of sections in the Acts. Knowledge is economic strength and India is losing out on this front due to lack of suitable protective legislations regarding the intellectual property.

The article traces the various provisions of all the acts and amendments thereof. Critical analysis highlights some issues which are paradoxical in nature.

A Patent may be defined as a grant by a sovereign or state to an inventor or to his assignee giving exclusive rights to make, use, exercise and vend the innovation for a limited period in exchange for disclosing it in a patent specification. This gives the owner the right to exclude others from using the patented product/ invention.

Patents are national rights and there is no such thing as a 'world patent' or an 'international patent' in the true sense of the term. However, a Patent Cooperation Treaty application is called an international application. Patents, therefore, must be applied for each of the countries where one seeks to have the innovation protected. The rights accrue only when the patent is granted.

Before the creation of the World Trade Organization in 1995, individual countries evolved their own patent laws. India earlier practicing the Indian Patents and Design Act of 1911, replaced it with the Patent Act 1970. The significance of evolving the Patents Act 1970 was in underlining various criteria for obtaining patents. The "Justice Ayyangar" report on the revision of patent law advised limiting patents to specific processes but not generally to products. Section 2 of the Patent Act 1970 defines 'invention' as anything useful, like art, process, method or manner of manufacture. Section 5 provides *inter alia* that in case of 'substance intended for use, or capable of being used, as food, medicine, or drug, while no patent shall be granted in respect of the claims for the substance themselves'; however the 'claim for the methods or processes of manufacture shall be patentable'. Thus the Indian law, till its amendment by patent Amendment Acts 1999 and 2000 (to give effect to the obligations under TRIPS) only recognized process patent and not product patent. Consequently, Indians unearthed knowledge par excellence and resolved many problems but failed to make a revenue model out of the same. Others succeeded in acquiring patents and increasing their asset value, while India quietly overlooked such gross theft or piracy done in the name of legal correctness.

India, despite being a rich country in the context of traditional knowledge and creations has not been able to gain in the manner of intellectual property. Most of the knowledge of the uses of various products especially as the ones falling into the bio-agricultural sector have been confined to oral tradition and are largely undocumented. This has given way to the entry of bio-pirates who are into mass patenting of Indian recognized herbs. Such bio-piracy of Indian generic products and processes is happening rampantly. Lack of protective legislation further hinders India's progression into the IP world.

Historically, the Indian legal system concerning Patents and the consequent Intellectual Property issue is coloured by the predecessors: The Act VI of 1856 on Protection of Inventions based on the British Patent Law of 1852; wherein certain exclusive privileges had been granted to inventors of new manufacturers for a period of 14 years; the Act of 1859 modified as Act XV; Patent monopolies called exclusive privileges (making, selling and using inventions in India and authorizing others to do so for 14 years from date of filing specifications); The Patents & Designs Protection Act of 1872; the Protection of Inventions Act of 1883 consolidated as the Inventions & Designs Act in 1888; and finally the Indian Patents & Designs Act 1911. All these Acts have played a crucial role in molding our concepts and concerns of the Intellectual property.

The Patent Act 1970

Soon after independence, with a view to ensure that the Patent system was more conducive to national interest the Govt of India appointed the Patent Enquiry Committee in 1949 under the chairmanship of Dr. Bakshi Tek Chand, a retired judge of Lahore High Court. The committee submitted the final report in April 1960. A bill based on these recommendations was introduced in the Parliament in 1963, but it lapsed due to dissolution of the Lok Sabha.

In 1957 the Govt of India further appointed Justice N Rajgopal Ayyangar to examine the nitty gritties of the Patent system and he submitted the report in Sept. 1959 recommending the preservation of the Patent System despite its shortcomings. The patent bill, 1965 based mainly on his recommendations was introduced in the lower house of parliament on 21st September 1965. It incorporated a few changes pertaining to the patents for food, drug, and medicines;

the Bill was referred to a joint committee of parliament on 25th November 1965. And it was formerly moved in Lower House of Parliament on 5th December 1966. This bill also eventually lapsed with the dissolution of Lok Sabha on 3rd March 1967. Finally, the Bill was cleared by the Parliament and became law known as the Patents Act 1970; being enforced from 20.4.1972. It contains 23 chapters which relate to patenting procedure, international arrangement and other miscellaneous matters.

The Patents Act 1970 in comparison with Indian Patents and Design Act 1911 has far-reaching effect in some areas of food, drug and medicines where all the patents granted under this category are deemed to be endorsed with the words 'license of right'. Many of the provisions are kept in line with the development of patent law in developed countries particularly Great Britain. The major departure is in the reduction of the term of patent for inventions relating to drugs, medicines and food and abolition of product patent per se for drugs, medicines, food and chemicals. The Act has a more elaborate definition of the term 'invention'. Product patents for drugs and medicines including certain class of chemicals which are produced by chemical reactions have been abolished. However, inventions relating to methods or processes of their manufacture are patentable. The area of search for novelty has also been extended to include documents published anywhere in the world. The provision for grant of compulsory license, license of right and revocation of patent on the ground of non-working has also been incorporated. International issues pertaining to international applications have been dealt with. India's membership in the Paris Convention and PCT w.e.f 7.12.1988 has enhanced this process and has made it more practical.

The Act under chapter IVA provides specific provisions for the grant of Exclusive Marketing Rights (EMR) with a view to fulfill its international obligations under the TRIPS agreement. Under the Act two types of patent applications have been classified: the patent applications under Patents Act 1970 and the International applications under PCT (Patent Cooperation Treaty).

This Act provides a detailed methodology under Sections 2 to 26; with a view to put in place a proper procedure to scrutinize all patent applications.

These processes also address delicate issues of wrong claims. First the patent examiners scrutinize the claims and are given adequate time not exceeding 18 months to do so; the complete specifications are made open for public inspection; any interested person can oppose the grant of patent on specified grounds; and finally, a patent is granted only after entertaining such opposition. The advantage of such a procedure is that any wrongful claims can be detected well in time before the patent is granted. For example, if only NCEs are eligible to get patents, then the pre-grant scrutiny can detect applications for secondary patents and protection can be denied. However, the Patent Ordinance has brought about such restriction in pre-grant objections: thereby diluting the procedure. Full scale proceedings for opposition to grant of patents can start only after the patent is granted. The Ordinance lists 11 grounds on which a patent can be opposed, but only after the patent has been granted. Opposition, prior to grant of the patent is restricted to only two grounds: "(i) Patentability, including novelty, inventive step and industrial applicability, or (ii) non-disclosure or wrongful mentioning in complete specification, source and geographical origin of biological material used in invention and anticipation of invention by the knowledge, oral or otherwise available within any local or indigenous community in India or elsewhere" (Section 25). Moreover, the Patent Rules 22 issued to implement the Ordinance also specifies time limits for making and giving cognizance to such opposition.

Overall, the Act has been instrumental in the development of the indigenous industry – to a point where the Indian pharmaceutical industry is the leader in the developing world. It has served its purpose well during the last two decades and has also catapulted the industrial growth. However, changes in the business world at large and national economy in particular nudge the settled issues to change too.

Amendments in the Patent Act 1970

India as member of WTO and as a global business player needs to make the necessary changes to comply with the treaties and agreements made on the international platforms. These changes can be visualized in the Patent Amendment Acts of 1999, 2002 and 2005. Obligations of TRIPS, namely those related to rights of patentee, term of patent protection, compulsory licensing, reversal of burden of proof and introduction of full product protection in all fields including pharmaceuticals have been the main objectives of these amendments.

The TRIPS agreement provides for a three stage frame for countries such as India which did not grant product patent rights earlier. The Patent (Amendment) Act 1999 has come into force with retrospective effect from 1st January, 1995. The important provision has been the introduction of a facility (mail box), to receive and hold product patent applications in the fields of pharmaceuticals, agricultural and chemicals. Such applications will not be processed for the grant of a patent until the end of 2004. However, Exclusive Marketing Rights (EMR) can be obtained for such application. All the product patent applications held in the mail box are required to be taken up for examination from January 1, 2005. S.24a of the Act allows the controller to give exclusive marketing rights (EMR) over inventions. This section authorizes the grant of an EMR for 5 years for inventions made in India on or after January 1, 1995 and for which a claim for process patent has been made and granted.

In the case of substances that can be used as medicines or drugs, S.24b(2) of the Patent (Amendment) Act 1999 provides that prior publication before the filing of claim for patent by the applicant either in India or in a convention country would not constitute EMR infringement.

Patent (Amendment) Act 2002

Another Bill was introduced in the Rajya Sabha in December 1999 which faced many hurdles and was referred to a joint parliamentary committee; they in turn submitted a revised bill in December 2001. This Bill with a few changes was approved by the Parliament and the Patents (Amendment) Act, 2002 was passed in May, 2002 and notified in June, 2003. The Act has been made effective from May, 2003 and has brought about lot of changes.

64 amendments in the Patent Act 1970 have been made vide the Patents (Amendment) Act, 2002. Main among them relate to terms of patents (20 years), exceptions to exclusive right and compulsory licensing.

Some significant features are as follows:

"Inventiveness" is a new criteria set up by the Patents (Amendment) Act 2002. Before which, the criteria followed was laid down by the jurisprudence in the case of Bishwanath Prasad Radhy Shyman vs. Hindustan Meta Industries, (AIR 1982 SCC 144). The criterion was that the invention must be the inventors own as opposed to a mere verification of what was already known before the date of the patent. Inventiveness is now linked with the word "novelty" and thereby the traditional test has now been changed.

Sec. 2(1)(j) of Patent (Amendment) Act 2002, defines the term "invention" as "a new product or process involving an inventive step and capable of industrial application" where 'inventive step' means a feature that makes the invention not obvious to person skilled in the art. Earlier 'invention' means any new and useful i) art, process method or manner of manufacture; ii) machine apparatus or other article; iii) substance produced by manufacture; and includes any new and useful improvement of any of them and an alleged invention. The source of geographical origin or the biological material used in invention is required to be disclosed in the specification. The declaration of inventorship on Form 5 has to be filed along with the complete specification.

It is clear that the definition of term invention in Patent Act, 2002 has enlarged the scope of protection. The controller has also been vested with the power to consider the question of obviousness of the invention disclosed while conducting the examination of application for considering the grant of a patent for the invention. In this context it should be noted that in the Patent Act 1970, the Controller had no direct power to consider the question of obviousness. The effect of this amendment is that it may not be possible to get a patent for trivial modifications.

The concept of 'unity of invention' has been broadened to include a group of inventions linked so as to form a single inventive concept. The claims in a specification should relate to a single invention or a group of invention linked to form a single inventive concept. Now, by this amendment it may be possible to claim more than one process in a single application if these processes fall under one group and are closely linked.

The 'term of patent' U/S 53 has been enlarged to twenty years for existing patents and patents granted on pending applications. This term is calculated from the date of filing of the application. Earlier, the term of patent for method or process of manufacture of substance (e.g. food, medicines, drugs etc.) was five years from the date of the sealing of the patent or seven years from the date of patent whichever period is shorter and in respect of any other invention, fourteen years from the date of the patent.

Time for restoration of a ceased patent, U/S 60 has now been increased from 12 months to 18 months.

A method or process of testing during the process of manufacture will now be patentable.

Process defined, U/S 3(i) in case of plants, are now patentable while a process for diagnostic and therapeutic has now been considered as non patentable, 18 months publication has been introduced, therefore, every patent (except in which a secrecy direction is given U/S 35) will now be published just after 18 months from the date of filing/priority and will be open for public on payment.

India has opted for a deferred system of examination of application under section 35. This means the Controller will not initiate examination of the application. Examination of an application will now be taken up only upon request by applicant with the application form and payment of requisite fees. The request is to be made within forty-eight months from the application filing date. The applicant or agents can also withdraw the application at any time (before the grant of the patent) after filing the application. The application of patent will now be examined in serial order in which the request for examination is filed.

U/S 39 persons are prohibited from filing application of patents in other foreign countries for an invention without first applying in India or without the written permission of the Central Government. If the applicant is not interested to secure a patent in India or the invention is not patentable according to the Indian law, he has to as per law, file an application for the said invention and has to wait for the expiry of six weeks after filing the application and only then file the corresponding application abroad for the same invention.

The date of every patent U/S 45 would be considered the date of filing the application for patent. According to The Patent Act 1970, the date of patent was the date of filing of complete specification. The date of patent gains significant importance while determining the full term of Patent.

As per Section 48, the rights can be considered as negative because the rights of patentee, in the case of product patent, prevent third parties without the consent of the patentee, from making, using, offering for sale, selling or importing into India; The rights in the case of process patent, prevent third parties without the consent of the patentee, from the act of using that process and offering for sale or selling in India or importing for those purposes the product directly obtained by that process, provided that the product obtained is not patentable under the Act.

The branch offices of the Patent office as per Rule 4 have been vested with more powers. Under Sec. 68 the actions such as making a request of sealing of patents, registration of assignment etc has to be made in the appropriate Branch offices of the Patent office and not at the Head Office as the case was earlier.

The overall judiciary processes to settle issues pertaining to complaints or enquires or wrongful claims have now been made less time consuming and less cumbersome.

Lately, the Indian Patent law has again been amended with the enactment of Patents (Amendment) Bill 2003. The amendment will take effect from January 1, 2005. The amendment has deleted Section 5 of IPA 1970 that specified that only methods or processes of manufacture are patentable for certain inventions, so as to allow product patent protection in all fields of technology including areas of foods, medicines and drugs. However, the new uses of known substances are still non-patentable unlike patent laws in other countries which afford protection for new uses. Considering Indian strengths in this area and its R&D capabilities it would have been appropriate if Utility Patents were allowed under the Indian Law.

Critical Analysis of the Amendments

The TRIPS compliant regime has settled in India. There has been extensive debate within the country about what the contours of India's Patent Laws should be.

Not surprisingly, the two largest parties in the country the BJP and the Congress are continuously debating on the issue and have succeeded in pushing for Amendments to India's Patents laws that actually go beyond what the TRIPS agreement provides for.

The "general principles" are very impressive and are in fact more elaborate than that in the Act of 1970. The general principles note that patents are granted to encourage inventions and to make the benefit of patented invention available at "reasonably affordable prices to the public", to secure that these are in operation in India, and not to enable patentees to enjoy monopoly power by importing. That the patent right is not abused by the patentee and the patentee does not "resort to practices which unreasonably restrain trade or adversely affect the international transfer of technology".

The Patents Act, 1970 had an important objective of eliminating the monopoly of the MNCs and removing the bottlenecks of the previous regime which prevented the indigenous firms from producing patented drugs. It was done through a very simple process of abolishing product patent protection in drugs. The Act of 1970 also had the restrictive provisions for compulsory licensing for pharmaceutical processes. In fact under Section 87 of the Act, any process patent related to pharmaceuticals was to be endorsed with the words "Licenses of right" within three years of the sealing of the patent. In such cases, anyone could ask for a license from the patent owner to use the patented process on mutually agreed terms. A compulsory license was redundant in the previous regime. Being free to produce the patented drugs, the indigenous firms could develop their own processes; However, with the advent of product patent regime, the indigenous firms will not be able to produce a patented drug even if they develop the processes of manufacturing the same unless they get a compulsory license. It is, therefore, fundamentally important that the compulsory licensing system is simple and easy to administer where in reality it has not been the case.

The basic problem with the amended Act is that it lacks any positive strategy. Overall, it appears that adequate attention has not been devoted to design the law to take advantage of the flexibilities which TRIPS provides. Since before the signing of the WTO agreement, and in the ensuing 10 years till date, globally as well as in the country, diverse contentions have emerged about the impact of TRIPS compliant Patent Laws on domestic industry – especially, in developing countries. There is, however, a wide consensus that domestic laws, while being TRIPS compliant, need to make full use of "flexibilities" available in the TRIPS agreement. This was reiterated in unequivocal terms by the WTO Doha Declaration on TRIPS Agreement and Public Health (2001), which, *inter alia*, commented that countries have the sovereign right to enact laws that safeguard domestic interests. It recognised the gravity of public health problems in developing countries and clearly provided that the member countries had the right to protect public health and to promote access to medicines for all. However, the entire amendment seems to have been carried out very mechanically. It starts with the relevant text of the Patents Act, 1970 followed by suitable changes to make it TRIPS compliant. This has been done by deleting some clauses of the 1970 Act (for example abolition of special license of right compulsory licensing provisions relating to pharmaceutical processes) and lifting some clauses from TRIPS and inserting these in the amended Act. In the process many negative aspects have remained in the amended Act, which could have been tackled without violating TRIPS. As Article 1 of TRIPS has made it clear, member countries are "not obliged to implement in their laws more extensive protection than is required by this Agreement..." But the government has adopted a stricter compulsory licensing regime than what is required under TRIPS. In the amended Act, an application for a compulsory license can be made under two sets of circumstances: under Section 84, three years after the sealing of the patent and under Section 92, anytime after the sealing of the patent with respect to a patent notified by the government as eligible for a compulsory license. The amended Act has elaborate provisions on compulsory licensing in Chapter XVI (Sections 82 to 94) thereby making it more complicated.

It is now sought to provide for product patent in respect of medicines and drugs. The provisions for the grant of 'Exclusive Marketing Rights' for pharmaceutical and Agrochemical products for a period of five years as well as for receipt of mailbox applications for the grant of patent have been incorporated as a consequence of the complaint filed by US and the ruling of the Dispute Settlement Body. The countries have agreed to amend its Patent Act within a period of fifteen months.

Representation for opposition will have to be made within three months of the date of publication of the patent application. The applicant will have to reply to the notice, if issued by the Controller within one month. The Controller of Patents will have to decide about the refusal/grant of patent ordinarily within one month from the completion of proceedings, which may include hearing, if requested (Rule 55). Thus, unlike as under the Patents Act 1970, a patent can be granted even when the issue of granting or otherwise is not convincingly settled. This obviously will speed up the process of grant of patents and which seems to be the objective and will prove favourable to the patentees. Since MNCs are the main innovators of new drugs, this favours the MNCs. They can continue to enjoy exclusive rights even when these are wrongfully claimed and granted, till the post-grant scrutiny establishes it and this may take years. With much greater access to financial resources, the MNCs can delay or influence the proceedings. To enjoy such monopoly power and charge high prices which would constitute abusing the patents rights. Since TRIPS does not impose any restrictions on what procedures WTO member countries can adopt, there is no need and justification for India to change the procedure of pre-grant scrutiny as provided in the Act of 1970.

Under the original 1970 Act, importing was not mentioned as an exclusive right. This has been amended (in Section 48) to conform to TRIPS. Unlike Article 28 of TRIPS, Section 48 of India's amended patents Act provides no qualification about exhaustion of patent rights. Instead another section (107A(b)) has been inserted which says that "importation of patented products by any person from a person who is duly authorised by the patentee to sell or distribute the product shall not be considered as an infringement of patent rights." This does permit parallel imports but only in some cases. As the Indian Drug Manufacturers Association (IDMA) has pointed out, the phrase "duly authorised by the patentee" may cause delay and difficulty. In accordance with the spirit of Article 28 of TRIPS, any import from any legitimate source even if not specifically authorized should be permitted.

Section 47 of the Patents Act, 1970, which has not been deleted in the recent amendments, provides other exceptions. The patented product/process may be made or used by any person for the "purpose merely of experiment or research including the imparting of instructions to pupils." As UNCTAD-ICTSD 2002 (p.101) has pointed out, the exception can not only be for scientific research with no commercial intent. It can also possibly lead to ambiguity, it should be clearly understood that the non-patentees can experiment with the patented product and develop their own processes of manufacturing for commercial purposes, (though they may not be able to actually use these unless they are authorized to do so).

Since 1995, the experience of countries who have implemented the TRIPS agreement show an increasing skewing in the balance between the rights of patent holders and consumers in favour of the former. The TRIPS agreement marks a fundamental shift in this balance, as well as a shift in global attitudes where private profits are put ahead of social benefits. This is further fueled by dependence of economies in the developed world on industries that require strong intellectual property protection. Of the fifteen most profitable industries today at the global level, six are from the pharmaceutical sector and five from the information technology sector – all of whom are dependent on strong Patent protection. It is also a reality and a paradox that intellectual property protection allows such industries to create monopolies, not only over production, but also in the control of knowledge.

The most dramatic effect is being felt in pharmaceutical sector. The net result of the TRIPS accord has been the high cost of medicines and the consequent denial of access to medicines to the income poor across the globe. Further, it has also led to a situation where medicines required to treat diseases that predominantly occur among the poor are not researched at all. Instead drugs that are being researched are drugs used for "lifestyle" diseases like impotence, baldness, obesity, etc. While the pharmaceutical industry claims that high prices are explained by the massive expenditure on R&D, the truth is that drugs they actually research have little relevance to real medicinal needs. Moreover, the kind of profits that big pharmaceutical MNCs generate are an indication of profiteering and not just legitimate profit making.

Contrary to widespread apprehensions, only a few applications for EMR have been filed in India. But the one granted to an MNC, Novartis, for an anti-cancer drug, imatinib mesylate (Novartis' brand name: Gleevec) has created a controversy.

Under Article 70(3) of TRIPS, a WTO member country has no obligation to provide protection (through patents or EMRs) for any subject matter which has fallen into the "public domain" before WTO came into being, i.e., before January 1, 1995. Patent information published in the US FDA Orange Book shows that Novartis' patent for the new chemical entity, imatinib mesylate was granted in USA before 1995. A number of Indian companies (Natco, Ranbaxy, Sun Pharma, Cipla, Emcure, Intas, Hetero) have been manufacturing and marketing generic versions before the EMR was granted to Novartis in November 2003. Compared to the price of Rs.1,20,000 per month for the Novartis's product, generic versions cost between Rs.9,000 and Rs.12,000. The EMR sought and granted to Novartis is for modification of the crystal form of imatinib mesylate (beta-crystal form). Novartis' EMR relates to this modified form for which it got patent and marketing approval in Australia during 2001-03. While Natco has challenged the grant of EMR to Novartis in the Delhi High Court, Novartis filed suits against the other generic companies in the Madras High Court. The latter has passed an interim order restraining six Indian companies from manufacturing and marketing imanitib mesylate. What is basically being contested is whether secondary patents obtained after 1995 for a new chemical entity patented before 1995 can be used to prevent generic companies from producing the drug. This has impending implications for grant of patents to the mailbox applications as well.

In contrast to the small number of EMR applications, more than 7000 applications for product patents for pharmaceutical and agro-chemical products are believed to have accumulated in the mail box. If and when a product patent is granted to any mailbox application, what are the consequences to the generic companies which may be producing the product?

A need for another amendment was found by the end of 2004 to replace the EMR system and to introduce product patent protection. A Bill (the Patent Amendment Bill 2003) was introduced in the parliament in December 2003. Although, a fact was that only two clauses were necessary to replace the EMR system and introduce product patents in all fields, the Bill actually included 70 other clauses. These were introduced to simplify the patent grant procedures so as to make it easier for the MNCs to get product patents. But this Bill could not be passed in the Parliament. And as a fact even without discussions in the Parliament a full fledged product patent regime has been introduced in India from January 1, 2005 through the presidential decree (the Patents Amendment Ordinance, 2004.) issued on December 26, 2004.

The Rajya Sabha has finally passed the Patent (Amendment) Bill 2005 on March 23, 2005, after a public debate. India now has product patents for pharmaceuticals, agricultural chemicals and special food products. It has struck a balance between the consumers' interest and that of innovators. The changes in the definition of patentability, restoration of pre-grant opposition and automatic license of right would help to maintain supply and prices of medicines currently manufactured in India. It would also allay fears of developing countries about the continuity of supply of low-cost medicines from India.

Conclusion

Under TRIPS, it is mandatory for all member countries of WTO to provide patent protection for all products including pharmaceuticals. But the protection of the rights of the patentees is not the sole concern of TRIPS. TRIPS, therefore, provides flexibility for governments to strike a balance between the private rights of patentees and the socio-economic needs and objectives of the country as a whole. The costs of high prices resulting from product patent protection may be tackled by:

(i) Resorting to parallel imports or granting compulsory licenses during the patent term, and

(ii) Ensuring that the entry of generics is not delayed after the expiry of patents.

The recent amendments to India's patent law provide for parallel imports and hence the country can shop around and import cheaper alternatives, if available. But considering the status which the generic companies in India have achieved, what is of greater importance in India is a proper compulsory licensing system. In a product patent regime, a proper compulsory licensing system is of vital importance in promoting competition while ensuring that patentees get compensation through royalties.

If the bias in the Patents Act, 1970, which did not provide product patent protection, was in favour of the non-patentees, the bias in the amended Act is clearly in favour of the patentees. No time limit has been specified for processing of compulsory licensing applications and a compulsory license can be used only after the appeals against the grant of such a license by the Controller of Patents are turned down following a detailed procedure. But in the case of applications for product patents, time limit has been specified and patents can be granted even before it is convincingly settled that it can be granted. Unlike in the case of compulsory licenses, full scale opposition proceedings can start only after the grant of patents. The aim for this stance appears to be, not to deprive the patentees of the exclusive patent rights except under very special cases. India as can be seen, has effectively provided a more extensive protection to patentees than what is required under TRIPS.

The Patents Ordinance of 2004 will have to be followed up with the necessary legislation. While this is deliberated in India's Parliament, it is still possible to incorporate the necessary provisions in India's patent law to suit the societal and economic requirements.

As regards the provision in the amended law allowing manufacture of a patented product for export by companies other than the innovator after 2005, MNC is reported to have taken a stand that import and export of a patented product (by some other than the innovator) is not TRIPS-compliant.

MNCs are also complaining about the provisions on compulsory licensing in the new law about third party access to patents who can apply for compulsory license on the ground that the reasonable requirements of public have not been satisfied, that the patented invention is not available to the public at a reasonably affordable price or that the patented invention has not worked in India.

There is a debatable situation revolving around the issue of what is 'novelty' because any 'invention' consists of 'novelty' and 'utility'. There is lack of novelty if there is publication, public use or public knowledge. There is no utility if it is not a new manufacture or does not include new and useful improvement. In considering whether the claim made by the inventor is an invention, it will have to be considered whether the subject matter is non-obvious and obviousness is to be judged by the standard of man skilled in the art convened. Therefore, with the passage of time and implementation of the Patent regime, India can look forward to more litigations and consequent judicial pronouncements than the number of sections in the Acts.

(Bharti Thakar is a faculty member in ICFAI Business School, Ahmedabad).

References

1. Andy Gibbs, Bob DeMatteis (2003), *Essentials of Patents,* John Wiley & Sons, Inc. USA.
2. Amiya Kumar, Bagchi, Parthasarathi Banerjee and Uttam Kumar Bhattacharya (1984), "Indian Patents Act and its Relation to Technological Development in India: A Preliminary Investigation." *Economic and Political Weekly,* February 18.
3. Sudip Chaudhuri, (2002), "TRIPS Agreement and Amendment Act in India," *EPW,* August 10.
4. A V Ganesan (1999), "The Implications of the Patents (Amendment) Ordinance 1999", New Delhi: Indian Council for Research on International Economic Relations.
5. Joint Committee, (2001), "*The Patents (Second Amendment) Bill, 1999 – Report of the Joint Committee*", New Delhi: Rajya Sabha Secretariat.
6. M B Rao, Manjula Guru (2003), "*Understanding TRIPS: Managing Knowledge in Developing Countries*", New Delhi Response Books, Sage Publications.
7. M D Nair (2004), *"Third Amendment to IPA (1970), Balancing TRIPS Obligations and Safeguarding Indian Interests"*, Patentmatics, online at: www.patentmatics.com/pub2004.
8. Prabuddha Ganguli (1998), "*Gearing up for Patents: The Indian Scenario*", Universities Press Hyderabad.
9. UNCTAD-ICTSD (2002), *TRIPS and Development: Resource Book, Part Two, Substantive Obligations, Patents,* Geneva; United Nations Conference on Trade and Development and International Centre for Trade and Sustainable Development (accessed from the website of the ICTSD: *www.iprsonline.org*).
10. UNCTAD-ICTSD (2003), *TRIPS and Development: Resource Book , Part Six, Transitional and Institutional Arrangements, Transitional Periods,* Geneva; United Nations Conference on Trade and Development and International Centre for Trade and Sustainable Development (accessed from the website of the ICTSD: *www.iprsonline.org*).
11. UNCTAD-ICTSD (2004), *TRIPS and Development: Resource Book , Part Six, Transitional and Institutional Arrangements, Transitional Periods,* Geneva; United Nations Conference on Trade and Development and International Centre for Trade and Sustainable Development (accessed from the website of the ICTSD: *www.iprsonline.org*).
12. Jayshree Watal (2001), *Intellectual Property Rights in the WTO and Developing Countries,* New Delhi: Oxford University Press.
13. *www.pharmabiz.com*

11

Indian Patent Regime vis-à-vis European Patent Regime – A Comparative Analysis

How Far are the Indian Patent Laws Lagging Behind their European Counterparts?

Deeptarag Mukherjee and Gaurav Dasgupta

This article analyses the present Indian position as per the Patents (Amendment) Act 2002. The European position under the European Patent Convention, 1973 has also been studied. The Indian and the European patents systems have been compared, specifically in relation to three areas namely "diagnostic method", "capable of industrial application", and "unity of invention". An attempt has been made towards a better understanding of whether the domestic Patent laws promote or suppress the Indian intellectual property through a comparative study and also locating the areas wherein the Indian laws lag behind the European Patent Convention.

Introduction

The topic has been studied in the specific context of patent laws. This article analyses the present Indian position as per the Patents (Amendment) Act 2002. The European position under the European Patent Convention, 1973 has also been studied. The Indian and the European patents systems have been compared, specifically in relation to three areas namely "diagnostic method", "capable of industrial application", and "unity of invention". An attempt has been made towards a better understanding of whether the domestic Patent laws promote or suppress the Indian intellectual property through a comparative study and also locating the areas wherein the Indian laws lag behind the European Patent Convention. Measures to rectify the present loopholes in the patent regime have also been suggested.

Patentability of Diagnostic Method

Section 3(i) of the Indian Patents Act, 1970 states that any process for the medicinal, surgical, curative, prophylactic or other treatment of human beings or any process for a similar treatment of animals or plants to render them free of disease or to increase their economic value are not patentable. Although with the advent of The Patents (Amendment) Act, 2002, any process for treatment of plants has now become patentable, the diagnostic or therapeutic process are still not considered to be patentable.[1]

The European Patent Convention contains a prohibition on the grant of patents for "methods of treatment of the human or animal body by surgery or therapy and diagnostic methods practised on the human or animal body". A 1987 Appeal Board decision, *Non-invasive measurement/Bruker*, held that the only diagnostic methods that are excluded from patent protection are those whose results immediately make it possible to decide a particular course of medical treatment. As a result of this, it had been held that methods, **which produce only interim results, are not barred** from patentability.

---

1 *See* http://www.patentoffice.nic.in/ipr/patent/salient_f.htm

In *Cygnus,Inc.*[2] it was held:

The Board is therefore convinced that the only diagnostic methods to be excluded from patent protection are those whose results ***immediately make it possible to decide*** *ovn a particular course of medical treatment.*

In *Joos vs. Commissioner of Patents,*[3] the vital issue of patentability in respect of methods of strict medical treatment was by-passed by Barwick C J when he said at p.63:

"...the only matter for consideration in this appeal is whether a process must be held not to be a proper subject for a grant simply because it is a process for 'treatment' of a part of the human body. For the purpose of deciding this question it may be granted that a process for the treatment of the human body as a means of curing or preventing a disease, correcting a malfunction or removing an incapacity is not a proper subject matter for grant of monopoly."

Therefore, instead of outright rejecting the diagnostic methods or therapeutic processes from patent protection, the Indian courts should apply the European approach in determining whether diagnostic methods are patentable and allow patentability of those diagnostic methods which produce only interim result without suggesting a particular course of medical treatment.

Capable of Industrial Application

Section 2(1)(j) of The Patents (Amendment) Act, 2002 defines invention as:

"invention" means a new product or process involving an inventive step and capable of industrial application.

According to this definition, irrespective of the fact that the subject matter is a method, machine, apparatus, or article, it would be considered an invention as long as it is new, useful and involves an aspect of manufacture.

The Patents Act 1970 (India), before the 2002 Amendment, did not have the requirement of 'capable of industrial application'. However, one of the requirements

---

2 Case No. T 964/99 of the EPO.

3 [1973] RPC 59.

of a patentable invention under the Act was that it should be useful.[4] Thus the Act, prior to the 2002 Amendment required satisfaction of the criteria of utility, which was substituted by the words 'capable of industrial application' as a result of the Patents (Amendment) Act 2002.

A mere reading of the two terms leads to the conclusion that the amendment has broadened the scope of what was previously a narrow term. 'Useful' previously was qualified with the end-result of the invention. It required the process of manufacture should result in a vendible product. This 'purpose' or 'result' has been further broadened by the 2002 amendment by inserting the words 'industrial application'. Now the situation is that even if the claim does not result in a vendible product, so long it is new and has **industrial application** (irrespective of the vendibility requirement), it can be patented. However, this 'industrial application' requirement is a very vague concept because no criteria has yet been evolved to determine what constitutes industrial application.

In the case of *Indian Vaccum Brake Co. Ltd.,*[5] it was held by a single Judge of the Calcutta High Court that the term 'utility' used in the Act has been used in a special sense. **Mere usefulness is not sufficient** to support the patent. Patent for making in-one-piece articles which were formerly prepared in two or more pieces could not be called to be a valid patent.

Industrial application may be an issue where a range of substances is claimed and it is argued that some do not do what is claimed. In *Chiron Corp vs. Murex Diagnostics Ltd,*[6] a range of polypeptides encoded by a genome of Hepatitis C virus was claimed. The defendant in an infringement action challenged the validity of the patent on the basis, *inter alia,* that the invention was not capable of industrial application because the claim included polypeptides unconnected with Hepatitis C virus. The polypeptides had no conceivable use at first instance. Aldous J held that the patent was capable of industrial application. He said:

---

4 *See* Section 2(1)(j): "invention means any new and useful..." (i) art, process, method or manner of manufacture; (ii) machine, apparatus or other article; (iii) substance produced by manufacturer, and includes any new and useful improvement of any of them, and an alleged invention."

5 AIR 1926 Cal 152.

6 [1996] RPC 535.

> *"Although the range of polypeptides falling within the claims...may be large, there is no evidence to suggest that once the sequence is known they could not be made by the industry."*[7]

The defendant appealed, claiming that Aldous J was wrong to substitute the word 'by' for 'in', arguing that the correct question was whether the invention could be **made or used *in* industry and not *by* industry**. The defendant submitted that there is no industry in making the useless. The plaintiff argued that whilst what was claimed must have some practical use, a claim in respect of practical things is not invalidated by the inclusion at the edge of the claim of something for which there is **no present or foreseeable use**. The Court of Appeal was unimpressed by that argument and Morritt L J said:

> *"We accept that the polypeptides claimed...can be made...[but it is required] that the invention can be **made or used 'in any kind of industry'** so as to be **'capable' or 'susceptible of industrial application'**."*

This approach by the European Patent Office is commendable. The EPO has interpreted 'capable of industrial application' in relation to its use in the industry, that is its feasibility to be used in the industry on the day when patent is claimed. The EPO has clearly denied any patent on mere assumption of utility by the industry in future. This objective criteria for determining industrial application should be incorporated by the Indian courts.

Unity of Invention

"Single Inventive Concept" has been incorporated in Section 10(5) of the Patents Act by The Patents (Amendment) Act, 2001. As per the current provision, claims of a patent specification can relate to a group of inventions linked so as to form a single inventive concept. The claims in a specification should relate to a single invention or a group of invention linked so as to form a single inventive concept. Now, by this amendment it may be possible to claim more than one process in a single application if these processes fall under one group and are closely linked.

The requirement for unity of invention is set forth in Article 82 of the European Patent Convention (EPC) 1973:

---

7 *Id.* at 575.

"The European patent application shall relate to one invention only or to a group of inventions so linked as to form a single general inventive concept."

Single inventive concept is defined in Rule 30(1) of the EPC as:

Where a group of inventions is claimed in one and the same European patent application, the requirement of unity of invention referred to in Article 82 shall be fulfilled only when there is a technical relationship among those inventions involving one or more of the same or corresponding special technical features. The expression "special technical features" shall mean those features which define a contribution which each of the claimed inventions considered as a whole makes over the prior art.

A single inventive concept may also be recognised between independent claims of same category. This is however limited to **specific cases**, such as:

1. *Several uses of a same product, such as a pharmaceutical use and a non-therapeutic use,*[8] *or a first medical use and a second medical use.*[9]
2. *Intermediate product(s) and final product deriving therefrom, provided they share a same essential structural element.*[10]

In *Canadian General Electric Co. Ltd. vs. Fada Radio Ltd.*,[11] it was held that:

"Sometimes it is the combination that is the invention; if the invention requires independent thought, ingenuity and skill, producing in a distinctive form a more efficient result, and uniting them all into apparatus which, taken as a whole is novel, there is a subject matter. A new combination of well known devices, and the application thereof to a new and useful purpose, may require invention to produce it and may be good subject matter for a patent."

Although the Indian Patents Act provides for combined application of independent product or processes (which are separately patentable), such a concept is yet to be in practice. This is so because it goes against the ossified

8 Case No. T 200/86 of the EPO.

9 Cases No.W 5/91, W 28/91.

10 Cases No. T /82, T 110/82, T 35/87, T 470/91.

11 AIR 1930 PC 1.

notion in the Indian Patent Offices that there must be a single patent application for one single invention.[12] Therefore, when two separate processes are involved, a single application for their patentability is rejected outright. This deliberate indifference in giving effect to the legal provisions should be corrected.

Conclusion

In conclusion, the Indian Patent system is lagging behind the European Patent Convention, due to its constricted approach towards patentability of various processes as well as the narrow interpretation given to various technical terms in the Patents Act. However, if the recommendations given in this paper are implemented, then the Indian Patent system will be at par with the international standards, thereby removing the disharmony presently existing and the suppression of the 'ambit of patents' resulting therefrom.

(Deeptarag Mukherjee is a former student and Gourav Dasgupta is a 4th year student of National University of Juridical Sciences (NUJS), Kolkata.)

---

12 *See* Section 7(1), The Patents Act, 1970 (India).

12

India: Intellectual Property Crime

Sudhir Ravindran and S A Chenthil Kumaran

Intellectual Property crime is more generally known as counterfeiting and piracy. During recent years the scope and scale of the problem has grown at a rate previously unknown. The counterfeit goods always incur a huge cost to the original manufacturer in terms of monetary loss and loss of goodwill. The article explains the difference between counterfeit products and copyright infringements. It gives a description of the above viewpoint from an Indian perspective.

Increasingly, the global economy is dependent upon the creation and distribution of intellectual property (IP) to drive economic growth.[1] However markets are plagued by fakes be it stamps, watches, cigarettes, cosmetics, pharmaceuticals, FMCG products, auto components, software, music, films etc., resulting in significant loss to companies, corresponding evasion of tax duties and violation of the rights of the consumer. Studies by industry associations bear this out, the CII Alliance[2] estimates that the FMCG sector loses approximately 15% of its revenue to counterfeit goods with several top brands losing up to 30%

1 The fight against Piracy and Counterfeiting of Intellectual Property: Prepared by the Commission on Intellectual Property of ICC, Paris and submitted to the 35th ICC World Congress, Marrakesh, June 7, 2004.

2 In order to strengthen further the enforcement of IPR in a focused manner, an Alliance in the name of CII Alliance for Anti-Counterfeiting/Piracy was formed with the leadership and initiatives of Indian industry and right holders who are affected by the counterfeiting/piracy menace in 2004.

Source: Global Business Solutions, January 7, 2005.

of their business due to IP crime. The nature of the crime, its size, diversity and scope has hindered the task of coordinating a dynamic response. Lack of consumer awareness and advancement of technology are the major factors which encourage counterfeiting which is further fuelled by lax enforcement laws which make things easy for counterfeiter. The continuity of socio-economic growth and industrial competitiveness depends upon high level of IP protection and enforcement[3] raising profound concerns of the rapidly growing piracy of IP rights and production of counterfeit goods.

IP Crime

IP crime is more generally known as counterfeiting and piracy. Counterfeiting is, wilful trademark infringement, while piracy involves, wilful copyright infringement. These are very similar and often overlapping crimes. IP crime is not a new phenomenon but due to globalisation and advances in technology counterfeiting and piracy has become big business.[4]

Overview of Problems

During recent years the scope and scale of the problem has grown at a rate previously unknown. The counterfeit traders with whom most people come into contact are small-scale operators or street vendors. However, such vendors are only the front end of much wider and more sophisticated networks. Although the term "organized crime" should be used with caution in describing the counterfeiting industry, Interpol states that "extensive evidence is now available which demonstrates that organized criminals and terrorists are heavily involved in planning and committing intellectual property related crimes."[5]

Further, online piracy is facilitated by increases in transmission speeds, since faster connections enable users to send and download larger files (such as software programs) more quickly. Without strong online copyright laws and enforcement of those laws, online piracy *via* spam, auction sites and P2P systems will continue to grow alongside increases in Internet usage.[6]

---

3 "The CII Alliance for Anti-Counterfeiting/Piracy", Confederation of Indian Industry. *www.ciionline.org*

4 "Counter Offensive: An IP Crime Strategy", a DTI service of the United Kingdom Patent Office DDU/93/IPID/7-04.

5 "Counterfeiting and Organized Crime: INTA Counterfeiting Special Report September 2004", *www.inta.org*.

6 "Piracy Study: First Annual BSA and IDC Global Software Piracy Study", July 04. Business Software Alliance, *www.bsa.org*.

There are four main factors contributing to the growth of IP crime:[7]

- Widespread availability of technology.
- Increased globalization of world trade; it is easier to manufacture in one geographic location and distribute elsewhere. The result of more open borders and more trade is that it is also easier for counterfeits to flow across borders.
- Legal penalties are low; if they exist at all.
- The influence of organized crime.

Counterfeiting and piracy have emerged as clear and serious threats to business, consumers and government. Counterfeiting is obviously a breach of consumer affairs, health, trade, and employment law. It is the negation of all the major legislation protecting individuals.[8] Without coordinated action and policy to clamp down on the criminals and to dissuade consumers by bringing about increased awareness, a cycle of economic destabilization occurs with control slipping to the criminals.

Costs to the Right Holder

Industries which find themselves in direct competition with counterfeiters suffer a *direct loss in sales*. Indeed, some markets are even dominated by counterfeiters, creating barriers of entry for the producers of the genuine product. Some would argue that the buyers of the fakes would not have bought the genuine item but that is a very narrow argument and can only apply to a small segment of luxury goods. Many counterfeit products today are of higher quality and compete directly with the genuine items. In addition, consumers who are deceived into believing that they bought a genuine article when it was in fact a fake, blame the manufacturer of the genuine product when it fails, creating a loss of goodwill. Even cheaper and obvious copies that are bought in good faith represent a serious threat to the company that wants its brands associated with quality and exclusivity. Beside direct losses of sales and goodwill, one should not forget the expenditure involved in *protecting and enforcing* intellectual property rights. The

7 *Surpa iv.*

8 "Counterfeiting & Organised Crime", Union des Fabricants Pour La Protection International De La Propriete Industrielle Et Artistique 2003.

right owner becomes involved in costly investigations and litigation when combating counterfeiters and may also have to spend further sums on product protection. The budget for anti-counterfeiting is rarely well-defined within an organization, but spans across several departments such as marketing, human resources, product development and legal departments.[9]

Legal Protection

A counterfeit product can infringe any, or all, of the main intellectual property rights, namely trademarks, patents, designs and copyrights. Counterfeiting predominately deals with trademarks whereas copyright infringements are referred to as piracy. Generally patents alone are not usually referred to as counterfeits or as piracy.

The difference between these rights should be understood. Both patents and copyrights are monopolies, granted by law. A trademark is not a monopoly. The proprietors of patents and copyrights can grant a license to others without conveying any real interest. A license in these situations is defined as a purchased right to act without the threat of suit by the Right's owner. The registration of all IP rights is a complex issue and companies that try to save money by not registering their rights run a great risk, even though they may feel that their products are not worthy of this protection. No matter how small the company, or the product, if it is successful then someone will imitate it. It is not a legal requirement to register trade marks but, to gain full benefit of the various courses of action available, it is strongly recommended.

While the necessary legal protection may exist, it can be said that consumer demand drives counterfeiting, which in turn harms numerous industries. Rising global over-capacity for the manufacture of discs is also key factor behind the spread of disc piracy, affecting music, film and computer software.[10] There can be no doubt that product counterfeiting is a serious and damaging economic crime.[11]

---

9 "The Economic Impact of Counterfeiting", Organisation for Economic Co-operation and Development, 1998.

10 Commercial Piracy Report, The recording industry International Federation of the Phonographic Industry (IFPI), July 2004, *www.ifpi.org*.

11 "Product Counterfeiting – Protecting your Good Name", Paul Carratu, Group Managing Director Carratu International, *www.carratu.com*.

There are definitely no "major" or "minor" counterfeits. Counterfeiting is a serious offence on a level with trafficking in weapons or drugs.[12] It is vital that the public understands that fake products carry with them a real safety hazard and not just the prospect of disappointing performance.[13] Because no industry sector is immune from attack by counterfeiters and no country is exempt from this type of criminal activity.[14] Finding ways to successfully combat it is an international challenge, and demands the participation not only of companies, but also members of the world's law enforcement agencies, and governments around the world. Each of these groups has a critical role to play if this challenge is to be met.[15]

Indian Perspective

India continues to remain on the priority watch list of the US Trade Representative, meaning that India is perceived as not providing adequate intellectual property rights protection or enforcement of laws protecting IPR. However, the admitted experience of IP crime in India is lower than in Asia-Pacific region and globally and is contrary to general perception of the relative incidence of IP crime in India.[16] While India does not have a separate legislation to address counterfeiting as in the US, it offers statutory remedies, both civil and criminal[17] which are embodied in the new Trademarks Act of 1999, The Copyright Act, 1957, The Patents Act 1970, The Designs Act 2000, The Geographical Indications of Goods (Registration and Protection) Act 1999, Custom & Border measures are provided in The Customs Act, 1962 which one can access through various IP statutes.

India has made important changes to its IP laws and more are in the pipeline, including changes in IP and Customs laws to implement border control measures as required by the TRIPs Agreement. India has signed Customs Mutual Assistance Agreement with most of its major trade partners including EU & USA. These

12 D Nazat, "The Counterfeiting of Toys", *International Criminal Police Review*, No. 464, 1997.

13 A practical guide for European Engineering Companies, Orgalime Guide Combating Counterfeiting with the support of the European Commission, October 2001.

14 "Counterfeiting and Theft of Tangible Intellectual Property: Challenges and Solutions" Written Testimony of Timothy P Trainer, President International Anti-Counterfeiting Coalition, Inc. (IACC) before the United States Senate Committee on the Judiciary Washington, DC March 23, 2004. *www.iacc.org*

15 "The Global Threat of Software Piracy", by Annmarie Levins, *International Criminal Police Review*, Official Publication of The International Criminal Police Organization, ICPR 476-477/1999. *www.interpol.int*

16 "Global Economic Crime Survey: India", PricewaterhouseCoopers 2003. *www.pwc.com.*

17 "How to tackle Counterfeiting in India", Ranjan Narula & Taj Kunwar Paul Rouse & Co International, *Managing Intellectual Property*, Euromoney Institutional Investor plc, February 2004.

treaties establish formal guidelines and allow officials to share intelligence and investigative data relating to IP violations. In addition, in the last five years the Indian courts have taken a more pragmatic approach to counterfeiting. Lobbying by various brand owners' associations, and more education programmes have resulted in increased awareness and a greater understanding of IP issues among law enforcement authorities.[18]

While crimes such as drug dealing and trafficking are viewed with great concern, the general perception in India of IP crime is that it is a "victimless crime". Consumers in India still appear to be relatively unconcerned because of a divergence of public perception and the lack of understanding about the effects of IP crime. Recently, there have been stronger signals with lengthier sentencing and higher penalties for those convicted of counterfeiting and piracy. However, mixed messages are still conveyed and lower penalties are more common than those imposed for more high profile criminal activities.

(Sudhir Ravindran is CEO and S A Chenthil Kumaran is a consultant of Global Business Solutions, #4, fourth floor, crown court, 128, Cathedral Road, Chennai - 600 086).

---

[18] *Supra xvii.*

13

How to Tackle Counterfeiting in India

Paul, Taj Kunwar and Narula, Ranjan

Today's India is globalized and open for foreign direct investment in almost every sector of the economy. A report on the Indian market produced by the brand protection committee of the Federation of Indian Chambers of Commerce and Industry showed that in the consumer goods sector, manufacturing goods such as soap, toothpaste and food items, had lost Rs.25 billion ($520 million) annually. Although, India does not have separate legislation to address counterfeiting in the same way as the US, statutory remedies, both civil and criminal, are now available in India. Theoretically, the jail sentences and fines provided under the TM Act, Copyright Act and IPC should have enough deterrent to check the flow of counterfeit products. A large volume of counterfeit goods from China that enter India's neighbouring countries actually end up being sold in India. INSET: Prevention is better than cure.

Today's India is globalized and open for foreign direct investment in almost every sector of the economy. This is not only good news for the foreign investors but also very advantageous for the Indian economy, as demonstrated by a 6% rise in the rate of economic growth in 2003. With the further globalization of the Indian economy, more and more foreign brands are entering the Indian market. Yet the irony is that before many foreign brands even enter the country, counterfeit versions are already entrenched in the market. The situation is becoming critical for brand owners. India, because it offers a cheap manufacturing base, is used by counterfeiters to produce goods not only for domestic sales but also for export. But now the counterfeit menace in India is growing, as local producers take advantage of rising consumerism and the increasing appetite for branded goods among the growing middle class.

A report on the Indian market produced by the brand protection committee of the Federation of Indian Chambers of Commerce and Industry showed that in the consumer goods sector, manufacturing goods such as soap, toothpaste and food items, had lost Rs.25 billion ($520 million) annually. And the government lost Rs.9 billion ($187 million) in taxes because of counterfeiting in the fast moving consumer goods industry alone.

According to the Manufacturers' Association of Information Technology, trade losses due to intellectual property theft, infringement and piracy reach Rs.2,160 million ($450 million) every year. The loss to the government exchequer on account of the grey market is estimated to be around Rs.400 million ($84 million) each year. It is estimated that the Indian music industry lost Rs.1.8 billion ($375 million) on account of music piracy in the three years from 2000 to 2002.

These figures show that the problem is big and growing. However, in many ways India is ready to tackle this crime. It has made important changes to its IP laws and more are in the pipeline, including changes in IP and Customs laws to implement border control measures as required by the TRIPs Agreement. The new Trademarks Act of 1999, which came into force on September 15, 2003, has increased the punishment and fine that counterfeiters face. Both civil and criminal remedies exist for combating counterfeiting. In addition, in the last five years the Indian courts have taken a more pragmatic approach to counterfeiting. Lobbying by various brand owners' associations, and more education programmes have resulted in increased awareness and a greater understanding of IP issues among law enforcement authorities.

Choosing a Strategy

Although India does not have separate legislation to address counterfeiting in the same way as the US, statutory remedies—both civil and criminal—are now available in India. Redress is available in the forms of *ex-parte* interlocutory injunctions, permanent injunctions, search and seizure orders, rendition of accounts, as well as common law relief in the form of claims for passing off. The new TrademarksAct has also introduced the theory of dilution in cases relating to well-known marks.

Criminal Remedies

The Trademarks Act, 1999

The long-awaited Trademarks Act, 1999 (the TM Act) is now in force and provides much stricter provisions to deal with counterfeiting of trademarks used for goods or services. The TM Act makes the offence cognizable (serious) in nature. Under the old Act, trademark offences fell into the non-cognizable category as well as being a bailable offence. As a result the police would not necessarily arrest the counterfeiter for dealing in counterfeit goods and police raids often only resulted in a loss of face for the counterfeiter. However, under the new TM Act, the offence is non-bailable and punishment and fines have been increased. Counterfeiters now face a minimum six month prison sentence and a fine of Rs.50,000 ($1,110) and a maximum of three years in jail and a fine of Rs.200,000 ($4,450). The TM Act has also given powers to deputy superintendents and assistant commissioners of police to search and seize counterfeit goods without a warrant.

Indian Penal Code

The Indian Penal Code (IPC) also has provisions to protect consumers from being deceived by traders or manufacturers who manufacture or sell counterfeit goods. A consumer can file a criminal complaint against the infringers on the grounds of cheating under Section 420 of IPC, for deceiving consumers, concealing the true trade origin of such goods and dishonestly inducing the public to buy the goods. Section 485 of the IPC makes it an offence to possess any counterfeit mark to be affixed to the goods, or to possess any kind of die, plate, or other instrument for the purpose of counterfeiting. The IPC also makes it an offence to sell or possess for sale any goods with a counterfeit property mark or to apply any false mark on a container. The court has the power to issue a general search warrant under

Section 93 of the Criminal Procedure Code, 1973, and to seize the counterfeit goods and other incriminating documents. IP holders can also use the provisions under the IPC to support their complaint under the Trademarks Act.

The Copyright Act, 1957

The Copyright Act also provides for both civil and criminal remedies to fight counterfeiting. It provides for imprisonment of six months to three years and a maximum fine of Rs.200,000 ($4,170). The Copyright Act also empowers a sub-inspector to search and seize infringing copies without warrant. The burden of proof, however, will lie with the prosecution. The Copyright Act is one of the most modern pieces of legislation in India. The offences under the Copyright Act are non-bailable. The Act provides for seizure not only of pirated work, but also plates and machinery used in production of counterfeit goods.

Theoretically, the jail sentences and fines provided under the TM Act, Copyright Act and IPC should have enough deterrent to check the flow of counterfeit products. However, in practice, slow prosecution and corruption makes criminal remedies a less attractive option. Often, criminal remedies are used by IP holders simply for their impact value. The fear created by a police raid on the premises of a counterfeiter coupled with the threat of arrest causes tremendous psychological discomfort.

Civil Remedies

In the last seven years, civil courts, and in particular High Courts, have come to the rescue of IP holders by granting *exparte ad-interim* relief in cases of counterfeiting. The courts have also been more liberal in granting IP holders' requests for specific directions to the local police for assistance in carrying out search and seizure at the infringer's premises.

The legislature has also taken into account the need to have quick and effective remedies to address the growing counterfeiting problem. It has introduced these changes in the new TM Act, and provided for *ex-parte* seizure orders.

IP owners have welcomed the new TM Act. The identity of the goods is now no longer necessary to invoke the statutory remedy of trademark infringement. In addition, the Act provides a wider definition of infringement. The definition covers use of a trademark as a trade name, or part of a trade name, if the party is dealing in goods or services for which the trademark is registered. This is a welcome step by the Indian legislators as there had been many cases in the past where the well-known brands were used as a trade name. Furthermore, under the TM Act, use of a registered mark in advertisements, business papers, packaging materials or labelling also constitutes trademark infringement.

Section 29 of the TM Act deals with infringement of registered trademarks. It provides that use of either an identical or similar mark for identical or similar goods constitutes infringement. It also says that the court would presume the likelihood of confusion in cases where a party uses a mark identical to a registered mark, and for identical goods and services covered by the registration. The TM Act also gives the court power to grant injunctions and award either damages or accounts for profits together with (or without) an order for delivery up of the infringing labels and/or marks for destruction in any suit related to infringement or passing off. The Act also provides that the order for injunction may include ex-parte injunction or any interlocutory order for delivery of documents or preservation of infringing goods, documents or other evidence.

The difficulties involved in working with the police have led many brand owners to prefer civil remedies. Over the years, the civil route has proved to be more cost effective and manageable and that is perhaps one of the reasons why the Business Software Alliance and Motion Pictures Association, who often rely on criminal remedies in other jurisdictions, have been using a mixture of civil and criminal remedies in India. The downside of civil action is that the concept of damages is not fully developed in India. As a result, there is no financial deterrence to counterfeiters. In cases, where a large quantity of goods are seized, there is a growing trend to engage the counterfeiter in settlement talks and to recover costs and damages as a part of a settlement.

The Customs Act, 1962

Unlike the strict Custom and Excise laws against counterfeiting that exist in many developed countries, India does not have too many provisions under the Customs Act to combat this crime.

Although, there are a handful of provisions under the Customs Act, it provides no protection against counterfeiting. The Customs authorities and the central government have the power to ban the import or export of goods under the Customs Act. The Customs authorities may also prohibit, either absolutely or subject to certain conditions, the import or export of goods to prevent deceptive practices and protect patents, trademarks and copyrights. However, until now there is no custom recordal process in India. Therefore, it is left to IP holders to keep track of shipments, develop intelligence and work with customs to seize goods.

Although the Customs authorities have the power to seize counterfeit goods, they have to make the rightful owner a party. Otherwise, the Customs authorities are obliged to release the seized goods. As a result, under the existing provisions, even if the customs authorities accept a complaint, they find it difficult to act proactively. Generally, they have to rely only on a permanent injunction from the court.

The influx of counterfeit goods from China is also becoming a problem in India. The counterfeit goods not only enter India through sea ports but also from Nepal, Bangladesh and Myanmar. India has long boundaries that it shares with its neighbouring countries and controlling the movement of persons, vehicles, and cargo across national land borders is a difficult task. Lax border control enables counterfeiters to expand their operations. A large volume of counterfeit goods from China that enter India's neighbouring countries actually end up being sold in India. India's porous borders remain a source of threat to the country's economy.

However, the government is trying to tackle counterfeiting more effectively. Reforms are on their way in line with TRIPs. A good example of initiatives by the Central Board of Excise & Customs is the co-operation and mutual administrative assistance agreement initialled in New Delhi by the head of the EU's delegation to India, Da Câmara Gomes and PRV Ramanan, a member of the Central Board of Excise Customs of India, on November 29, 2003. Formal conclusion of the agreement is due to take place in early 2004.

This agreement will simplify Customs procedures and develop trade facilitation actions in Customs matters in accordance with international standards. As a part of the agreement, mechanisms of mutual administrative assistance for exchanging information and carrying out inquiries are due to be set up. These should improve the effectiveness of the fight against fraud and counterfeiting while guaranteeing the confidentiality of information, and respecting the purpose for which the data was collected.

As in any other developing county, working with law enforcement authorities and courts is quite challenging in India. However, so long as IP holders have designed their objectives and a strategy that suits their requirements, then achieving good results is not a difficult task.

(Paul, Taj Kumar and Narula, Ranjan are IP Consultants with Rouse & Co. International.)

Prevention is Better Than Cure

India's archaic laws often make the road to justice a long and winding one, with the nation's understaffed courts groaning under the weight of thousands of undecided cases that take years to settle.

A series of measures taken by the government—including amending the IP laws to make them TRIPs compliant and the creation of special IP protection cells within the police force—has helped to address the problem. However, much remains to be done. Indian laws and regulations need to be amended and updated to cope with the new realities. But of course, prevention is always better than cure and the preventive measures outlined below can help to address the problem more effectively.

Secure your rights: Although well-known marks have statutory protection, it is always advisable to have the mark registered with the Indian Trade Marks Registry taking into account your present and future business plans.

Keep a well-informed brand protection team: The people in a company's anti-counterfeiting team should be well-equipped and well-informed. It is vital to set up reporting lines. People, whether internal or external resources, who are on the look out for counterfeits should know what to do when they find them. This will ensure speedier decision-making once counterfeit operations are found.

Invest in investigations: Reliable and timely information is key to effective enforcement. An investigating agency can play a vital role in effective enforcement by identifying production and storage sites where counterfeit material can be found and seized during a 'raid' action.

Watertight agreements: A sound agreement between the local distributors, manufacturers, joint venture partners and the IP holders minimizes the risk of counterfeiting.

Timely actions: Usually, in cases where small time manufacturers are engaged in counterfeit offences, the IP owners are reluctant to take action, assuming that their production volumes will not have any major impact on their sales. However, it is important to take early and timely steps to curtail counterfeiting at an early stage to protect the brand and to deter more small players becoming organized.

<u>Section III</u>

IPR: Global Perspectives

14

Recent International Developments in the Area of Intellectual Property Rights

Carlos M CORREA

This paper examines some of the recent international developments in the area of IPRs: the interim implementation of paragraph 6 of the Doha Declaration on the TRIPS Agreement and Public Health, copyright and the expansion of "open access" options, the negotiations on the harmonization of substantive patent law, and the protection of traditional knowledge (TK). It does not address other equally relevant issues, such as the proliferation of TRIPS-plus bilateral and regional agreements, which have been dealt with elsewhere[1], nor issues still subject to negotiation in WTO, such as geographical indications and the review of Article 27.3 (b) of the TRIPS Agreement.

I. IPRs and Public Health

The relationship between TRIPS and public health has dominated the agenda of the TRIPS Council since 2001. Patents are particularly important for the pharmaceutical industry and their interests are well represented by some

1 See, e.g., US bullying on drug patents: One year after Doha, Oxfam Briefing Paper 33, November 2002.

governments in that Council.[2] At the same time, many developing countries have realized that the broad and strong IPRs protection in that field, and the aggressive patenting and enforcement strategies of large pharmaceutical companies, generates costs that had not been duly anticipated at the time of the adoption of the Agreement.

The Doha Declaration on the TRIPS Agreement and the Public Health, adopted in November 2001, was one of the most important international developments in the area of IPRs in WTO since the adoption of the Agreement in 1994.

The Declaration has indicated that in cases of conflict between IPRs and public health, the former should not be an obstacle to the realization of the latter. In affirming that the TRIPS Agreement, "can and should be interpreted and implemented in a manner supportive of WTO Members' right to protect public health and, in particular, to promote access to medicines for all", paragraph 4 gives guidance to panels and the Appellate Body for the interpretation of the Agreement's provisions in cases involving public health issues. In doing so, Members have developed a specific rule of interpretation that gives content to the general interpretive provisions of the Vienna Convention on the Law of the Treaties on which GATT/WTO jurisprudence has been built up.

The confirmation that the TRIPS Agreement has left room for flexibility at the national level, namely with regard to the determination of the grounds for compulsory licensing and the admission of parallel imports, has important political and legal implications. It indicates that the pressures exerted by some developed countries to impede the use of available flexibilities run counter to the spirit and purpose of the TRIPS Agreement, especially in the light of the recognized "gravity of the problems"[3] faced in the area of public health by developing countries and LDCs. In legal terms, such confirmation means that panels and the Appellate Body must interpret the Agreement and the laws and regulations adopted to implement it in light of the public health needs of individual Member States. Therefore, in cases of ambiguity, or where more than one interpretation of a

---

2 As illustrated by the USA rejection to the Chair's proposed solution for the problem described in para 6 of the Doha Declaration on TRIPS and Public Health, due to US pharmaceutical industry's concerns about the scope of the mechanism to be approved under that paragraph.

3 See paragraph 1 of the Declaration.

provision is possible, panels and the Appellate Body should opt for the interpretation that is effectively "supportive of WTO Members' right to protect public health".

The Doha Declaration instructed the Council for TRIPS to address a delicate issue: how can Members lacking or with insufficient manufacturing capacities make effective use of compulsory licensing. The Declaration requested the Council for TRIPS "to find an expeditious solution to this problem and to report to the General Council before the end of 2002" (paragraph 6).

On August 30, 2003, an agreement was reached at the Council for TRIPS[4] for the implementation of its paragraph 6. This "solution" is based on a compromise developed by the Chair of the Council and on a "Statement by the Chair" requested by the USA as a condition to accept the compromise. The Decision takes the form of an *interim* waiver, which allows countries producing patented products under compulsory licenses to export the products to eligible importing countries, provided that a compulsory license has also been granted in the importing country and that various other conditions are met. The waiver would last until the TRIPS Agreement is amended.

The conditions established in both the text of the Decision and the Statement for allowing exports of patented medicines, are hardly compatible with the idea of an "expeditious" solution (see Box 1).

Box 1: Conditions for the Operation of the "Solution" Under Paragraph 6

In order to get the supply of drugs under this mechanism the following steps must be followed[5]:

(1) unless the prior request of a voluntary license does not apply, an entity in the importing country must seek a voluntary license from the patent owner;

(2) failing this, an application for a compulsory license must be submitted and the license be obtained in the importing country;

(3) the importing country must assess its generic industry's capacity to produce the medicine locally;

Contd...

[4] See IP/C/W/405.

[5] See e.g., Brook K. Baker, "Vows of Poverty, Shrunken Markets, Burdensome Manufacturing and Other Nonsense at the WTO", Health GAP, Sept. 27, 2003.

Contd...

(4) if capacity is insufficient, it must notify the WTO of its decision to use the paragraph 6 "solution";

(5) the interested importing country or party must identify a potential exporter;

(6) that exporter must in turn, seek a voluntary license on commercially reasonable terms for a commercially reasonable period of time;

(7) if the voluntary license were refused, the potential exporter must seek a compulsory license (to be granted on a single-supply basis) from its own government;

(8) if a license is granted, the exporter will have to develop the chemistry and formulate the drug (when produced by the licensee for the first time), and to investigate products' shape, coloring, labeling and packaging of the patent-holder's product in the importing country in order to differentiate the product for export;

(9) the exporter will also need to seek product registration and prove it's bio-equivalence base and bioavailability, when required by national law[6];

(10) if in the importing country exclusivity (as promoted by the USA and EU) is granted with regard to data submitted for the registration of a medicine, the supplier will have to obtain authorization by the possessor of those data to use them, or to develop its own studies about toxicity and efficacy, unless the use of such data is included in the compulsory license;

(11) before shipment begins, the licensee shall post on a website information about the quantities being supplied and the distinguishing features of the product;

(12) the exporting Member must notify the Council for TRIPS of the grant of the license, including the conditions attached to it.

The process described in Box 1 must be fulfilled over and over since only the amount necessary to meet the needs of one particular eligible importing Member may be manufactured under the licence, and the entirety of this production shall be exported to the Member that has notified its needs to the Council for TRIPS.

In addition to all these steps, and as a pre-condition for the operation of the system, eligible countries may have to amend their national patent laws to allow the granting of licenses for export, or for import. The waiver of the obligations under Article 31(f) only means that a *WTO Member* will not complain against another Member using the system, but it does not prevent a *private party* from

6 If in the importing country exclusivity (as promoted by the USA and EU) is granted with regard to data submitted for the registration of a medicine, the supplier will have to obtain authorization by the possessor of those data to use them, or to develop its own clinical studies.

blocking the exportation or importation of drugs, if the national laws do not specifically permit such exports or imports under compulsory licenses.

Though the intent of the majority of the WTO Members in drafting the Decision was to facilitate the export of affordable drugs produced under compulsory license, the Chair's Statement added further constraints to the already cumbersome Decision. The Statement indicates that the special conditions (as set out in paragraph 2(b)(ii) of the Decision) apply not only to formulated pharmaceuticals but also to active ingredients produced and supplied under the system and to finished products produced using such active ingredients. The Statement also adds (though there is no evidence to support this statement), that it "is the understanding of Members that in general, special packaging and/or special colouring or shaping should not have a significant impact on the price of pharmaceuticals. In addition, the Statement introduces a monitoring system clearly aimed at facilitating challenges to another Member's use of the system, including monitoring how the Member in question has established that it has insufficient or no manufacturing capacities in the pharmaceutical sector.

The Statement also indicates that Members recognize that the system "should be used in good faith to protect public health and, without prejudice to paragraph 6 of the Decision, not be an instrument to pursue industrial or commercial policy objectives". This ignores that the only sustainable way of providing a credible alternative to the supply by patent owners is the creation of incentives for other commercial companies to supply the required drugs and, ultimately, the development of a viable domestic industry.

As discussed elsewhere,[7] in order to be effective, a solution to the problem described in paragraph 6 should be economically viable, and not only diplomatically acceptable. This agreement fails to provide an effective means of increasing competition and lowering drug prices. The adopted "solution" is so cumbersome for potential suppliers that they will be hardly encouraged to use the Decision, "because it is so designed that no generic manufacturer would be able or willing to comply with its provisions".[8] Such a complex and burdensome

---

7 See e.g., Carlos Correa, "Implications of the Doha declaration on the trips agreement and public health", World Health Organization, Geneva (2002) at 33; Commission on Intellectual Property Rights, Integrating Intellectual Property Rights and Development Policy London, 2002 (available at *www.iprcommission.org*).

8 Comments by D G Shah, Indian Pharmaceutical Alliance (mail of August 26, 2003, on file with the author).

system does not create a serious risk to the patent owners' position; hence, they will have little or no incentive to lower their prices or to negotiate voluntary licenses.

In sum, the adopted "solution" is largely symbolic in view of the multiple conditions required for its application. It is unlikely to lead to any significant increase in the supply of medicines, particularly for the poor. In any case, developing countries now face two important tasks in relation to the adopted Decision:

1. Developing an interpretation of the Decision and Statement that clarify both the constraints and the flexibilities for the application of this "solution". Many ambiguities in the text, as well as the legal status of the "Statement" need to be clarified.
2. Elaborating and proposing a *permanent* solution to the problem affecting countries with limited or without manufacturing capacities in this field, in order to reach an amendment of the TRIPS Agreement, as necessary. Such an amendment may be based on a fresh conceptual start, including a possible clarification to Article 30 of the Agreement. It should aim at a simple and effective solution both in legal and economic terms.

Finally, it should be noted that *paragraph 6 only describes one of the problems* arising in the context of the TRIPS Agreement with regard to public health. The IPRs protection of pharmaceutical will continue to pose significant challenges to public health policies in developing countries, even if the agreed "solution" were proven to be viable and effective. The agreement on paragraph 6 does not mean an end to the controversies around IPRs and public health. They are likely to continue, especially as developed countries seek TRIPS-plus protection *via* interpretation[9] or the negotiation of bilateral and regional agreements,[10] and as patents on marginal or trivial developments (sometimes called "ever-greening" patents) are granted and used to block or delay generic competition.[11]

9 The USTR, for instance, interprets that Article 39.3 of the Agreement requires the granting of an exclusive period of protection for data submitted for the marketing approval of pharmaceuticals and agrochemicals.

10 See e.g., the recent US-Chile and US-Singapore bilateral agreements.

11 See e.g., Carlos Correa (2001), Trends in Drug Patenting. Case Studies, Corregidor, Buenos Aires.

II. Developments in Patent Law

Important developments (albeit with unpredictable outcomes) are taken place in the area of patent law. In September 2001, the WIPO Assemblies approved an initiative by the Director-General aimed at simplifying the acquisition of patent rights globally and at the further harmonization of patent law. The 'WIPO Patent Agenda' includes three components ultimately oriented to develop a framework for a "global patent":

(a) efforts to promote the ratification of the Patent Law Treaty (PLT), which harmonized procedures for patent applications;

(b) the reform of the Patent Cooperation Treaty (PCT); and

(c) negotiations on a Substantive Patent Law Treaty (SPLT).

The Patent Agenda is supposed to address the failure of the system to adequately respond to the international nature of business activities, the high costs of obtaining patents, the workload crisis in patent offices and time consuming procedures.[12]

While the reform of the PCT is intended to reduce patent offices' overload, it would also blur the separation between Chapter I (international search) and Chapter II (international assessment of patentability) and extend the period for initiating the national phase of patent applications.

The SPLT, if adopted, may have far reaching consequences for developing countries, as it may dramatically limit the space available for designing patent policies at the national level. The TRIPS Agreement left great flexibility with regard to the crucial issues of what is patentable and how the requirements for patentability are defined and applied. This flexibility would disappear or be substantially eroded if the harmonization exercise is successful.

The TRIPS Agreement, in effect, only indicates what the requirements of patentability are (novelty, inventive step or non-obviousness, and industrial applicability or usefulness),[13] but it neither defines such concepts nor what an

---

12 See Memorandum of the Director General, Agenda for Development of the International Patent System, August 2001, WIPO A/36/14, Geneva, para. 17–28.

13 See Article 27.1 of TRIPS.

"invention" is. TRIPS, moreover, does not contain rules on the modalities and interpretation of patent claims, which are essential to establish the scope of protection.

Discussions on the SPLT include, *inter alia*, key issues such as whether an invention should show a "technical character" in order to be patentable.[14] The United States seeks to internationalize its legislative model, which does not require such a character and thereby allows the patenting of computer programs, business methods[15] and research tools.[16] Proposals have also been made to establish a harmonized standard of inventive activity based on the *general* knowledge of a person skilled in the art (as obtained, for instance from handbooks)[17], and for the adoption of a "doctrine of equivalents" in a form that significantly limits the scope for inventing around a patented invention.

Progress towards the possible harmonization of the patent law may be blocked by differences between USA and EU on issues such as the grace period and the technical effect of patents. If these differences were overcome, however, developing countries would face the risk of being under pressure to adopt harmonized rules that would limit the possibility of defining what an invention is, applying strict standards of patentability and designing, according to their interests and levels of development, other aspects of substantive patent law.

III. Copyright and the Challenge of Open Access

The TRIPS Agreement reinforced the protection of copyright, especially for computer programs and data bases. It also strengthened the protection of neighboring rights, particularly in relation to phonograms. However, the copyright section of the Agreement did not go as far as other sections (like the section on patents) in terms of developing new international standards of protection. Shortly after the adoption of the Agreement, two international

---

[14] See SCP/6/9, para. 184.

[15] "Business Methods" include methods applied to business activities such as buying and selling, marketing techniques, financial schemes and strategies, generally supported on computer software and networks.

[16] "Research Tools" are methods or substances (such as Expressed Sequence Tags – ESTs) used to undertake research, notably in the biological field.

[17] This means that specialized journals should not necessarily be taken into account to assess inventiveness.

conventions on copyright-related issues were successfully negotiated under the auspices of WIPO.[18]

While these conventions were designed to expand and strengthen copyright protection, several initiatives have been launched since the 1990's on the basis of the concept of "open access". They include, for instance,[19] the initiative for a freely accessible software under a legal mechanism called "copyleft". This mechanism aims at protecting free available software from being modified and then protected by a third party under IPRs.

Open access initiatives may be particularly appropriate in fields where decentralized creation is efficient, like in academic research and software development. It may also be applied in agriculture, where the improvement of seeds may be leveraged by access to a wide pool of materials. Farmers have, in fact, traditionally improved seeds and shared them with other farmers for cultivation, multiplication and further improvement.

Open access offers an alternative to the restricted access model based on the exercise of IPRs. It is gaining a growing number of adepts in the software area. In the United States, the European Union and many developing countries, governments are considering measures to encourage the public procurement of open-source software, such as the Linux operating system, already adopted by major hardware producers.

Creators or innovators under an open access model have no expectation of direct monetary gain. Access is easy and the dissemination of information/products is faster and more cost-effective than under IPRs. Open access, however, operates within the current legal framework of copyright law. It deals with information susceptible of appropriation under IPRs, that is made openly and freely available by the right holder who retains some or all of the exclusive property rights that

---

18 WIPO Copyright Treaty and WIPO Treaty on Performances and Phonograms (1996). WIPO also convened a Diplomatic Conference to develop a treaty on databases in December 1996. One of the basic proposals considered by the Conference was the protection of non-original databases the production of which entailed a "substantial investment" (see document WIPO CRNR/DC/6, 30.8.96). This initiative, however, has found considerable resistance (including from the scientific and librarian communities in the USA) and no further negotiations have taken place so far.

19 The "Budapest Open Access Initiative", the "Scholarly Publishing and Academic Resources Coalition" (SPARC) and, most notably, the Human Genome Project, are also examples of free access schemes.

are granted under statutory IP laws.[20] Despite the fact that open access is based on a restricted use of IPRs, WIPO has refused to deal with this kind of initiatives.[21]

IV. Traditional Knowledge

WIPO's General Assembly established in 2000, an Intergovernmental Committee on Intellectual Property and Genetic Resources, Traditional Knowledge and Folklore (ICGRTKF), with the mandate of discussing (a) access to genetic resources and benefit sharing, (b) protection of TK and (c) protection of expressions of folklore. The IGCGRTKF held five sessions that provided an opportunity for discussion of legal, policy, economic and scientific issues relating to TK protection, including the analysis of *sui generis* forms for TK protection.[22]

While informative and technically solid, the analysis undertaken by the WIPO Secretariat for the IGCGRTKF has attempted to explain traditional and indigenous practices of conservation and transmission of knowledge under established IP concepts,[23] thereby ignoring the traditional and indigenous communities' views on the creation, use and sharing of knowledge.

WIPO has addressed the possible development of a *sui generis* regime for TK. The recognition and enforcement of customary law as a form of protection that respects cultural diversity, has been largely overlooked. For instance, a draft legislation prepared by the WIPO Secretariat for Venezuela proposes the granting of a set of exclusive rights essentially similar to those required under article 28 for patents, and makes protection of TK dependent on a disclosure requirement and the registration of knowledge.[24] A similar approach inspired the law for the

20 See e.g., Paul Uhlir (The National Academies), summary report of the Meeting on Copyright, Science, and the Public Interest, Science and Intellectual Property in the Public Interest (SIPPI), Directorate for Science and Policy Programs, American Association for the Advancement of Science (AAAS), (Washington DC, 20 June 2003).

21 WIPO Secretariat accepted last July a suggestion from a group of lawyers and economists to convene an international meeting on the subject in 2004. The US Patent and Trademark Office objected the decision (thereby echoing the opposition of some US software companies and the Business Software Alliance). It argued that open-source software was contrary to WIPO's mission to promote intellectual property rights, and that to hold a meeting to disclaim or waive such rights would be "contrary to the goals of WIPO". WIPO Secretariat subsequently announced that the meeting will not be convened. See Declan Butler NATURE|VOL 424|28AUGUST 2003 *www.nature.com*.

22 For a summary of the IGC's discussions, see WIPO, Overview of Activities and Outcomes on the Intergovernmental Committee (WIPO/GRTKF/IC/5/12).

23 See, e.g., WIPO, Intellectual property needs and expectations of traditional knowledge holders, Geneva, 2001.

24 See Secretaría de la OMPI, "Proyecto de ley sobre la protección de los conocimientos tradicionales de los pueblos indígenas de la República Bolivariana de Venezuelay comentarios de las principales disposiciones".

protection of TK adopted by Panama (Law No. 20, June 26, 2000 and Executive Decree No.12, March 20, 2001).

In order to be protectable, TK[25] must be capable of commercial use (Law, Article 1) and based upon tradition, although it need not be 'old' (Law, Article 15). The knowledge must be registered and published, and protection is granted upon examination. Collective rights under the Panama's law are exclusive. They allow titleholders to authorize or prevent use and commercialization (Article 15) and industrial reproduction (Law, Article 20), for an indefinite time.

The extent to which WIPO Secretariat approach to the protection of TK would serve the interests of its intended beneficiaries is doubtful. Little consideration seems to have been given, in addition, to the *costs* that such a system would create, if operative. For instance, the granting of exclusive rights on products used in traditional medicine (TRM) systems may have high social costs *via* a reduction of access to medicines and treatment.

There are also other limitations and gaps in WIPO's work on the matter. For instance, no serious analysis has been made of the standards for patentability applied by WIPO members (such as the differential novelty standard applied in the USA with regard to inventions disclosed in non-written form outside the country) which allow the patenting of genetic resources and TK. Work done has also overlooked the role of customary law as a basis for TK protection.

During the fifth (and last) session of the IGCGRTKF (July 7-15. 2003), a very clear split between developed and developing countries emerged about the possible renewal of the Committee's mandate. Developed countries aimed at prolonging the current mandate, limited to technical analysis, for another two-years period or more. The USA, in particular, proposed to prolong the current mandate unchanged for another 4 years. The African Group, in contrast, demanded an immediate start of negotiations on "a legally binding international instrument on genetic resources, traditional knowledge and folklore". Developing

25 The law protects customs, traditions, beliefs, spirituality, cosmovision, folkloric expressions, artistic manifestations, traditional knowledge and any other type of traditional expressions of indigenous communities, which are part of their cultural assets (cultural heritage) (Law, Article 2). It also covers TK embodied in creations such as inventions, models, designs and drawings, innovations contained in images, figures, graphic symbols, petroglyphs and other material, cultural elements of history, music, arts and traditional artistic expressions (Decree, Article 1).

countries form Asia and Latin America did not go so far, and suggested an action-oriented agenda, not limited to further studies, aiming at "norm-setting" of some kind, in particular to develop rules about bio-piracy and misappropriation of TK. The final decision is to be taken late this year by WIPO's General Assembly. A likely outcome is that it will simply prolong the mandate for another two years without major change.[26]

The indigenous organisations that intervened at the last Committee meeting presented a coherent message. They supported the developing countries' request to pass from analysis to action, but "strongly emphasised the limited relevance of IPRs to the protection of TK, and consequently that any future work must 1) involve other intergovernmental organisations with more relevant mandates, and 2) take customary law rather than intellectual property law as a starting point".[27]

Depending, in totality, on the decision to be taken later this year about the future of the IGCGRTKF, it may continue as a forum of discussion and study, as it was so far, or evolved into a negotiating or standard setting forum, as requested by some developing countries. Both options present some advantages and disadvantages. On the one hand, the extension of the mandate of the Committee as a discussion and study forum, may neutralize developments in other organizations, as some developed countries argue that work on TK should wait for the outcomes of the IGCGRTKF.[28] These outcomes may not be expected soon, given the complexity of the issues under consideration and the broad mandate of the Committee.

On the other, the negotiating or standard-setting option may allow the development of international rules on the matter. It is unclear, however, whether developing countries have a clear strategy and an articulated position to initiate negotiations. A logical approach would be, as suggested by some countries during the Committee's meeting, to concentrate as a first step on the development of

26 See Peter Einarsson (2003), Report WIPO GRTKF5 (mimeo).

27 Ibid.

28 For instance, the EC and its Member States have stated that they "support the development of an international model for the legal protection of traditional knowledge" and expressed their hope that the issue be taken by the WIPO Intergovernmental Committee referred above in cooperation with the CBD, and that "once a model is in place, attention can then be focused on how and to what extent the protection of traditional knowledge can be included in the TRIPS Agreement". See IP/C/W/254, 3.4.01.

misappropriation rules. While developing countries' governments have actively proposed the protection of TK, it is unclear to what extent there has been sufficient dialogue between governments and traditional/indigenous communities so as to ensure that their vision and customary law approaches are duly taken into account.

There is also a risk that the general philosophy of WIPO and its narrow mandate to promote intellectual property, influence such development in a way that ignores the multiple facets and implications of intellectual property protection, such as the restrictions on access to TRM and derived products, and the ensuing consequences for equity and human development. WIPO has been strongly led by a legalistic approach, without adequately consider other equivalent economic and social dimensions.

(Professor Carlos Correa is the Director of the University of Buenos Aires' Masters Programme on Science and Technology Policy and Management. Trained as both a lawyer and an economist, he has acted as a consultant to numerous international agencies.)

[The publication has been produced under the ICTSD Programme on IPRs and Sustainable Development. Readers are encouraged to quote and reproduce this material for education, non-profit purposes, provided the source is acknowledged. http://www.iprsonline.org]

15

New Conciliation and Arbitration Initiative for IP Disputes

Woranuch Periera and Edward J Kelly

In Thailand, a large volume of cases relating to Dispute on Intellectual Property is submitted every year to the Intellectual Property (IP) and Information Technology (IT) court. This has evoked a formidable concern in Thailand's administration and has thrown a challenge to the IP regime. The Department of Intellectual Property (DIP) under the Ministry of Commerce in Thailand has risen to the occasion and issued measures to put an end to the disputes involving intellectual property by means of Arbitration, including Arbitration and Conciliation of IP-related disputes. The authors in this article have highlighted the rules and procedures of the two categories of the alternate dispute resolution system relating to the intellectual property disputes. The method of dispute resolution by way of Arbitration is conducted in accordance with the 'Rule of Arbitration' as stipulated by the Department of Intellectual Property.

Source: ICFAI Journal of International Business Law, October 2003.

Introduction

Disputes regarding intellectual property have been significantly increasing in Thailand. This has had a critical impact on Thailand's administration and the development of an effective intellectual property regime and has also acted as a drag on the overall economic development of the country.

For the aforementioned reasons, the Department of Intellectual Property (DIP) under the Ministry of Commerce of Thailand, the organization charged with the administration and protection of intellectual property, has issued measures to help prevent and end disputes involving intellectual property arbitration, including arbitration and mediation of IP-related disputes. These measures will be useful to all parties in disputes and will help to make the settlement process of such disputes more effective, prompt, economic, and fair.

The above-mentioned measures, which were designed to deal with intellectual property disputes that can be settled out of court, will reduce the backlog on the docket of the Intellectual Property and International Trade Court (IP&IT Court) by screening and preventing certain intellectual property disputes from reaching the IP&IT Court.

The Ministry of Commerce has classified these measures into two categories, namely, conciliation and arbitration, and has established two sets of rules accordingly:

- Rules on the Conciliation Intellectual Property Disputes.
- Rules on the Arbitration of Intellectual Property Disputes.

Rules on the Conciliation of Intellectual Property Disputes ("Conciliation Rules")

These rules will be applied to the conciliation of disputes arising out of a contract or related to a contract or other formal legal relationship where the intention has been expressed that the concerned parties desire to settle out of court under the supervision of the DIP.

Before submitting the dispute for conciliation, the concerned parties shall have a meeting for possible negotiation and settlement of the dispute. In the event that the Director General of the DIP thinks it is necessary and the concerned parties so agree; one or more persons will be appointed to handle the conciliation procedure. At any time, the concerned parties may agree to exempt or change any conciliation rules by written agreement, but such exemption or change will not affect the validity of the results of the conciliation. However, if there is any difference between the amended conciliation rules and the laws governing public order and good morals, the laws shall apply.

The conciliation of a dispute will start when a concerned party sends a written notice to another party offering to settle the disputes by conciliation procedures in accordance with the Conciliation Rules. If the other party accepts such an offer, he must send notice of acceptance in writing within 30 days after receiving the offering notice; otherwise, the offering party may treat the lack of response as a rejection of the offer.

Normally, one conciliator is appointed to conciliate the dispute, unless the concerned parties agree to appoint more than one conciliator. The parties concerned may appoint the conciliator themselves or request the Director General of the DIP to recommend or appoint the conciliator. After a conciliator is appointed, each party shall submit his dispute in writing to the conciliator describing the nature and issues of the dispute, with copy of such written sub-mission to the other party. During the conciliation procedure, the conciliator may ask the concerned parties to provide additional facts for consideration.

In the conciliation procedure, the conciliator shall proceed as follows:

1. The conciliator will assist the concerned parties in reaching a compromise agreement fairly and without bias.
2. The conciliator shall apply the principle of justice by considering the rights and obligations of the parties in dispute, the customs of trade, and other circumstances, including the past practices of the parties concerned.
3. In the event that either party thinks it necessary, the conciliator, upon request, may allow such party to produce a witness for hearing, but the principle of prompt conciliation must be taken into account.

4. At any stage of the conciliation procedure, the conciliator may prepare an offer for conciliation of the dispute to the concerned parties. Such an offer may be made verbally without giving any reasons for such offer.

In the event that the concerned parties can agree and settle the dispute, the conciliator shall prepare a draft settlement agreement for the parties to sign. In such a settlement agreement, if the parties desire, a contractual term may be inserted providing for arbitration procedure to settle the disputes arising out of such agreement.

The conciliation procedure will end when:

1. The concerned parties sign the settlement agreement.
2. The conciliator makes a written declaration that the conciliation procedure has ended because the conciliation process has reached an impasse.
3. The concerned parties agree to end the conciliation procedure by written agreement.
4. Either party sends written notice to the other party and the conciliator expressing a wish to end the conciliation procedure.

Rules on Arbitration for Intellectual Property Disputes ("Arbitration Rules")

An Arbitration Committee will be composed of the Director General of the DIP as chairman and other members appointed by the Minister who are qualified in IP matters. The number of members shall not exceed six persons.

A panel of eligible hearing officers or "conciliators and arbitrators", will be established as recommended and approved by the Committee and registered by the DIP. Other conciliators and arbitrators are not named as part of the official panel may nevertheless be appointed by agreement of the parties in dispute. Any person who is appointed to act as a "conciliator" for any dispute may not also be appointed as an "arbitrator" in the same dispute.

Prior to proposing disputes for arbitration, the parties shall first meet for negotiation and an attempt at amicable settlement. If necessary, the Director General of the DIP may appoint one conciliator or more as deemed appropriate by the parties. The Rules of Conciliation shall be applied for the conciliation in this step.

Application of Rule of Arbitration

The Rule of Arbitration ("the Rule") shall be applied to an arbitration arranged by the DIP. The parties may agree otherwise in writing so long as the Director General approves.

In the event where an unforeseen situation arises that has not been provided for in the Rule, action must proceed in accordance with the parties' agreement, or the arbitrator's consideration as deemed appropriate, or the Arbitration Act B.E. 2545 (A.D. 2002) on a case-by-case basis.

Procedures for Dispute Settlement

1. A proposal for dispute settlement must be made in writing and submitted to the Director General of the DIP in the official form, comprising the following details:
   - Application for dispute settlement by arbitration.
   - Name and address of disputing parties.
   - Rule of arbitration or agreement for dispute settlement by arbitration that will be applied to the parties.
   - Agreement or other legal relationship or other basis for the IP dispute.
   - Factual information that is the basis for claim and amount of claim.
   - Claim and application for arbitration award.
   - Number of arbitrators, one or three, if the disputing parties have not agreed.
2. If the written proposal for arbitration meets with the official's approval, the official will, without delay, send a copy to the other party in the dispute by registered mail or other means as deemed appropriate.
3. A deposit for costs and expenses may be required if deemed appropriate.
4. Upon receipt of the copy of the proposal, the other party is entitled to file a written opposition and countered claim with the official within 15 days

from the date of receipt of the copy of proposal for arbitration. The aforesaid procedure also applies to any reply to the counterclaim.

5. The parties may appoint legal representatives or any other person to assist them in the arbitration proceeding. The parties shall notify the Director General in writing of the name and address of such representative or person.

Appointment of Arbitrator

Unless the parties agree otherwise, the number of arbitrators can either be one or three.

Arbitration Procedures

Unless otherwise provided by the parties' agreement, the arbitrator shall be empowered to conduct any such proceedings as deemed appropriate in accordance with the principles of justice and in order to give sufficient opportunity to the parties to present evidence supporting their claims.

Unless otherwise agreed upon by the parties, the taking of evidence proceeds as follows:

1. Both parties have to submit documentary evidence in support of their claims to the arbitrator on the date of the first hearing.
2. Hearing of witnesses shall be conducted by the arbitrator. The arbitrator shall briefly record the testimony of such witnesses along with the witnesses' signatures, as evidence, and keep this in the arbitrator's case file.
3. The arbitrator may request that the official assist in recording the witness hearing.
4. Taking of evidence shall be in camera.

The arbitrator may request any expert to provide a report pertaining to the dispute. In this case, the parties shall provide the relevant facts as required by such an expert.

Upon receipt of the expert's report, the official will notify the parties of the details of the report. A copy of the report will be available to the parties upon request.

The parties may file an application for interrogatories from the expert. If approved by the arbitrator, the taking of evidence as above mentioned shall apply *mutatis mutandis.*

Award

The award shall be made within 90 days from the date of appointment of the last arbitrator. If necessary, this deadline may be extended for a reasonable period of time, but not exceeding an additional 90 days.

The decision, order, and award in a dispute shall be determined by the majority of the arbitrators. It cannot exceed the scope of the arbitration agreement or the parties' applications, except in the fixation of expenses in the arbitration stage or remuneration for the arbitrator or for the award in accordance with the agreement or amicable settlement between the parties.

The arbitrator shall decide the dispute in accordance with the principles of law and justice. In interpreting any agreement, the arbitrator may also take into account market conditions, commercial realities, and trade practices.

Conclusion

At present, a large volume of cases is submitted annually to the IP&IT Court. More than four thousand cases were filed in the year 2002 alone. The advantages of proceeding to arbitration consist essentially of saving of time and expense, and also the availability of hearing officers with practical experience in the subject matters of the dispute. Moreover, as the hearings are in camera, the reputation of a company, its policies, and trade secrets or confidential information may be maintained and kept confidential.

(Woranuch Periera is an Attorney, Copyright and IP Licensing Specialist, Intellectual Property Department. Edward J Kelly is a Partner, Intellectual Property Department, Enforcement, Licensing & Transactions).

Arbitrating Intellectual Property Licensing Disputes

The number of patents being licensed has been increasing and along with it the disputes too. Litigations concerning disputes on the terms and norms of the agreement of the patenting licenses between the two parties have increased manifold over the last few years. Consequently, the parties to the agreement have now found an easier way to resolve the disputes rather than knocking the doors of the judiciary which is time consuming. The easier and quicker method is arbitration. It is considered to be the most advantageous way for the resolution of an intellectual property dispute. An arbitration clause is entered in the license agreement itself. Arbitration clause creates a forum for resolving disputes privately instead of going to the courts. This forum is generally in an arbitration hearing room in the lawyer's office or at a place offered by an Alternative Dispute Resolution provider. This helps the parties to the dispute to maintain privacy and decorum. The parties also have the freedom to restrict the disclosure of information during arbitration. It is also a cheaper and faster means of resolving the dispute as compared to the litigation process. The parties also have the right to select a person who has specialized expertise in the specific fields as an arbitrator.

American Arbitration Association (AAA) has also formulated a set of rules which apply unless otherwise provided by the parties. These help to select the rules and also provide specific clauses wherever needed. The critical issue in the whole process is the selection of right arbitrators; since the responsibility of the outcome of the dispute rests on their shoulders.

16

Music Piracy and iTunes

Hansa Iyengar

Since the late 1990s, the global music industry had been plagued by rampant piracy. By 2001, with 40% of all music sold being pirated, piracy was rapidly turning into a major threat to the industry's survival. The industry fought back with a slew of lawsuits and co-ordinated raids to close down several websites providing free downloads along with scores of illegal CD manufacturing units across the world. Still piracy continued unabated. During these tumultuous times, Apple Computers came up with its iTunes Music Store, which promised to change the fortunes of the beleaguered industry. But, iTunes also had its limitations and was up against serious competition.

The global music industry had been facing a serious onslaught of piracy that threatened its very existence since the late 1990s. Pirated Compact Discs (CDs), mass manufactured across the world, were being marketed at lower prices than the originals. Rewritable CDs or CD-Rs were also getting manufactured with the help of music downloaded from the Internet. Further, the Internet allowed sharing of unauthorised music files between the users of services like 'Napster'. According to the 'International Federation of Phonographic Industries' (IFPI),

40% of CDs and cassettes sold in 2001 were pirated versions.[1] Organised criminal gangs had also entered the CD pirating business.

The industry bodies like the IFPI and 'Recording Industries Association of America' (RIAA) retaliated by suing the online services that provided free downloads. They set up an online anti-piracy software called 'Songbird' that allowed them to monitor the transfer of unauthorised music files across services like Napster. They also collaborated with the law enforcement authorities of various countries and shut down many illegal CD manufacturing units across the world. Major music companies started their own online subscription service that allowed users to purchase songs online for a small fee.

Despite these measures, piracy continued, with sites like 'KaZaA' and 'Grokster' replacing Napster. In 2002, the number of music files available for free downloads soared from 500 million to 900 million.[2] The first half of 2003 saw the pre-recorded market fall by 10.9%[3] as compared to the same period of the previous year.

Under such formidable circumstances, Apple launched its online music store, 'iTunes' in early 2003. It was launched especially for Mac users and it sold songs online for 99 cents per song. With two million songs[4] sold during the first two weeks, iTunes was an instant hit. The iTunes version for 'Windows' PCs was launched in late 2003. It was followed by a slew of promotional campaigns that endorsed iTune, which was hailed as the turning point for the music industry.

Despite its huge popularity, iTunes had a few inherent flaws. Besides, with the entry of services like 'Rhapsody' and 'BuyMusic' offering downloads at lower rates as compared to iTunes, the threat of existing sites like KaZaA offering free downloads and the intention of online retailers like 'Amazon' and 'eBay' to sell music online, the future for iTunes was paved with challenges.

The Piracy Menace...

The emergence of new technologies in recording and shaping the music that reached the listeners, influenced the development of the music industry. The compactness of the cassette player (tape recorder) as compared to the Gramophone and the affordability of cassettes coupled with a steady growth in the various genres of music, led to the development of a global market for pre-recorded music during the 1960s and 1970s. Between 1989 and 1998, CD became the most preferred form of music record due to its compactness, ability to store a larger number of songs and better sound quality when compared to the cassette. In 1998, CD sales crossed the 800 million-unit mark [Exhibit 1]. The late 1990s saw the emergence of the Internet as a popular medium of communication. New software was developed which could convert music into digital form using MP3 technology. The same period also saw the rise of web services that enabled free downloading and sharing of music on the Internet using file-sharing technologies.

Exhibit 1: Sales of LP Records, Cassettes and CDs (in million units) for the Period between 1989-1998

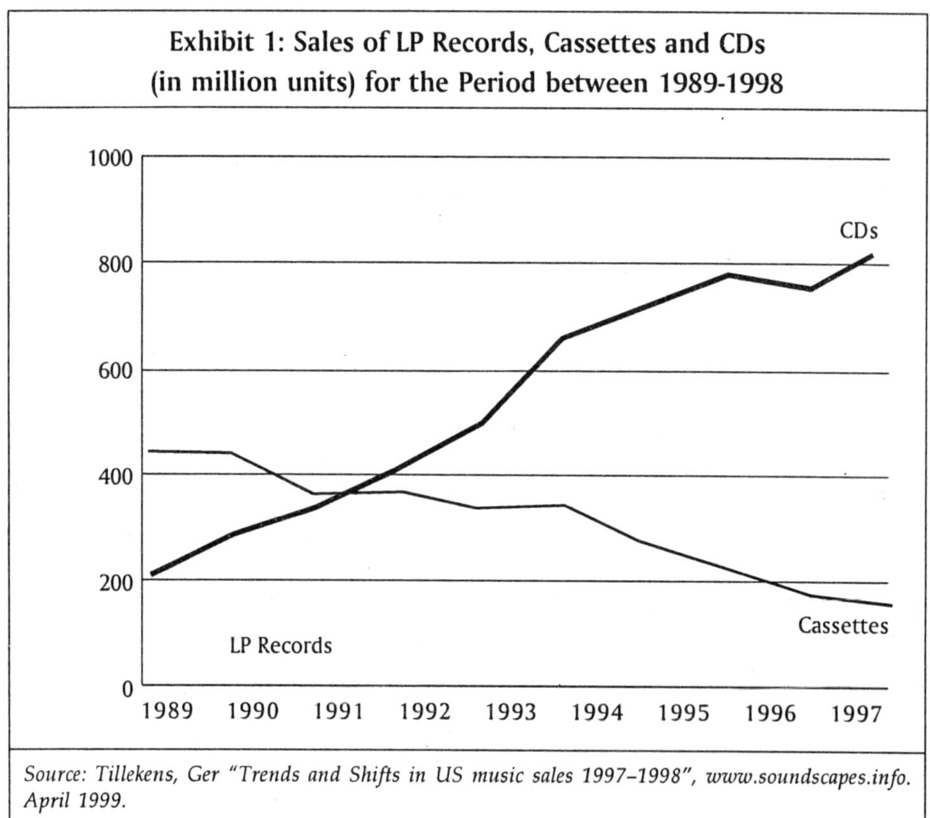

Source: Tillekens, Ger "Trends and Shifts in US music sales 1997–1998", www.soundscapes.info. April 1999.

This file sharing technology, popularly known as Peer-2-Peer (P2P), became very popular among the Internet users and millions of tunes were downloaded and exchanged. Ingenuous music pirates then copied these songs onto CDs and the pirated CD-Rs were sold at very cheap rates. A report by IFPI estimated that out of 510 million pirated discs sold in 1999, 60 million[5] were CD-Rs copied from MP3 downloads. In 2000, the global pirated music market reached 1.8 billion units totalling $4.2 billion in value[6] with CDs and CD-Rs constituting 35% of all pirated music sales [Exhibit 2]. The Napster service, a website dedicated to providing free music downloads, took the industry by storm in 2000 and in February 2001, 2.8 billion songs[7] were exchanged between the users. Global music sales fell to $33.7 billion[8] in the first half of 2001, a decline of 5% as compared to the same period the previous year (2000).

Exhibit 2: Composition of Pirate Market – 2000 & 2001

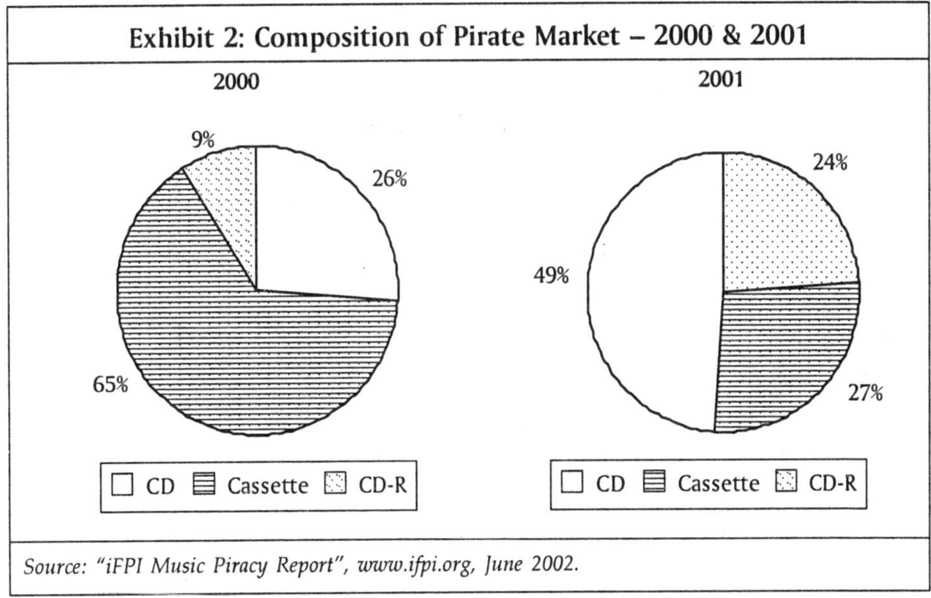

Source: "iFPI Music Piracy Report", www.ifpi.org, June 2002.

The global pirated CD market reached sales of 950 million units in 2001, with CD-Rs constituting 450 million.[9] The value of the pirated market rose marginally to $4.3 billion.[10] Domestic piracy levels around the world increased to unprecedented levels in 2001 [Annexure 1] and 2002 [Annexure 2] with millions of locally manufactured CDs flooding the market. In 2002, disc piracy (CDs and CD-Rs) rose to an all time high of 1.1 billion units and $4.6 billion.[11] At any given time in May 2002, there were 500 million unauthorised files and three million users of P2P services worldwide.[12]

By late 1990s, organised criminal gangs entered the pirated CD business to utilise the profits generated from this business to fund more serious crimes. While in Russia, CD counterfeiters were involved in credit card fraud, in Ireland, CD piracy was found to have links with terrorist factions like the "Real IRA". In Greece, authorities arrested members of a crime racket, which financed production of explosives with profits from the CD piracy trade. An illegal firearms factory was discovered alongside a hi-tech CD-R facility in Taiwan. Latin American pirates used the profits from CD piracy to fund the narcotics and prostitution rackets.

The Industry Strikes Back...

Recording industry associations, RIAA and IFPI collaborated several national governments to bring the rampant piracy under control. In 1999, authorities raided seven illegal CD manufacturing plants in different parts of the world that had a potential to manufacture 25 million CDs. In 2000, 20 plants with a capacity to churn out 70 million CDs were closed.[13]

The RIAA and the IFPI filed lawsuits in 2000 against MP3.com and Napster, two of the major websites offering free downloads. MP3.com was asked to pay $170 million[14] as damages for infringement of copyright. Napster was also found guilty of knowingly infringing copyright material and was ordered to block such material and monitor its online service for illegal downloads. Industry bodies also collaborated with local authorities of various countries and were successful in closing 15,000 sites and 300,000 illegal music files available on the Internet in 2000.[15] The 'World Intellectual Property Organisation' (WIPO) brought in treaties for protecting the rights of intellectual properties on the Internet, which were endorsed by many countries and came into effect in 2001.

The music industry started realising that digital technology was the major cause of the ever-increasing piracy problem. In May 2001, the industry organisations launched an anti-piracy software on the Internet called 'Songbird', which could identify the existence of unauthorised files on a large scale and allowed industry users to scan Napster's database of songs and identify the illegal music files. Furthermore, two web services offering paid downloads came into being in 2001. 'AOL', 'EMI', 'BMG', 'Warner' and 'RealNetworks' launched their service 'MusicNet' while 'Yahoo!', 'Universal' and 'Sony' launched 'Duet'. MP3.com was acquired by Vivendi Universal and converted into a paid service. The Napster service was taken offline in June 2001. During the year, 9.6 million pirated

CD-R discs and 19 million blank discs meant for illegal CD-R labs were seized. Authorities shut down 42 illegal CD manufacturing units in Indonesia, Malaysia and Philippines, which had a total capacity to process 200 million CDs annually.[16]

In 2002, EMI set up its own online service and tied up with other subscription based services like 'FullAudio', 'Rhapsody', 'StreamWaves' and 'MusicNet' to market its services while Sony and BMG launched their paid website 'PressPlay'. The year also saw 50 million pirated discs being seized; of which half were illegally copied CD-Rs. Various raids also uncovered 7000 CD copying machines that could have copied 250 million pirated discs per annum. Several hundred CD-R burners and blank CDs were uncovered in Spain and Philippines.[17]

Still...

Piracy continued unabated despite such efforts by the music industry. Other sites like 'KaZaA', 'Grokster' and 'MusicCity' that offered free downloads replaced Napster. These sites provided P2P file sharing software and gave users a platform for sharing their music files. The main source of revenue for such sites came from pop-up advertisements, making the service totally free for users. In 2001, 1.7 million users[18] had downloaded the software required to access MusicCity alone. The number of music files available on sites providing free downloads skyrocketed from 500 million to 900 million in 2002.[19] The year 2002 saw the market for recorded music falling by 7% to $32 billion.[20] As compared to the first half of 2002, the market for pre-recorded music fell by 10.9% in the first half of 2003 to $12.7 billion.[21]

iTunes – Taking the Industry by Storm...

The paid sites launched by the big music companies allowed users to 'burn' or write songs onto a CD for a subscription fee. But the major drawback of these sites was the narrow repertoire of songs that were made available. The reasons being that the companies were worried about online sales affecting the sales of CDs. They also found it difficult to provide free downloads due to their huge investments in the production and promotion of music. This, in turn, prompted music fans to flock to sites that offered a large number of songs for free.

In this scenario, Apple computers announced the launch of its web service iTunes in April 2003. The iTunes Music Store was developed with the idea of providing music downloads at a rate of 99 cents for a single song and $9.95 for an entire album. It featured a collection of more than 400,000 songs. The product was initially released for 'Mac' users and allowed the tunes to be transferred between any three pre-nominated Mac PCs. It had a few user-friendly features like 'Smart Playlists'. The user had to set a few rules and the playlist would be automatically filled with songs that matched the rules. Another feature was 'Sound Check', which analysed the sound files and automatically adjusted the volume when one song faded into another. A special feature allowed parents to set up a pre-paid account for their children with specific credit limits. The iTunes playlists could be synchronised with Apple's digital music player, iPod [Annexure 3]. "The unbeatable combination of iPod and iTunes offers music lovers a seamless experience for buying, managing and listening to their digital music collections anywhere,"[22] said Apple CEO, Steve Jobs, on the launch of the service by Apple. All these added features contributed to the increasing popularity of iTunes. In the first two weeks, iTunes sold over two million downloads.[23] This was despite the fact that Mac users formed less than 5% of the global PC market.

To reach a larger audience, Apple launched iTunes for Windows users in October 2003 with the tunes being transferable between three pre-designated computers that could be any combination of Mac and Windows PCs. Within a week of the launch, iTunes had sold more than a million tunes and by the end of October, it had sold 14 million songs online.[24] iTunes proved that people were ready to pay for music and was hailed as the service that could turn the industry around. Ted Cohen, Vice President of digital development and distribution at EMI said, "Apple was a wake up call that if you properly market, there is [business]."[25] Of the 99 cents charged per song, 65 cents were paid to the music label. It was also observed that some people who downloaded songs online also bought the CD of their favourite album. This added to the industry's optimism.

In October 2003, Jobs announced a massive music promotion campaign with Pepsi sponsoring a giveaway of 100 million tunes at the time of the 2004 Super Bowl. Under the campaign, winning Pepsi bottle caps carried a number inside and these numbers were redeemable on iTunes for a song. On the eve of launching the scheme, Steve Jobs said, "This historic promotion to legally give away 100 million free songs will go down in history as igniting the legal download market".[26]

In November 2003, fast food chain McDonald's also announced its plans for giving away a billion tunes from iTunes. Both Pepsi and McDonald's had agreed to pay iTunes' full price of 99 cents per tune.[27] These plans by two of the largest consumer goods companies to spend a significant amount of promotional money on music sharing was hailed as a validation of Apple's revolutionary iTunes service and endorsement for the beleaguered music industry.

Future Challenges

iTunes proved that most of the users preferred to download single songs rather than entire albums with 12 single songs being sold against every album on iTunes.[28] But Apple had to face tough competition from the new Napster service that had been re-launched as a paid service by 'Roxio Inc' with a collection of 500,000 songs in its database. Microsoft was also planning to sell songs through its MSN unit. Another service *'BuyMusic.com'* launched its website with 315,000 songs with rates ranging from 79 cents to $1.14 per song.[29] Rhapsody Digital Service owned by RealNetworks Inc. offered a catalogue of 30,000 albums and charged a subscription fee of $9.95 per month and allowed songs to be copied to CDs for an additional 79 cents per song. Rhapsody recorded sales of 28 million songs in October 2003.[30] In October 2003, MusicMatch launched its own online store with a collection of 250,000 songs, which were transferable to portable music players or CDs. It also provided online 24-hour radio stations for various artists. Huge online retailers like Amazon and eBay also planned to enter the online music market with low cost offerings of their own.

One of the major drawbacks of the iTunes service was the limited repertoire of songs available as compared to the millions of songs available at sites like KaZaA. Many users also found that the compressed file format used by iTunes reduced the quality of the sound as compared to the regular CDs and services like Napster. Album connoisseurs preferred to purchase CDs of their favourite artists' albums as a collector's item that would allow them to burn as many copies of the songs, transfer them to their PC or iPod and retain the sound quality. The price of the iTunes service was also perceived to be more expensive than that offered by services like PressPlay and EMusic [Exhibit 3].

Exhibit 3: Online Music Services at a Glance

Service	E'Music	PressPlay	KaZaA	Apple
Cost	$9.99/month for unlimited downloads (12 months) $14.99/month for unlimited downloads (3 months)	$9.95/month for unlimited streaming/downloads $17.95/month for unlimited streaming/ downloads + 10 portable downloads	Free	99 cents per track; $9.99 for most albums
Songs in library	200,000	300,000	Millions	200,000
Audio format(s)	MP3	WMA	MP3, WMA, and others	AAC only
Strong points	File freedom (burn, transfer, keep); speedy and reliable downloads; good, album-oriented Web interface; good for jazz, classical, alternative, and electronica fans	Many popular tracks; speedy and reliable downloads and streams; software interface is clean and deep; community element	It's free; vast selection of songs and other files	30-second file preview; file freedom (burn, transfer, keep); speedy and reliable downloads; excellent integration with iTunes; well-organized, well-edited interface

Source: Kim, James, "Apple's iTunes Music Store", *www.techtv.com, April 28th 2003.*

EMI's Vice President of digital development and distribution, Ted Cohen called iTunes and the excitement related to it "a big halo effect" and predicted that a number of digital music stores could open in the next few months. "Its not unique to Apple; it can spread rapidly", he said. Jeff Somers, Head of music merchandising at *Amazon.com*, commented, "It's very clearly a new day for music, very exciting but creates a lot of trash in the marketplace."[31]

(Hansa Iyengear is the team leader of ICBR, Banglore.)

Endnotes

1. "IFPI Music Piracy Report", *www.ifpi.org*, June 2002.
2. Matheson, Clare "Mixing up the Music Industry", *www.bbc.co.uk*, November 19th 2003.
3. "Global Sales of Recorded Music Down 10.9% in first half of 2003", *www.ifpi.org*, October 2003.
4. Weaver, Jane "Internet Names Scramble to Match iTunes", *www.msnbc.com*, May 22nd 2003.
5. "Commercial Piracy Report 2003", *www.ifpi.org*, June 2003.
6. "Commercial Piracy Report 2001", *www.ifpi.org*, June 2001.
7. Ibid.
8. "Global Music Sales Down 5% in 2001", *www.ifpi.org*, April 2001.
9. "Commercial Piracy Report 2003", *www.ifpi.org*, June 2003.
10. op.cit, "IFPI Music Piracy Report."
11. "Commercial Piracy Report 2003", *www.ifpi.org*, June 2003.
12. Ibid.
13. "IFPI Music Piracy Report2001", *www.ifpi.org*, June 2001.
14. Ibid.
15. Ibid.
16. "IFPI Music Piracy Report 2002", *www.ifpi.org*, June 2002.
17. "Commercial Piracy Report 2003", *www.ifpi.org*, 2003.
18. "In a Spin", *www.economist.com*, October 11th 2001.
19. Matheson, Clare "Mixing up the Music Industry", *www.bbc.co.uk*, November 19th 2003.
20. "Commercial Piracy Report 2003", *www.ifpi.org*, 2003.
21. "Global Sales of Recorded Music Down 10.9% in First Half of 2003", *www.ifpi.org*, October 2003.

22. *www.apple.com*
23. Weaver, Jane "Internet Names Scramble to Match iTunes", *www.msnbc.com*, May 22nd 2003.
24. "Upbeat", *www.economist.com*, October 30th 2003.
25. Weaver, Jane "Internet Names Scramble to Match iTunes", *www.msnbc.com*, May 22nd 2003.
26. Arango, Tim "McDonald's Spins Billion-song iTunes Giveaway", *www.nypost.com*, November 6th 2003.
27. Ibid.
28. "Upbeat", *www.economist.com*, October 30th, 2003.
29. "Music Industry Reluctantly Yielding to Internet Reality", *www.bizreport.com*, November 27th 2003.
30. Ibid.
31. Weaver, Jane "Internet Names Scramble to Match iTunes", *www.msnbc.com*, May 22nd, 2003.

Annexure 1: Domestic Music Piracy Levels around the World in 2001 (units)

	Over 50%	25-50%	10-25%	Less than 10%
North America				Canada USA
Europe	Bulgaria CIS (other) Estonia Greece Latvia Lithuania Romania Russia Ukraine	Cyprus Czech Republic Italy Poland Slovakia Spain	Croatia Finland Hungary Netherlands Slovenia Turkey	Austria Belgium Denmark France Germany Iceland Ireland Norway Portugal Sweden Switzerland UK
Asia	China Indonesia	India Philippines	Hong Kong Singapore	Japan

Contd...

Contd...				
	Malaysia Pakistan	Taiwan Thailand	South Korea	
Latin America	Bolivia Brazil Central America Colombia Ecuador Mexico Paraguay Peru Venezuela	Argentina Chile Uruguay		
Australasia				Australia New Zealand
Middle East	Egypt	Israel Kuwait Lebanon Saudi Arabia	Bahrain Oman Qatar	UAE
Africa	Kenya Nigeria		Ghana South Africa Zimbabwe	
Source: "IFPI Music Piracy Report", www.ifpi.org, June 2002.				

Annexure 2: Domestic Music Piracy Levels around the World in 2002 (units)

	Over 50%	25-50%	10-25%	Less than 10%
North America				Canada USA
Western Europe	Greece	Cyprus Italy Portugal Spain	Belgium Finland Netherlands	Austria Denmark France Germany Iceland

Contd...

Contd...				
				Ireland Norway Sweden Switzerland UK
Eastern Europe	Bulgaria Estonia	Croatia Czech Republic	Turkey Slovenia	
	Latvia Lithuania Romania Russia Ukraine	Hungary Poland Slovakia		
Asia	China Indonesia Malaysia Pakistan	Hong Kong India Philippines Taiwan Thailand	Singapore South Korea	Japan
Latin America	Argentina Bolivia Brazil Colombia Ecuador Mexico Paraguay Peru Uruguay Venezuela	Chile Costa Rica		
Middle East	Egypt Israel Lebanon	Kuwait Saudi Arabia	Bahrain Oman Qatar	UAE
Australasia				Australia New Zealand
Africa		South Africa	Zimbabwe	

Source: "Commercial Piracy Report 2003", www.ifpi.org, 2003.

Annexure 3

The iPod

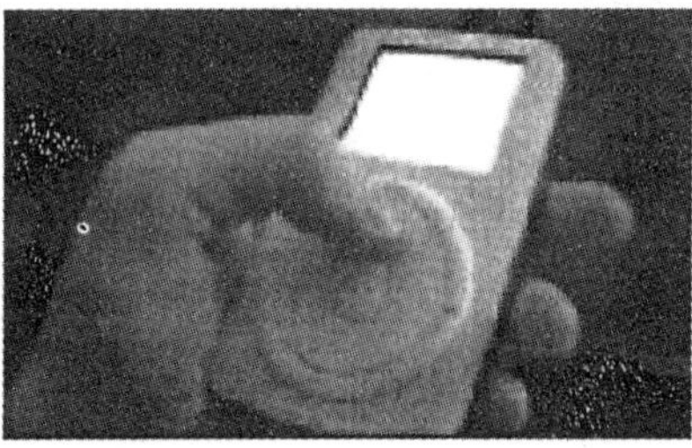

The iPod was developed by Apple Computers and was launched in 2000. It rapidly became a must-have gadget for music lovers. **iPod's features:**

- Same size as a deck of playing cards.
- Weighed less than 2 CDs.
- Came in variations of 20GB or 40GB drives.
- Had the capacity to hold up to 10,000 songs and thousands of digital photos.
- Could be synchronised with iTunes to download any number of tunes.
- Had a built-in voice recorder and a digital media recorder that enables the user to store thousands of digital photographs.
- Featured an LCD screen and buttons that feature a backlight for clear visibility in low-light conditions. Uses touch wheel technology for scrolling through the menus.
- The iPod delivered the highest sound quality from input to output. It supported the most popular audio formats including MP3, MP3 Variable Bit Rate (VBR), and was the only portable digital music player that supported the AAC format used by the iTunes Music Store for Mac and Windows.
- Also had the feature of games, and the functionality of a portable calendar with built-in alarm system and sleep timer. It also allowed text downloads which could be viewed on the LCD display.
- Prices ranged from $300 to $500 depending on memory.

Compiled by IBS-CDC from www.apple.com.

The File-Sharing Litigation

A litigation was filed against the company Napster Inc. with regard to the new digital file sharing technology. The company allowed the users to download music files through internet at no cost or at a very minimal cost. It was found that no change in the contents of the file was done and was delivered in the same mode. Again its usage was fairly commercial. It was held that the distribution of a file to an anonymous user cannot be considered as a personal use and would not fall into the purview of fair use. Napster users were found to be involved in illegal copying and the entire reproduction of a material was done without any payment.

During the proceedings, a similar version of other such file sharing litigation was cited. The case was between Sony Corporation of America vs. Universal City Studios Inc. Sony used to earn revenue primarily from the advertisements that were telecast during the programs. During that period a new device called home tape recorders were existent in the market. Sony brought about a copyright infringement action trying to stop the sale of home video tape recorders, because these devices would enable the owner of the device to record the programs aired on channel and thus provided the facility to fast-forward the advertisements or even not to record them at all. The viewer could watch the serial or the show at his own leisure and ease. However in this case, the Supreme Court held that any instance of copying for home use cannot infringe a copyright holder's exclusive rights for the television programs.

17

Copyright and Intellectual Property Rights: A Case Study from the Web Face

William Kilbride

This case is about a mega company Bertelsmann Music Group which entered into a contract with another company Napster, which was in the business of music exchange. The company had a motive to acquire the company but did not do so. This decision was challenged in the court of law and BMG was accused of facilitating the process of copyright infringement by users. The case highlights how one company succumbed to infringement of copyrights through another company without being directly involved. The case gives an account of intellectual property and rights issues relating to an online research archive.

Introduction

This short case study gives an account of intellectual property and rights issues relating to an online research archive. It describes the licensing regime in place to protect the creators and publishers of the data, and provides a case study of actions taken to stop unlicensed re-publication of data by a third party. It concludes

Source: Arts and Humanities Data Service (www.ads.ahds.ac.uk). © William Kilbride. Reprinted with permission.

that clarity is essential in the protection of intellectual property rights and that effort taken at an early stage will be rewarded in the long-term.

Context

The Archaeology Data Service (ADS)/Arts and Humanities Data Service Centre for Archaeology (AHDS Archaeology) supports research learning and teaching in archaeology in the UK by promoting good practice in the use of IT, by preserving important digital research archives for the long term, and by making a large amount of data available online. At the time of writing, ArchSearch *(http://ads.ahds.ac.uk/catalogue/)*, our online catalogue of archaeological resources, provides details of some 600,000 sites, monuments and research projects in the UK and wherever UK-based archaeologists work. In many cases, short descriptive records provide access to rich and detailed archives that may contain any form of digital object associated with archaeological research. Archives include very large quantities of text—theses, monographs and journal articles are in digital form—as well as unpublished 'grey literature'. They include database files, images, CAD plans, geophysical and topographic survey, virtual realities, animations and statistical data. The vast majority of this data is supplied to us from external agencies who license us to distribute and preserve data on their behalf. This non-exclusive licence specifies the conditions under which we can distribute data, and has provision for digital preservation but does not transfer ownership of copyright.

Access

ArchSearch is free to users, and has few of the restrictions to access encountered in other online services. Archaeological information is the result of very many years of fieldwork and research—much of it is funded through the public purse and explicitly to encourage and sustain a better understanding of the historic environment. It seldom has significant commercial value. Users of the data are not required to provide any personal details in advance, nor are they required to remember a password or login. There is no authentication system restricting access to registered IP addresses. Moreover, because we provide access to authentic archival materials, it would be prejudicial to the integrity of the resource, were we to brand digital objects with copyright or other fingerprints. In some cases—especially print quality images—we present only screen grade images on the understanding that users can ask for higher quality originals: this is partly to protect copyright of depositors, and also because these files can be very large and require high capacity bandwidth to access them.

This light regime places an extra responsibility to protect the intellectual property rights of material entrusted to us. Consequently, access to collections is covered by a generous but clear series of copyright, liability and access statements (see *http://ads.ahds.ac.uk/cap.html* and *http://ads.ahds.ac.uk/copy.html*). The copyright and liability statements form a common agreement that are shared across the AHDS. So, users are licensed to use resources for their own *bona fide* teaching, learning and research; they waive any liabilities that may result from use of the collections; and they are required to acknowledge the source of material. These statements are asserted repeatedly within ArchSearch. Moreover, a copyright challenge for use of the system explicitly requires that users agree to these conditions. This challenge sets a cookie which expires after 15 minutes, thus ensuring that users have little ground for objecting that they are unaware of the access conditions.

Preservation through Documentation

Digital preservation is a specialist and demanding task, of which rights management is only one aspect. It is particularly important for the discipline of archaeology that, through the process of excavation, systematically destroys its own primary evidence. In such circumstances the preservation of notes of excavation—termed preservation by record—is of critical importance (Richards and Robinson 2000). Excavations in the crypt of Christ Church, Spitalfields in London in the 1980s provide an example of the need for such recording, the problems that arise from the creation of such documentation, and complications that can arise in relation to intellectual property rights from this process.

The excavations were undertaken under the auspices of the Greater London Council on behalf of the Parish and Friends of Christ Church Spitalfields who sought to turn the crypt of the church into a homeless shelter. Scientific interest in this unusual project ensured that a range of leading agencies and individuals collaborated to undertake the project and complete the painstaking laboratory research that followed. This included the Natural History Museum, the Nuffield Foundation, the Ministry of Works (subsequently English Heritage), as well as the architectural practice that was responsible for the conversion. Project staff were recruited on an occasional basis. Some stayed with the project for a long period of time, while sickness and attendance records suggest that some may have stayed for little more than a day.

Though published in generous detail (Reeves and Adams 1993, Molleson and Cox 1993, Cox 1996), much of the research is now only available by inspecting the site archives. The notebooks, photographs, drawings and recording sheets in the archive provide a meticulous account of the excavation and thus represent the primary source. A long held desire to digitise a representative sample of this data was fulfilled in 2000 with the start of an online teaching and learning project that drew attention to the interdisciplinary nature of this type of study.

Yet digitising this material presented a familiar problem for intellectual property rights (Dunning 2004). Specifically, it was far from clear who owned the copyright associated with the various files and documents that we digitised. It rapidly became clear that, while conventional archives are licensed *via* a single exchange of documents from the project team; in this case, the project team no longer existed. The numerous agencies and staff involved in the excavations would have to be contacted and their approval sought individually. Amongst these, English Heritage, the Nuffield Foundation and the Natural History Museum had provided funding and in-kind support to the project. Each was asked to sign a standard deposit licence allowing ADS to distribute and preserve the data (but retain their copyright in the data. For more on this process, with an example licence see *http://ads.ahds.ac.uk/copy.html*). These three were joined by a fourth licence provided by the Christ Church Parish and the 'Friends of Christ Church Spitalfields'—a voluntary group that supports the work of the Parish. These were recognised as the most important 'inheritors' of the project and the data that resulted from it. In addition, the project team made strenuous efforts to contact all of the individuals involved in the project, to inform them of our plans and to seek their advice and approval, and to offer them a deposit licence, should they wish to sign. None in the end objected, but a consensus emerged that individual contributors would only be happy if the Parish and Friends of Christ Church Spitalfields also approved.

Archaeology and Human Remains

Parallel to legal concerns over copyright were ethical and quasi-legal concerns over the explicit nature of some of the archive. Christ Church Spitalfields was remarkable for the degree of preservation associated with many of the individuals recovered from the crypt. Soft tissue and fabric—seldom recovered from archaeological contexts—was present in significant quantities. This material became an important reference collection for forensic archaeology far beyond the context of eighteenth and nineteenth century London. Moreover, identification of individuals through name plates and other inscriptions made it possible to cross reference forensic pathology with biographic details disclosed in historical sources. Consequently, much of the post excavation research concentrated on refining methodologies for analysing and identifying individuals from challenging archaeological contexts—such as may be found on battlefields or anonymous mass graves.

However, the handling and study of human remains for archaeological study is not unproblematic (for a discussion see Downes and Pollard 1999). Strict legal requirements exist, in part reflecting a number of ethical principles, such as a desire not to cause offence. It can be seen that digital images of partially decomposed human remains are appropriate tools in archaeological research and teaching. However, Internet access raises the possibility that material can be lifted out of context and used easily for inappropriate purposes. Consequently, the project team took particular pains to warn users about what they were likely to find in the archive. In this way the project team sought to avoid offence and to ensure that publication of the archive did not bring any of the agencies involved into disrepute. This desire was further amplified by creators of the data in their responses to the invitation to comment on the archive. In addition, senior independent advisors were asked for their opinions. All concurred that the archive should be both, fit for the purpose and appropriate for use before it was released to the public.

Thus, after an extended process of licensing and review, the digital archive from Christ Church Spitalfields was released under the standard terms and conditions that apply to the whole of ArchSearch.

Research Data Online

The launch of the research archive, with the associated teaching and learning materials, has largely been a success. Patterns of use show that the archive has been among the most used resources within ArchSearch: in 2002-03 and again in 2003-04 the archive was the single most popular excavation archive available within the system (ADS 2004). The tutorial has been used in teaching in contexts that we previously could not have envisaged (Kilbride *et al.* 2002), and we have received a number of requests for further data such as contact details for how to obtain access to the rest of the research archive. This represents a success within the operational plan of the organisation.

Late in 2003, routine monitoring of our systems showed an unusual amount of activity of use in the archive. Further analysis of this activity led to the identification of a website which had re-published some of the more explicit—and thus potentially offensive—images from the archive. This new context in which the images had been embedded was a breach of the access agreement and copyright statements which users are required to accept before using these archives. Moreover, having seen this infringement, it would have been negligent to allow this unlawful republication to continue. Given the legitimate concerns of data creators and those who licensed the data to us, it was imperative that we act swiftly and successfully.

Action Plan and Procedure

This is the first time since their creation that our Access Agreement and Copyright Statement had been invoked to protect the intellectual property rights of depositors. Though, we hoped that the matter could be resolved without aggressive legal action, it was clear that we needed to imagine a 'worst case scenario', in which our host institution would have to take more formal legal action. Envisaging such a scenario, we first had to be certain that the material was indeed copied from our web server and that the Access Agreement and Copyright statement had indeed been breached.

Both were straightforward. The project team had digitised the images from the original slides and still had them in our possession: the data could not have been obtained from any other source. The Access Agreement is explicit in only allowing users to pass on information to approved users—i.e. under the same terms and conditions by which they had been supplied to them—while the Copyright Statement offers a 'non-transferable' licence to users to use within their own research learning and teaching. Republication on a third party website is clearly beyond the scope of both documents. Moreover, the Access Agreement entitles us to terminate the licence they have to use the data, and makes it explicit that users risk legal action should they breach any of the conditions.

Having established this, we then approached senior managers to ensure that they supported our request to have the material removed—aware of the 'worst case scenario'. At this point we also consulted various legal authorities—in particular JISC Legal for their advice. This advice confirmed our view that we should begin with a relatively low key approach to the webmaster of the offending site, but also identified an alternative course of action which could be pursued through the website's Internet Service Provider (ISP). A recent case—Godfrey *vs.* Demon Internet Ltd., suggests that ISPs share liabilities in relation to material they publish (Charlesworth 2000).

The result of these consultations was to devise a simple decision tree that we should follow in the event of our requests being ignored or denied. This may be extensible to similar cases, so if is published here should others find themselves in the same situation in the future. It is now our own agreed protocol of how to respond to future incidents of this kind, and might best be thought of as a flowchart with 5 steps each of which takes 14 days. It ends in either the offending material being removed or in more formal legal action. One would hope that it is resolved before the end point, which is 70 days from the first email.

1. ('Day 0') Contact webmaster identifying clearly the areas of concern, identifying the terms and conditions breached, specifying changes to be made, requesting an immediate acknowledgement and requesting that changes be completed within 14 days from the dispatch of the first email.
2. ('Day 14') If the matter has not been resolved in 14 days, contact the webmaster again making clear the legal implications and our intention to proceed to court if changes were not completed within 14 days of the dispatch of the second email. Send copy of this email to the Internet Service Provider.

3. ('Day 28') If the matter has not been resolved in 28 days, contact the ISP pointing out the infringement and requesting that they intervene to have the offending material removed from their domain within 14 days of the dispatch of the third email.
4. ('Day 42') If the matter has not been resolved by this point, write again to the ISP making clear the legal implications for them and our intention to proceed to court if changes were not completed within 14 days of the dispatch of the fourth email.
5. ('Day 56') If the matter has still not been resolved, obtain letters from the university lawyers to the webmaster and to the ISP making clear the infringement and requesting changes within 14 days of the postmark of the letter.
6. ('Day 70') If the matter has still not been resolved, take further legal advice and begin legal proceedings.

Resolution and Conclusion

In the end we were pleased not to have to proceed beyond the first stage in our decision tree. The offending material was removed within a few hours of the first contact being made and the matter was closed.

At first inspection, threatening legal action seems an excessive and risky policy to resolve a breach of copyright. In this case, however, we were confident in our approach for a number of reasons, mainly to do with clarity. We had a very extensive documentation trail that showed conclusively where copyright resided. The Access Agreement and Copyright Statement were well drafted so the nature of the infringement was clear. We could spell out in simple terms the infringement that had occurred and what action we required. In fact these modifications required relatively trivial amounts of work: so we did not have to make onerous demands. In addition, one suspects that the relatively generous access conditions also worked to our advantage. It could hardly be argued that we were restricting access to information or protecting special intellectual privilege. All of these gave us confidence to act decisively.

Thus, clarity in intellectual property rights management was core to the protection of open access, web-based research materials. The effort at the start associated with licensing materials and ensuring that users are aware of conditions of use, has proven to be time well spent. Our experience suggests that protecting IPR needn't require complicated mechanisms of authentication and authorisation: especially in contexts where resources have limited commercial value. But without clarity no regime—however sophisticated—is likely to be viable.

(Dr. William Kilbride is an assistant director, Archaeology Data Service/Arts and Humanities Data Service Centre for Archaeology, University of York. He can be reached at wgk1@york.ac.uk).

Bibliography

ADS 2004 Archaeology Data Service/AHDS Archaeology Annual Report 2004, online at *http://ads.ahds.ac.uk/project/annrpts/2004.html*

Cox, M 1996, "Life and Death in Spitalfields 1700 to 1850", Council for British Archaeology Occasional Paper 21.

Downes J and Pollard T (1999), "The Loved Body's Corruption: Archaeological Contributions to the Study of Human Mortality", Cruithne, Glasgow.

Dunning, A (2004), Copyright and Other Rights Issues in Digitisation, AHDS Information Paper online at *http://ahds.ac.uk/creating/information-papers/copyright-introduction* last visited 13/09/04.

Charlesworth, A (2000), New Developments in UK Internet Law, JISC Senior Management Briefing Paper 10.

Kilbride, W G, Fernie K M, McKinney P, Richards, JD (2002), 'Contexts of Learning: The PATOIS Project and Internet-based Teaching and Learning in Higher Education' in Internet Archaeology 12, online at *http://intarch.ac.uk/journal/issue12/patois_toc.html* last visited 12/03/04.

Molleson, T and Cox, M (1993), *The Spitalfields Project, Volume 2: The Anthropology—The Middling Sort,* Council for British Archaeology Research Report No 86.

Reeves, J and Adams, M (1993), *The Spitalfields Project. Volume 1: The Archaeology—Across the Styx,* Council for British Archaeology Research Report No 85.

Richards JD and Robinson DJ (2000), *Digital Archives from Excavation and Fieldwork: A Guide to Good Practice* (Second Edition) Arts and Humanities Data Service, London (online at *http://ads.ahds.ac.uk/project/goodguides/excavation/*).